Stanza
My
Stone

G Is it to hear the blatter of grackles and say
Invisible priest; is it to eject, to pull
The day to pieces and cry *stanza my stone?*
Where was it one first heard of the truth? The the. ꓷ

Stanza
My
Stone

Wallace Stevens
and the
Hermetic
Tradition

Leonora
Woodman

Purdue University Press
West Lafayette, Indiana

Library of Congress Catalog Card Number 82-81679
International Standard Book Number 0-911198-68-7
Printed in the United States of America

For Harold

⚅ Contents ⚅

Acknowledgments

A book so long in the making accumulates many debts. Its genesis may perhaps be traced to Roger K. Meiners, who first introduced me to Stevens' work. In the course of meditating, writing, and — inevitably — revising my many drafts, I profited from the advice and encouragement of my colleagues at Purdue University: Thomas P. Adler, John J. Contreni, Chester E. Eisinger, Felix N. Stefanile, G. Richard Thompson, and Harold H. Watts. Two summer research grants from the Purdue Research Foundation allowed me to work at the Huntington Library, the Library of Congress, and the Charles Patterson Van Pelt Library of the University of Pennsylvania. My thanks to the staff of each of these superb libraries. My thanks, too, to Ann Hedgecough, who typed my manuscript with her usual dispatch and accuracy.

I wish to thank *Texas Studies in Literature and Language* for permission to print part of an essay that first appeared in its pages. I am grateful to Alfred A. Knopf, Inc. for permission to quote from the following copyrighted editions of the works of Wallace Stevens: *The Necessary Angel: Essays on Reality and the Imagination* (1951); *The Collected Poems of Wallace Stevens* (1954); *Opus Posthumous*, edited, with an introduction by Samuel French Morse (1957); and *Letters of Wallace Stevens*, selected and edited by Holly Stevens (1966).

I owe my greatest debt to my husband, Harold, whose spirited and pointed comments helped to shape my work at every stage.

_____ *Key to Abbreviations* _____

Volumes frequently cited within the text of this work have been assigned abbreviations as follows:

The Necessary Angel: Essays on Reality and the Imagination (NA)
The Collected Poems of Wallace Stevens (CP)
Opus Posthumous (OP)
Letters of Wallace Stevens (L)

☾ *Introduction* ☾

Shortly before his death, Stevens wrote to a friend that his was a quiet existence, punctuated only by "meditation and prayer" (L, 841). No gloss accompanies this assertion of devotional activity—the only such reference in the letters of Stevens' mature years. We might well be puzzled; coupled as they are, the words bear a distinct religious ring that ill accords with Stevens' disdain for traditional religious orthodoxies. We are perhaps further mystified when we encounter in another late letter further testimony to some kind of religious belief, again left cryptic and unexplained. Evidently stung by a critic's view that he had "surrendered all residual belief in religion,"[1] Stevens writes to Sister Bernetta Quinn that his critic engages in "oversimplifications." "I am not an atheist," he continues, "although I do not believe to-day in the same God in whom I believed when I was a boy" (L, 735).

Oblique references, to be sure, but enough to give us pause especially since critical estimates, no matter how diverse, have assumed the secular nature of Stevens' vision. Even those who have probed the unmistakable idealist strain in his thought have done so provisionally, conceding from the outset that Stevens' lifelong celebration of the human imagination is innocent of transcendental sanction. Indeed, how could it be otherwise? A poet who greets the dissolution of the gods with glee; who repeatedly scorns the church and all received belief; who vigorously asserts man's autonomy; and who, above all, embraces the earth with passionate intensity, claiming it as a sufficient and altogether satisfying substitute for heaven—such a poet is hardly to be conceded a religious vision, no matter how broadly we define the religious impulse.

And yet, there is room for doubt that naturalism alone is an adequate guide, especially to the later poetry, where Stevens repeatedly invokes a potential realm of order as yet but dimly known. At times this elusive order seems to embrace the whole of life; at other

1

times, it appears to point particularly to poetry. Often there is the suggestion of finality, as if the poet were seeking some fundamental and unalterable substratum of reality governing both life and the poem. Sometimes, Stevens approaches this realm tentatively, using the method of rhetorical question that nevertheless asserts the possibility of what it seeks:

> And in what covert may we, naked, be
> Beyond the knowledge of nakedness, as part
> Of reality, beyond the knowledge of what
> Is real, part of a land beyond the mind?
>
> (CP, 252)

Elsewhere, modulating into a more assertive declarative mood, he predicts a future "final order," foreseeing "A life beyond this present knowing, / A life lighter than this present splendor" (OP, 101).

This persistent stretching for an elusive "beyond" is paralleled by the poet's search for an "ultimate poem" or a "central poem" or a "poem of pure reality," terms that suggest a potential absolute cleansed of the adventitious and contingent. The significance of this theme is underscored by the complementary theme of disguise—the belief that the true nature of the phenomenal world is veiled and hidden, leading the poet to lament that man grasps "never the thing but the version of the thing" (CP, 332) and sending him in quest of the "savage transparence" lying just beyond the "pediment of appearance" (CP, 361).

These disconcerting transcendental themes, implying another order of life now but vaguely known, present a formidable problem to the student of Stevens, who must reconcile them to Stevens' putative naturalism. On the one hand, Stevens seems to celebrate objective reality, yearning to record it accurately and faithfully, but on the other, he appears to suggest another and superior order of reality, leading him to scorn facticity in favor of piercing the "mere objectiveness of things" (CP, 531). The demand might be understandable in view of Stevens' celebration of the imagination's metamorphic powers, yet strangely he appears to denigrate both art and imagination as a means of approaching his evanescent realm, insisting that the "poem of pure reality" be sought directly without the aid of mediate forms—"untouched / By trope or deviation" (CP, 471). Indeed, the compelling attractions of "the thing itself" appear to be "Pure corus-

cations, that lie beyond / The imagination, intact / And unattained"
(CP, 349).

The difficulty of adjusting a naturalist perspective to these assuredly transcendental themes is further compounded by a vocabulary
reminiscent of mysticism. Terms like "being" and "nothingness" and
"abstract" and, above all, the "center"—repeatedly invoked from
Harmonium to "The Rock"—belong less to an earthbound vision than
to the tradition of mystical communion, where they imply the soul's
union with the divine image encountered in the course of meditation.
When to this we add the distinct eschatological tone of a good many of
the later poems, which either hover around a faintly ascertainable "inherent order active to be / Itself" (CP, 442) or yearn for a "fixed
heaven, / Not subject to change" (CP, 520) or even predict a "central
arrival" (CP, 516), we may, perhaps, allow that naturalism, as it is
commonly understood, will not suffice.

How, then, are we to consider a poet whose allegiance to the
earth or "reality" is beyond dispute but who, at the same time,
suggests an "ultimate" reality that cannot be attributed to a transcendent source or divorced from an earthly setting, since for Stevens,
the gods are dead, and happily so? How, moreover, to account for a
vision that, in the absence of the gods, celebrates the era of "the idea
of man" but that refuses the humanist label the phrase suggests,[2] proposing as alternative the image of a hero aggrandized as "substance
and non-substance" (CP, 297), "The bread and wine of the mind"
(CP, 275), a "central man" (CP, 250), a "prodigious person" (CP,
443)—epithets that bear the unmistakable ring of divinity? And how,
if the hero is the paradigmatic imagination, as is commonly assumed,
may we assess a view that confirms the imagination's metamorphic
powers at the same as it scorns and dismisses its products—indeed, its
very being—seeking in its place "a land beyond the mind"?

We can of course adopt the familiar view that consistency is not
to be sought in Stevens' thought; that, indeed, he reflects the dilemma
that accrues to lapsed belief. The argument here, for the most part, is
confined to Stevens' putative dualism—his perpetual alternation between imagination and reality, the two conceived as Cartesian opposites. Accordingly, Stevens' vacillation is perceived as the consequence
of division "between the self (or, in Stevens' more usual terms, the
imagination, or the mind) and a reality which is not part of that self
but must be brought into its purview, composed, and so (as it were)
re-created."[3] Denied the consolation of traditional faith, the mind, in

this view, must seek its own validation by exercising its synthetic powers, so to probe the self's ambiguous and uncertain relations to the world. Activity and search, rather than conviction and certainty, define this act of existential consciousness; hence, the poetry offers to our view a mind in the very process of self-definition, in the course of which it deliberates, weighs, accepts, and discards alternative versions of its selfhood. In this exploration, poetry occupies a central place; often considered the poet's major subject, it stands as synecdoche for the possibilities that inhere in the mind engaged in creating itself, even as it creates its art.

The view is convenient, for in absolving the poet of fixed belief, it is broad enough to include the multiple, and often contradictory, perspectives that appear in his thought. And, indeed, as between imagination and reality, the poet appears wedded to uncertainty, so that for some readers, drawn to Stevens' idealist strain, his work testifies to "the power of *thinking* . . . the constructive power of deliberate choice."[4] Others, mindful of Stevens' attachment to the physical world, prefer to see him as a thoroughgoing nominalist, faithfully recording the phenomenology of sensation. As J. Hillis Miller remarks of this ostensible ambivalence, "It is impossible to find a single systematic theory of poetry and life in Stevens."[5]

Miller's view, widely shared, is persuasive so long as we accept the equally popular view that Stevens is an "atheist"[6] whose poetry reflects "the firm dignity of merely natural man."[7] Such a view, however, is open to question if, in addition to the marked transcendental strain of many of the later poems, we take seriously Stevens' disavowal of godlessness, though, to be sure, the God whom Stevens' acknowledges is not the God of traditional religious orthodoxy. Indeed, the poet's brief but honest profession of belief may serve as epigraph to this study, which maintains that Stevens is a deeply religious poet whose work is as consistent and systematic as any rigorous reader might wish, once we recognize his spiritual purpose. Stevens, I shall urge, held a vision of spiritual regeneration which he repeatedly outlined in many of his poems. His subject is not "natural" man but transcendental man—or at least the possibility of transcendental man—and it belongs to the venerable and well-defined Hermetic tradition which not only nourished his creative genius but gave him a rich and abundant storehouse of image and symbol—even, in many instances, the very architecture of his poems. Since, for reasons I shall later explore, Stevens offered this vision of human transformation in the vocabulary of aesthetics, my first concern will be to examine the textual evidence that clarifies the meaning of "pure poetry" and the "ultimate poem," phrases Stevens sometimes used to distinguish two levels of poetry. I turn next to "Owl's Clover," Stevens' longest poem and the one in which he most clearly defined mankind's "common god" (OP, 59), synonymous in the poet's arbitrary lexicon with "pure poetry" and equivalent to the transcendental Man of the Hermetic tradition. Chapter 3 considers this tradition in detail, outlining its premises and symbols to clarify the uses Stevens made of them. Succeeding chapters consider the relation of the Hermetic Man to the "supreme fiction"; the spiritual reciprocity between imagination and reality—variations of the Hermetic doctrine of correspondence; the decreation and recreation of self and nature that constitute the metamorphic stages of Hermetic meditation; and the Hermetic theory of transcendental perception that lies at the core of Stevens' account of human transformation. In the final chapter, I turn to Stevens' native Pennsylvania, in order, thereby, to suggest the means by which he encountered the Rosicrucian tradition (the corporate form of modern Hermetism) that appears to have profoundly influenced his creative life.

PART ONE

Disguised Pronunciamento: Stevens' Two Poetries

Chapter 1

The Ultimate Poem

That other one wanted to think his way to life,
Sure that the ultimate poem was the mind . . .

To begin a study of Stevens' work by exploring the sense of the "ultimate poem," a phrase that appears in the poetry only twice and even then does not arise until midpoint in the corpus, may strike the reader as somewhat eccentric. And well it might, if the phrase were viewed as singular—and aberrant intrusion bearing little or no relation to Stevens' work as a whole. This, of course, is questionable on two counts: the "poem" that Stevens invokes is one of his major motifs— indeed, as Samuel French Morse reminds us, Stevens' work "from the very beginning . . . [was] 'about' poetry; it is the one real subject of *Harmonium* and all the later work" (OP, xiv)—and the epithet is likewise representative, for in its suggestion of something fundamental and without peer, it is close in meaning to "supreme," "absolute," and "essential," frequently used in the poetry to suggest unconditioned rank. Indeed, the "supreme fiction," a major theme generally thought to mean poetry, bears a signification akin to that of the "ultimate poem." We may thus assume on both counts that the "ultimate poem," however seldom it arises, represents one of Stevens' major concerns.

The meaning Stevens intends in this perplexing phrase may be sought by attending to the sense of "ultimate," an hierarchical term implying degree. For an "ultimate poem" to exist, there must be "lesser" poems; and, indeed, this distinction between two levels of poetry is claimed in "A Primitive Like an Orb," a poem of the forties which offers for consideration a "central poem" that is "seen and known in lesser poems" (CP, 440). The sense that a lower form of poetry exists in which a higher form may be discerned or from which it may arise is similarly implied in a passage in "Notes toward a Supreme Fiction," where the poet foresees the "fiction of an absolute" (something perfect and whole, the sense of "absolute") which is expected to arise from "crude compoundings" (CP, 404), a phrase which suggests an impure amalgam from which something pure, presumably the poem or "fiction," is to be refined.

9

The notion of two levels of poetry—related, to be sure, but ultimately distinct—is crucial to the meaning Stevens intends when he proposes an "ultimate poem" that is somehow to evolve from "lesser poems." For it suggests, at the very least, a kind of linguistic legerdemain—a suspicion that the poet intends for the word "poetry" at least one meaning superior to its ordinary sense; and, at the very most, a sense that there exists for the poetic act a *terminus ad quem*—a conclusion beyond which it cannot go.

These distinctions appear in "Extracts from Addresses to the Academy of Fine Ideas," the only poem in which the "ultimate poem" is mentioned in the poetic text itself. (The phrase also appears in the title of the late poem, "The Ultimate Poem Is Abstract.") Its appearance is embedded in the poet's consideration of two aspects of the mind, the first dismissed as merely "systematic thinking," the other offered as the "ultimate poem":

> That other one wanted to think his way to life,
> Sure that the ultimate poem was the mind,
> Or of the mind . . .
>
> (CP, 256)

Affirmed as "the mind, / Or of the mind," the "ultimate poem" suggests both process and product—the mind that creates and the thing created. Except for the epithet, we might well concede that Stevens is proposing the "poem" in its ordinary sense, using as etymological guide for its double reference the Greek *poiein* which means "to make" and from which descends the modern meaning of "poem." When, however, the "poem" is prefaced by an epithet bearing the sense of stasis, we encounter the perplexing suggestion of a making— a process—which concludes in a product or "poem" beyond which there can be no further making. In short, "ultimate" suggests a closure that collides with the notion of process in which it lies embedded.

This perhaps overly-fastidious attention to Stevens' language has its point, namely, that when Stevens offers the "poem" or "poetry" qualified by "ultimate" or by equivalent epithets such as "central" or "high" or "pure"; or when, in another analogous construction, he suggests a "poem of pure reality" (CP, 471), he is not, I shall urge, concerned with the poem as it is commonly understood, but is rather celebrating a spiritual entity which he chose to veil in the language of aesthetics. Poetry in its "ultimate" sense had a special meaning for

Stevens, considerably different from what is usually referred to by that linguistic symbol; indeed, in Stevens' lexicon, "poetry" and the "idea of man" are synonymous, but not for the humanistic reasons commonly offered. Rather, Stevens believed in the evolution of a qualitatively different man shaped in the image of an archetypal prototype; and because art or the "lesser" poem expressed the features of this archetype—indeed, was the very medium which gave rise to his being—Stevens claimed him as the "ultimate poem."[1] The linguistic means Stevens used to adapt the word *poetry* to his private purpose may be seen in his letters, essays, and the "Adagia," his commonplace book, where certain recurring concepts will provide the initial textual evidence for the thesis of this study.

Ᏻ Ᏻ Ꮞ Ꮞ

We can best approach Stevens' "ultimate poem" by seeking the meaning of "pure poetry," a phrase that recurs with some frequency in his prose. Early references in several letters of the mid-thirties betray some uneasiness with the phrase. Not only does Stevens use it retrospectively, as if it were a concept once held but since discarded, but he appears to associate it with the first and apparently inferior half of a literature-life dichotomy. Asked by a correspondent whether the poems of *Harmonium* were "essentially decorative," he replies that he was on the point of responding negatively when he remembered his delight during the writing of *Harmonium* in the sensuous image and the musical phrase: "there was a time when I liked the idea of images and images alone, or images and the music of verse together. I then believed in *pure poetry*, as it was called" (L, 288). However, he continues, "life means a good deal more to us now-a-days than literature does. In the period of which I have just spoken, I thought literature meant most" (L, 288). Several months later he makes a distinction between "pure poetry" and "didactic poetry" but appears to assume that, while "pure poetry" remains his ultimate objective, "didactic poetry" or "didacticism in poetry" is a necessary stage in its evolution (L, 303).

By the end of the thirties, Stevens' skepticism regarding the value of "pure poetry" seems to have been resolved, for he confidently announces to one correspondent that "I am, in the long run, interested in pure poetry" (L, 340) and writes to another that "pure poetry" should be "the highest objective of the poet" (L, 369). At the same time the phrase crops up in several essays and in glosses to two major poems. In these later references, however, Stevens uses the phrase in a different sense from the one noted above. There "pure poetry" is discussed in a commonly accepted linguistic context: that is, "pure poetry," however its formal and aesthetic properties may differ from "impure" poetry, designates something that has achieved an objective form. Stevens' subsequent references, however, subtly alter this meaning; not only does he refuse to identify "pure poetry" with the affective components of image and music, but he consistently distinguishes it from the poem itself.

The distinction may be seen in the gloss Stevens provided in 1940 to poem xxii of "The Man with the Blue Guitar": "Poetry is the spirit, as the poem is the body. Crudely stated, poetry is the imagination. But here poetry is used as the poetic, without the slightest pejorative innuendo. I have in mind pure poetry. The purpose of writing poetry is to attain pure poetry" (L, 363).

What is striking here are the shifting and distinctly different meanings Stevens attaches to poetry. In the first set of equivalencies—poetry=spirit=imagination—the meaning of poetry is internalized, becoming synonymous with an attribute of the human mind—the imagination. In the second set of equivalencies, Stevens departs from grammatical logic to propose that poetry (noun)=poetic (adjective)=pure poetry (adjective, noun). Stevens refuses to locate his evaluative adjective, but clearly he means to establish "poetic" as distinct from either poetry as imagination or poetry as poem. Finally, poetry is used as a referent for the poem, but the process (writing) of poetry is conceived instrumentally: that is, one writes poetry to attain pure poetry, an achievement further complicated by the fact that if, indeed, the "poetic" and "pure poetry" are synonymous, the goal of writing poetry is not the poem but a state produced by the poem.

Since Stevens identifies "pure poetry" with the "poetic," our task is next to trace the word "poetic" to see what can be further established about "pure poetry." Here we are led to a major Stevensian theme, his eagerness to develop a "theory of poetry" that would expand its relatively narrow, specialized meaning to one embracing the whole of human activity. This is the sense of his proposition that "the theory / Of poetry is the theory of life" (CP, 486). His hope that such a venture would "disclose the truth about poetry" (L, 383) led Stevens in 1940 to urge a wealthy friend to establish a chair of poetry at Harvard for the study of "the history of poetic thought and of the theory of poetry" (L, 358), elaborated in a subsequent "Memorandum" (L, 377). His proposal clearly relegates poetry as genre to a minor place. A theory of poetry, he writes, should not confine itself to "specimens" of the genre that "are merely parts of a great whole," but should concern itself with the "poetic side of life, of the abstraction and the theory" (L, 383). "It [theory of poetry] does not mean verse any more than philosophy means prose. The subject-matter of poetry is the thing to be ascertained" (L, 377). The distinction between "poetic" and poetry as poem is repeated in the "Adagia": "The poetic view of life is larger than any of its poems (a larger thing than any poem); and to recognize this is the beginning of the recognition of the poetic spirit" (OP, 174). Evidently, Stevens regarded poetry as genre as an instance of a larger principle transcending the literary form. Indeed, he seems to have held a hierarchical view of poetry, according "the poetic view of life" or "pure poetry" a generic status subsuming poetry as poem.

Although the "poetic view of life" is still vague (Stevens acknowledged that it "sounds rather mussy" [L, 383]), Stevens provides a significant clue when he narrows its appearance in poetry to subject-matter, leading us to consider what he regarded as appropriate content for poetry. Here, the "Memorandum" may still suffice as text. It appears that the "poetic view of life" that depends on an "abstraction" is related in Stevens' mind to the idea of God, "the major poetic idea in the world" (L, 378). Acknowledging that current skepticism requires some modification of the traditional idea of God, he suggests that "the poetry that created the idea of God will either adapt it to our different intelligence, or create a substitute for it, or make it unnecessary" (L, 378). But in any case, he continues, the idea of God remains the primary "knowledge of poetry" (L, 378) as well as of philosophy and science.

The idea of God appears, then, to be linked to Stevens' concept of the "poetic" or "pure poetry." Let us investigate the precise relationship. Apparently disappointed in his effort to establish the study of the theory of poetry as a scholarly enterprise, Stevens attempted a formulation of his own, writing "A Collect of Philosophy" in 1951 as an example of what he meant by the "poetic view of life." Drawing on notes sent him by distinguished friends and a student's handbook of philosophy, Stevens sets out in this essay to demonstrate that the philosopher and the poet, however different their method and purpose, often "think alike" (OP, 186) by virtue of the "inherently poetic" ideas they treat—that it is conception rather than form, or idea (abstraction) rather than mode of discourse, that unites two such seemingly contrasting pursuits.

No doubt Stevens' reading of philosophy is eccentric (one critic notes that he had "read in almost every modern philosopher and . . . understood almost none"),[2] but to seek an accurate exposition of philosophical ideas in this essay is to miss Stevens' intent. Stevens is solely interested in developing his notion that the imagination of the philosopher, like the imagination of the poet, contains an innate reservoir of poetic ideas (an "enormous a priori" in the mind, he says, is a potential "poetic . . . concept" [OP, 194]), which compels the loftiest abstractions, chief of which is the idea of God. His purpose is not to argue ontologically for God's existence but rather to illustrate how the idea of God, as a purely psychic phenomenon, has inspired poetic ideas objectified in philosophical systems, and so he reads his philosophers in terms of this overriding objective. Thus, according to Stevens, Leibniz "thought like a poet" (OP, 186) because "Monad by monad . . . he achieved God" (OP, 185). Similarly, he reads Schopenhauer's *The World as Will* as a "cosmic poem of the ascent into heaven" (OP, 193). Both, it appears, are examples of "ideas that are inherently poetic" (OP, 183) because they agitate the imagination to conceive of an escape from human limitation—even, indeed, to aspire to godhead: "in a system of monads, we come, in the end, to a man who is not only a man but sea and mountain, too, and to a God who is not only all these: man and sea and mountain but a God as well' (OP, 185). *The World as Will* permits a similar escape: "it is precisely the faults of life that this poem enables us to leave behind" (OP, 193). Therefore, if the poem of the ascent into heaven is "unimpeachably divine," it is but a step removed from God, "the ultimate poetic idea" (OP, 193). Indeed, Stevens clearly identifies poetry with the idea of God unwittingly discovered by the philosopher:

> Essentially what I intend is that it shall be as if the philosophers
> had no knowledge of poetry and suddenly discovered it in their
> search for whatever it is that they are searching for and gave the

name of poetry to that which they discovered. Whether one arrives at the idea of God as a philosopher or as a poet matters greatly. (OP, 190)

And it is precisely because the idea of God—the supreme abstraction—derives from the imagination rather than from man's logical or cognitive capacities, that Stevens urges the imagination's ascendancy over reason:

> Does not philosophy carry us to a point at which there is nothing left except the imagination? If we rely on the imagination (or, say, intuition), to carry us beyond that point, and if the imagination succeeds in carrying us beyond that point (as in respect to the idea of God, if we conceive of the idea of God as this world's capital idea), then the imagination is supreme, because its powers have shown themselves to be greater than the powers of the reason. (OP, 200)

Even the most casual reading of Stevens' prose will reveal how extraordinarily drawn he was to the idea of God, yet the significance of this obsessive theme has never been fully appreciated.[3] An aesthetic interpretation suggests that is it merely a metaphor for the creative possibilities of the imagination and, by synecdoche, of poetry, inasmuch as poetry provides the fulfilling integration—the order, or the search for the ideal—that the idea of God had formerly sustained. Such an interpretation seems compelling, given Stevens' hostility to traditional Christianity and his persistent effort to replace religious orthodoxy with something he called poetry. Nevertheless, the evidence appears to indicate otherwise: according to Stevens, the idea of God is an innate constituent of the imagination variously but compellingly objectified not only by the poet but by the philosopher and scientist as well. Any discourse that reveals the idea of God is, by this definition, "poetry," a word now so broadly conceived as to apply to any number of human pursuits.

Stevens' preoccupation with the idea of God as the supreme "poetic idea" accounts for his multiple definitions for poetry. He distinguishes the "poetic" from the poem *qua* poem because he wishes to separate form (poetry as genre) from content (poetry as poetic concept), as when he proposes that a poem is composed of "several poetries": "Poetry is a poetic conception, however expressed. A poem is poetry expressed in words. But in a poem there is a poetry of words.

Obviously, a poem may consist of several poetries" (OP, 163). The "Adagia" provides another example of this double event in the life of the poem: "Every poem is a poem within a poem: the poem of the idea within the poem of the words" (OP, 174). The "poetic conception" and the "poem of the idea" echo the sense of the texts already explored, but another observation, provided in the essay "The Irrational Element in Poetry," clearly indicates that Stevens regarded the "poetic," "pure poetry," and the idea of God as closely related: "pure poetry is a term that has grown to be descriptive of poetry in which not the true subject but the poetry of the subject is paramount. All mystics approach God through the irrational. Pure poetry is both mystical and irrational" (OP, 222).

Here we move forward considerably. Though Stevens has ostensibly shifted to the poem as artifact, he is, in fact, still insisting on the poem's doubleness, repeating his view that "pure poetry" arises only when the "poetry of the subject" or the idea of God is "paramount." It appears, moreover, that the idea of God is an irrational, noncognitive abstraction arising from largely instinctive and unconscious psychic realms. If this is so, and if we take seriously Stevens' belief that the idea of God is an imaginative abstraction that reveals the imagination's supremacy over reason, then we must assume that the imagination is also a largely unconscious psychic function.

A summary will clarify these relationships. Initially Stevens identified "pure poetry" with the "poetic." The "poetic," as elaborated in the "Memorandum" and elsewhere, provided an added set of equivalencies: the poetic=poetic view of life=abstraction=subject-matter=poetry of the subject=idea of God. These equivalencies were repeated in "A Collect of Philosophy," with the addition of the imagination. If, to borrow a Euclidean axiom, things equal to the same thing are equal to each other, we may conclude that "pure poetry" equals the imagination, the source of the idea of God. Furthermore, it should be stressed that at no point did Stevens identify "pure poetry" with the poem as objective artifact. When he refers to the poem he either conceives it instrumentally ("the purpose of writing poetry is to attain pure poetry"), or as an element subordinate to the "poetic view of life," or as a vehicle embodying a "poetic conception." "Pure poetry," according to Stevens' definitions, is consistently internalized, becoming synonymous with a construct of the imagination and eventually with the imagination itself.

ᘓ ᘓ ᘔ ᘔ

In 1936 Stevens published his longest poem, "Owl's Clover," and later provided an extensive gloss to the poem in a series of letters to Hi Simons. These glosses provide the fullest explanation of what Stevens meant by "pure poetry," and, accordingly, I turn to them before examining the poem.

In his gloss to "The Greenest Continent," the third canto of "Owl's Clover," Stevens has this to say of "pure poetry":

> One way of explaining this poem is to say that it concerns the difficulty of imposing the imagination on those that do not share it. The idea of God is a thing of the imagination. We no longer think that God was, but was imagined. The idea of pure poetry, essential imagination, as the highest objective of the poet, appears to be, at least potentially, as great as the idea of God, and, for that matter, greater, if the idea of God is only one of the things of the imagination. (L, 369)

Of signal importance here is that Stevens is proposing *two levels of the imagination* in a hierarchy of ascending value. The secondary imagination constructs the myriad ideas of God, each of which convinces the believer of its absolute authority and compels him to reject a different view of the divine. However, as Stevens says here and was often to repeat, the idea of God is merely a human (imaginative) construct pointing not to God's objective existence but to a compelling human need to propose an object of veneration. Unfortunately, man has misunderstood this psychic need, converting it into a projected divine image when in reality he alone is the source and object of faith. The proof that the idea of God is merely the "idea of man," Stevens elsewhere says, lies in the fact that an objectified God always assumes an anthropomorphic form: "the gods of Greece are always Greeks and . . . all gods are created in the images of their creators" (OP, 211). But in truth the gods are only projections of man's inner life, testifying to "the fundamental glory of men and women, who being in need of it create it, elevate it, without too much searching of its identity" (OP, 208).

What this perpetual deification points to is not the form itself but the psychic structure that produced it. Man can entertain the idea of God because the image of divinity arises out of inherent qualities of the human mind for which no corresponding objective analogue need be postulated. The "essential imagination"—"pure poetry"—is thus the fountainhead of deity from which all images of deity—shadows of itself—spring.

In the second section of the gloss, Stevens further clarifies the distinction between the "idea of God" and "pure poetry." Since the idea of God, he writes, "partakes of consciousness," it unavoidably embodies extraneous and adventitious elements introduced by self-awareness, and so assumes multiple forms reflecting the peculiarities of race and nation. In contrast, the "essential imagination" is that deeper, irrational God the Father common to all: "This [idea of pure poetry] would be universally true if the imagination was the simple thing that it is commonly regarded as being. However, the imagination partakes of consciousness, and as the consciousness of West (Europe) differs from the consciousness of South (Africa), etc., so the imagination of West differs from that of South, and so the idea of God and the idea of pure poetry, etc. differ" (L, 369).

This distinction between two levels of the imagination accounts for Stevens' paradoxical view of divinity, excoriated on the one hand as merely a "postulate of the ego" (OP, 171) and aggrandized on the other as the god within: "God is in me or else is not at all (does not exist)" (OP, 172). The first proposition rejects the spurious objectified phantasies of the secondary imagination in favor of the inner "essential imagination"—man himself. The process by which Stevens arrived at this conclusion is given quasi-syllogistic form in the "Adagia": "Proposita: 1. God and the imagination are one. 2. The thing imagined is the imaginer. The second equals the thing imagined and the imaginer are one. Hence, I suppose, the imaginer is God" (OP, 178).

Stevens' reluctance to identify "pure poetry" with poetry as poem is now understandable. "Pure poetry," or the "essential imagination," cannot be poetry as object but must be poetry as subject: man himself is "pure poetry" because his unconscious "essential imagination" that produces the "idea of God" is itself the prototype of all the gods. The need is thus to divert man from worshipping the "fictions" created by his imagination to worshipping the imagination itself, conceived as an archetypal principle of deity. But, as Stevens admits, this has "its difficulties." Logically, he writes, he "ought to believe in essential imagination" divested of all symbolic representations (logically, of course, the unconscious is a *Ding-an-Sich* that cannot be objectified), but since "it is easier to believe in a thing created by the imagination" (L, 370), he will offer a substitute "fiction" to represent the "essential imagination." This substitute "fiction," Stevens writes, is the mythological Ananke, mankind's "common god" introduced at the end of the third canto of "Owl's Clover":

> Yet, the poem concludes with what is its point, that, if ideas of God are in conflict, the idea of pure poetry: imagination, extended beyond local consciousness, may be an idea to be held in common by South, West, North and East. It would be a beginning, since the heaven in Europe is empty, to recognize Ananke, who, now more than ever, is the world's "starless crown." (L, 370)

In the final gloss to the "The Greenest Continent," Stevens writes that Ananke is both created by and a symbol of the "essential imagination," that he is a substitute for the God that has been abjured, belief being necessary, and that he is a form of the fiction with which Stevens was grappling at the time (1940) the gloss was written (L, 370).[4]

It is my view that Ananke, Stevens' explicit symbol for the primary "essential imagination" (and for "pure poetry"), represents the single, most important element of Stevens' thought. This is not to say that this mythic figure receives extensive and explicit attention in the poetry. Indeed, apart from "Owl's Clover," Ananke appears in his specific form only twice, first in a cryptic parable in "Like Decorations in a Nigger Cemetery," included in the 1935 *Ideas of Order*, and later in an excised stanza intended for "Examination of the Hero in a Time of War," a poem that appeared in the 1942 *Parts of a World*. Nevertheless, Ananke casts his shadow over all of Stevens' creative life.

The textual examples provided were written over a period of some sixteen years, yet they exhibit a remarkable uniformity in language and conception. Stevens' insistence on more than one kind of poetry, his repeated use of "poetic conception," "poetic ideas," "poetic view of life," his recurring attraction to the idea of God, all serve to make these observations timeless, so that violating his chronology does not distort his meaning. Consequently, when an investigation of "pure poetry" leads ultimately to Ananke, clearly identified as "pure poetry" and said to be "the highest objective of the poet," we may safely conclude that Ananke is the presiding assumption of Stevens' later effort to define this important concept.

There is further reason to insist on Ananke's importance. It is apparent that Stevens' use of the word "poetry" is decidedly various, bearing in its ultimate sense—"pure poetry"—only a tangential relationship to poetry as artifact. In this connection, Stevens' identification of "pure poetry" with Ananke casts considerable doubt on many of the assumptions that have governed the criticism of Stevens' poetry. I have noted that Stevens' proposition that "the theory / Of poetry is the theory of life" is closely linked to his concept of "pure poetry." If, indeed, this belief is a central and informing doctrine in the poetry, it would appear that Stevens' poems are primarily concerned with Ananke and only peripherally concerned with aesthetics (aesthetics is a minor concern, as I shall shortly note). Furthermore, without explicitly acknowledging that Ananke is the fiction with which he is currently preoccupied, Stevens nevertheless implies in his gloss that Ananke is a form of the fiction. The consequences of this admission are again significant, inasmuch as Stevens' "supreme fiction" is another poetic theme that spans a considerable portion of his poetic career. Finally, there is good reason to believe, given Stevens' lexical arbitrariness, that when he universalizes poetry by suggesting that it is to supplant religion ("Poetry / Exceeding music must take the place / Of empty heaven and its hymns" [CP, 167]), or when he particularizes it as his poetic subject ("Poetry is the subject of the poem" [CP, 176]), he is not talking about an art form at all but is referring to the deification of man's unconscious life—the "ultimate poem"—which is to supplant the obsolete idea of God. This may be illustrated more precisely.

In "Sombre Figuration," the final canto of "Owl's Clover," Stevens introduces an Ananke surrogate, a shadowy "subman" who is clearly a symbol of the subterranean collective unconscious said to be eternal and absolute:

> There is a man whom rhapsodies of change,
> Of which he is the cause, have never changed
> And never will, a subman under all
> The rest, to whom in the end the rest return,
> The man below the man below the man,
> Steeped in night's opium, evading day.
>
> (OP, 66)

Now, if Ananke represents the "essential imagination" subsuming the secondary imagination that "partakes of consciousness," then plainly he and the subman are identical forces intended to represent the archaic contents of man's racial memory. This is what Stevens says of his "subman" in the gloss to "Sombre Figuration":

> The sub-conscious is assumed to be our beginning and end (I). It follows that it is the beginning and end of the conscious. Thus, the conscious is a lesser thing than the sub-conscious. The conscious is, therefore, inadequate. In another note I said that the imagination partakes of the conscious. Here it is treated as an activity of the sub-conscious: the imagination is the subconscious. (L, 373)

The importance of this gloss is not merely that Stevens identifies his Ananke-subman with the collective unconscious (subconscious) but that he invests him with eschatological significance. If the subconscious is that fundamental psychic stratum that inspires the "lesser" secondary imagination, then it and not its shadow is the master of man's psychic life, destined eventually to reassert its hegemony. In short, Ananke is the goal of human aspiration: "our beginning and end." When Stevens, therefore, writes that the "purpose of writing poetry is to attain pure poery," we can only assume that Ananke and not the poem is the *terminus ad quem* of the poetic act. Roy Harvey Pearce has observed of Stevens' late poems that "poetry, in being poetry, manifests the existence of a poetry beyond poetry."[5] Precisely. If man's Ananke-subconscious is "pure poetry," then it is towards Ananke as a principle of being that all human objectifications (projections of Ananke) actively strive and yearn. It is not merely that Ananke inspires all human endeavor but that all human endeavor actively strains to realize Ananke as a principle of life. We write poetry because we are compelled to express our desire to *be* Ananke, an assumption that led Stevens to the conclusion that a theory of poetry that would account for Ananke's preeminence would also be a "theory of life."

"Owl's Clover" is a visionary poem, as William Van O'Connor has correctly noted.[6] The word *future* appears twelve times, and where explicit statement will not do, Stevens resorts to the future-like infinitive "to be" or the predictive modal auxiliary "would be" to prefigure a vision that seems imminent but as yet inaccessible.[7] Moreover, the poem is suffused with the rhetoric of prophetic exaltation: a mysterious portent appears in the sky adumbrating "the form / Of a generation that does not know itself" (OP, 68); "eternal vistas" appear on the horizon; "celestial paramours" perform ritualistic dances of religious obeisance. Indeed, there is a persistent oracular quality about the poem that leads one to suspect that it is intended as a testament of faith.

Inspired by a Marxist critic's charge that *Ideas of Order* had failed to concern itself with the grave social and economic issues of the depression, "Owl's Clover" is Stevens' testimony that he was indeed concerned but that his concern and his solution were of an altogether different order.[8] Consequently, he refused to acknowledge his critic's assumptions that man's malaise stemmed from social and economic dislocations that the socially committed poet was morally bound to note and treat, and proposed instead that man's difficulties were to be traced to a far more archetypal event for which contemporary problems were but instances. That event, in Stevens' mind, was closely related to the origin and function of art; hence, each of the five cantos hovers around a ring of white marble horses, a central symbol sometimes intended as a symbol for art.

Ananke, however, is Stevens' principal subject; this important personification of "pure poetry" provides the key to the whole of "Owl's Clover." Most readers, following Ananke's mythological original, have seen him as an external god, "an utterly objective, transcendental force."[9] Precedent exists of course for such an interpretation. The inflexible order Ananke (a female divinity) represents in Parmenides and Plato suggests a transcendent, immutable world of Being distinct from the sensible and transitory world of human experience. However, W. K. C. Guthrie reminds us that the early natural philosophers often associated the principle of necessity with the concept of *physis*: "*Physis* in the eyes of these men is a natural necessity inherent in each separate thing or substance, not a law of interaction between them. With each thing moving as its own *physis* dictates, the clashes between them will be fortuitous though caused by necessity."[10]

In this sense, Ananke is an internal principle of necessity, compelling the organism to assert its inexorable nature. That Stevens considers him equivalent to the "essential imagination" similarly confirms him as a peerless interior god. Mythological precedent, then, gives warrant for Ananke's two-fold domain: he is at once an invincible outer deity controlling the destiny of the cosmos, and an equally "fateful" (Stevens' instructive epithet) inner force directing the affairs of men.[11]

Clearly, Stevens intends his Ananke to symbolize a first principle subject to no other. Predictably, too, he appears at the end of a canto whose focus is Africa. As the "Sultan of African sultans," Ananke represents the primitive and savage energy of man's instinctive life, revealed in the half-brute "jaguar-men" and "lion-men" who populate the primeval jungles of "The Greenest Continent." Predictably, too, the canto focuses on the idea of God, beginning with a rhetorical question on the nature of divine hegemony eventually answered in the minatory and aggressive declaratives signalling Ananke's appearance:

> Large-leaved and many-footed shadowing,
> What god rules over Africa, what shape,
> What avuncular cloud-man beamier than spears?
>
> (OP, 52)

> Fatal Ananke is the common god.
>
> (OP, 59)

> Sultan of African sultans, starless crown.
>
> (OP, 60)

Ananke certainly satisfies all the requirements of divinity: he is almighty, omniscient and eternal, totally without human frailty, and invulnerable to human desire. Much like the sovereign God of Stevens' Protestant forebears, Ananke sits in "ether flamed" (OP, 59), an "unmerciful pontifex" (OP, 60) whose "ubiquitous will" (OP, 59) directs human destiny. This universal god of Africa subsumes the myriad transitory gods worshipped in his name:

> He is that obdurate ruler who ordains
> For races, not for men, powerful beyond
> A grace to nature, a changeless element.
>
> (OP, 59)

Evidently Stevens believed in an original and powerful substratum of the human psyche that he thought once enjoyed total hegemony. The "essential imagination" represents not only the universal or archetypal imagination, as some commentators have noted, but a unified condition of life antedating the development of consciousness. Ananke is the vestigial memory of that former life, arising when human consciousness severed man's organic ties. As a result, man assuaged his loneliness and fear by inventing compensatory gods, but in reality these gods are merely Ananke's voice in another guise expressing man's sense of loss. Consequently, Stevens hammers at epithets of estrangement:

> He dwells below, the man below, in less
> Than body and in less than mind, ogre,
> Inhabitant, in less than shape, of shapes
> That are dissembled in vague memory
> Yet still retain resemblances, remain
> Remembrances, a place of a field of lights . . .
>
> (OP, 67)

Ananke is the force that agitates the imagination to retrieve its lost paradise. A portent of the future introduced in the final canto illustrates Stevens' regressive hopes. Said to be inspired by the "subman" ("An image of his making" [OP, 69]), the portent is a Janus image, embodying both past and future, memory and time to come:

> The portent may itself be memory,
> And memory may itself be time to come
> . . . .
> And memory's lord is the lord of prophecy . . .
>
> (OP, 70)

Stevens' gloss to this passage further emphasizes his conviction that mankind's future is closely tied to the contents of the collective unconscious: "The future must bear within it every past, not least the pasts that have become submerged in the sub-conscious, things in the experience of races" (L, 373).

From the belief that man's unconscious prods him to recapture a past condition of life, it is but a step to the further belief that man's imaginative constructions—his art and myth—objectify such yearnings. Evidently Stevens felt that mankind's expressive need and religious sentiment (the two are really one) arose only after the birth of consciousness, impelled by a consequent sense of isolation and solitariness. However, the imaginative constructions arising from these needs are derivative, originating in the reduced but germinal seeds of memory incubating in the subconscious. Thus art and myth have a single source of inspiration—vestigial memory, or Ananke:

> He thinks of the noble lives
> Of the gods and, for him, a thousand litanies
> Are like the perpetual verses in a poet's mind.
>
> (OP, 59)

Therefore, the ubiquitous statue of "Owl's Clover" is said to be "A ring of horses rising from memory" (OP, 57) and is directly attributed to Ananke's importunacy: "He, only, caused the statue to be made / And he shall fix the place where it will stand" (OP, 60).

Since Ananke is a dynamic symbol important for the change he presages and initiates, the art that incarnates his image is equally an instrument of change. Hence, the statue of "Owl's Clover" in some instances represents man's *redemptive* imagination—the role Stevens assigned to the constructs of the secondary imagination. Art functions in this manner because it is animated by an idea of God (actually the idea of man) that agitates and revives a corresponding idea in the mind of its audience. Consequently, each imaginative construct has extraordinary significance, for behind its plastic or verbal facade lies the compelling Ananke-musician whose music "mimics" man's inner life:

> He turns us into scholars, studying
> The masks of music. We perceive each mask
> To be the musician's own and, thence, become
> An audience to mimics glistening
> With meanings, doubled by the closest sound,
> Mimics that play on instruments discerned
> In the beat of the blood.
>
> (OP, 67)

Consequently, art has a job to do. It is functional rather than decorative, instructive rather than merely entertaining, the initially necessary but ultimately dispensable means of reawakening the "child asleep in its own life" (OP, 104). Its instrumental function is clearly defined in the body of the poem.

"Owl's Clover" opens with a description of a ring of white, winged, marble horses arrested in mid-flight. Forelegs taut, bodies "contorted," poised for the "vivid plunge," the horses are charged with an extraordinary vigor on the point of exploding into motion. The image is an appropriate one, for Stevens means the statue to represent man's Ananke temporarily imprisoned in the lifeless artifact. Its dynamism, however, expresses the latent power of man's unconscious straining for the leap that is to assure Ananke's hegemony. Immediately after this description, Stevens introduces an Old Woman, a strange and haggard figure who represents man's current estrangement from his Ananke and his consequent sense of desolation. She is, however, searching for an alternative, which finds its focus in the "atmosphere" generated by the statue, but it is only after the statue's strange and sudden collapse that she experiences it as an exact duplication of her own agitations: "A change so felt, a fear in her so known, / Now felt, now known as this" (OP, 45).

Stevens prepares us for the Old Woman's transformation through the incremental repetition of "black" and the destruction of the statue, both of which can be understood only in the context of his apotheosis of the collective unconscious. Stevens consistently uses black and its temporal analogue night to characterize his Ananke-subman-portent: the "dark-skinned" Ananke-serpent presides over Stevens' restored paradise, "the black sublime" (OP, 55); the "subman" is "Steeped in night's opium" (OP, 66); the form his portent takes "bears all darkness in its bulk" (OP, 68). The final gloss to "Sombre Figuration" explicitly identifies night with the subconscious: "as the portent sank in the night of the sub-conscious, the night in which the trees were full of farewells became the perennial night of the sub-conscious" (L, 375). Therefore, when Stevens writes that the Old Woman's "musty mind / Lay black and full of black misshapen" (OP, 44) and that her alteration in the wake of the statue's collapse takes the form of unity with night, he intends to affirm the latent power of the subconscious eventually asserting its supremacy.

The collapse of the statue also follows logically from Stevens' psychological assumptions. Stevens insists that the "atmosphere" of the statue corresponds to the "atmosphere" of the Old Woman's "musty mind" because he wishes to stress the abstraction embedded in the statue. He assumes that Ananke is the animating principle of art, but art is only incidental to Ananke. Indeed, art is only a kind of allegory—the "pinchings of an idea" (CP, 276)—representing once removed the splendors of man's original divinity. True, its function is initially necessary; as paradigm it incarnates, however faintly, man's original perfection; as catalyst, it impels the psychological transformation necessary for retrieval. Once it initiates the reconciliation of man to his Ananke, however, it loses its efficacy and rationale, collapsing to "marble hulk."

Thus, the collapse of the statue in the fourth section of the first canto merely presages its unique resurrection in the fifth section, for its destruction marks the annihilation of art and the beginning of human renewal. Characteristically turning to the future, Stevens predicts a state "beyond imagined trees" (OP, 45) in which "the horses would rise again" (OP, 46), this time not as a symbol of incipient and unconsummated power arrested in the static artifact, but as living beings finally capable of flight. The horses "Would flash in air" (OP, 46), their hoofs would grind, their muscular bodies strain, until all would explode into motion as "The light wings lifted through the crystal space / Of night" (OP, 46). No longer imprisoned in the cold and inanimate marbles of man's imaginative surrogates, the horses, vivid examples of Stevens' belief that "the theory / Of poetry is the theory of life," are now symbols of liberated mankind. The splendid powers of Ananke formerly projected onto the artifact have been redeemed; art has yielded to experience; and man himself is now the "ultimate poem."

The second canto, "Mr. Burnshaw and the Statue," further develops Stevens' regressive cosmology. This time the statue is the symbol of a moribund civilization, part of an "immense detritus" (OP, 49) to be swept aside in favor of "a hopeful waste to come" (OP, 49). But first its former powers must be exorcised; once a symbol of the viable artistic artifact, the statue is now an incubus discouraging the full maturation of man's inner divine life. Thus Stevens' mordant tone, the acrimony and contempt with which he speaks of art. The statue is, he writes, a paltry thing concocted by an artist-cook "that never rode the back / Of his angel through the skies" (OP, 46). Con-

tinuing, he flays the statue as the product of insignificant men—
"moonlit muckers" (OP, 46) who fashioned "crepuscular images" (OP,
46) as surrogates for "a life they never lived" (OP, 46). The horses
"should go clattering" (OP, 47), infinitely nobler in life than as the
frozen mementoes of "the sculptor's foppishness" (OP, 47). Indeed,
the statue is the product of man's "dank imagination" (OP, 47), as
"idea" considerably inferior to the original instinctive life it represents:

> much below
> Our crusted outlines hot and huge with fact,
> Ugly as an idea, not beautiful
> As sequels without thought.
>
> (OP, 47)

The destruction of the statue is completed in a dance of exorcism
performed by a group of "celestial paramours" whose dual function is
to destroy the old order and usher in the new. Hence, they chant
"sibilant requiems" (OP, 47) while performing a "ballet infantine"
(OP, 47), meanwhile turning their backs on the statue now characterized as an "effigy" (OP, 47). Foretelling a new day "Astral and
Shelleyan" (OP, 47), the dancers slowly circle the statue, symbolically
enacting the transference of art into life; and as they circle, the exchange takes place: "the statue falls, / The heads are severed, topple,
tumble, tip" (OP, 51), and men become "marble men" (OP, 52), ap-
pointing to themselves the power of their artifacts. The epitaph in-
scribed on the statue once and for all removes art from the realm of
human experience:

> The stones
> That will replace it shall be carved, *"The Mass
> Appoints These Marbles Of Itself To Be
> Itself."* No more than that, no subterfuge,
> No memorable muffing, bare and blunt.
>
> (OP, 48; Stevens' emphasis)

Between exorcism and annunciation Stevens predicts a modern
Gomorrah called "the end of the world" (OP, 49). It appears that not
only must man's art be destroyed to pave the way for Stevens' "new
reality," but so too must all the earmarks of his present culture. Thus,
the world is reduced to a "trash can" (OP, 49); buzzards feed on the
carrion of the rich and poor alike; both sculptor and statue lie decapi-
tated among the debris.

Having treated man in his fallen state (the metaphor of the Fall is of course naturalistically rather than Christologically defined) and his consequent redemptive struggle given form and focus in the statue, Stevens turns in his third and central poetic sequence, "The Greenest Continent," to Africa, the symbol for mankind's original paradise. Here man is ruled by the natural god of the instinctive self, offered in the image of a serpent whose province is "death":[12]

> That was never the heaven of Africa, which had
> No heaven, had death without a heaven, death
> In a heaven of death. Beneath the heavy foils,
> Beneath the spangling greens, fear might placate
> And the serpent might become a god, quick-eyed,
> Rising from indolent coils.
>
> (OP, 54)

This "heaven of death" deifies no abstract, external god: the "black sublime" of Africa is twice invaded in the course of the canto, once by the missionary "angels" of Europe who would impose their idea of God as mythology, once by the statue of Europe, which would impose its idea of God as aesthetic object. Neither survives. The missionaries return to "their tabernacles" (OP, 55), the statue to the "northern sky" (OP, 54). Twice returning to the subject of art, Stevens asks whether the statue could survive in primitive Africa, only to confirm the hostility of the earlier cantos. If it were indeed possible for the statue to arise in Africa, it would be quickly destroyed by man's serpent-Ananke, who has no need of it. Only where human life is characterized by a cultivated consciousness does it become necessary to project the idea of God in an artifact:

> If the statue rose,
> If once the statue were to rise, if it stood,
> Thinly, among the elephantine palms,
> Sleekly the serpent would draw himself across.
> The horses are part of a northern sky
> Too starkly pallid for the jaguar's light . . .
>
> (OP, 54)

"A Duck for Dinner," the fourth and most explicitly social canto, addresses itself to the twin themes of change and the future, in both of which the artist and his artifact have a significant and central function. Here, however, Stevens' revolutionary ardor is tempered, his mood evolutionary rather than apocalyptic. Confident that in contrast to socialist ideology—a "Profound/Abortion" (OP, 62)—the future promised by Ananke had universal validity, Stevens constructs his version of "everyman . . . rapt round / By dense unreason" (OP, 62) whom he sees rising "inch/By inch, Sunday by Sunday, many men" (OP, 60). His masses act in concert, obedient to their Ananke who guarantees their psychic unity and identity of purpose:

> Is each man thinking his separate thoughts or, for once,
> Are all men thinking together as one, thinking
> Each other's thoughts, thinking a single thought,
> Disclosed in everything, transcended, poised
> For the syllable, poised for the touch?
>
> (OP, 62)

While Stevens believes in universal change, he is yet doubtful about the capacity of "this mob" (OP, 63) to effect change without the dynamic leadership of an authoritative figure—a "super-animal" who is to "dictate our fates." The man most likely to fulfill this function, it appears, is the orator-poet, upon whom the "future depends":

> What man of folk-lore shall rebuild the world,
> What lesser man shall measure sun and moon,
> What super-animal dictate our fates?
> . . . .
> It may be the future depends on an orator . . .
>
> (OP, 63)

The language used here is instructive. Ananke, it will be recalled, wields absolute power: he is "fatal" and "fateful," our death and destiny. The "super-animal," then, cannot be other than Ananke in the guise of his most sensitive agent, the orator-poet. Hence, Stevens apotheosizes the poet in much the same hyperbolic rhetoric reserved for Ananke. Embodying sexual energy, tribal authority, and *Erde* mystique, the poet is a vatic figure whose "clairvoyant eye" discerns the shape of things to come:

> Don Juan turned furious divinity,
> Ethereal compounder, pater patriae,
> Great mud-ancestor, oozer and Abraham,
> Progenitor wearing the diamond crown of crowns,
> He from whose beard the future springs, elect.
>
> (OP, 64)

Since the poet's special task is to erase the legacy of estrangement by uniting the man to "the man below," he is indeed a figure of enormous prestige, like Ananke worthy of being crowned with the royal diadem. Not surprisingly, Stevens addresses him as "Great mud-ancestor, oozer and Abraham," deliberately regressive images recalling the Ananke-god who arose when man became a "pale alien of the mud." For the artist, Ananke's most sensitive instrument, provides the articulated link between man and his original paradise.

The statue serves a similar instrumental function. More than an artifact designed to give aesthetic pleasure, it rather objectifies the aspirations of man's instinctive life, focusing in an explicit image of the idea of God what had previously rested on the threshold of consciousness. To its observers, it reflects:

> The metropolitan of mind, they feel
> The central of the composition, in which
> They live. They see and feel themselves, seeing
> And feeling the world in which they live.
>
> (OP, 64)

Predictably, the statue adumbrates the future appearance of "another race, / Above our race, yet of ourselves transformed" (OP, 64). Art, in short, is Stevens' intermediate version of the Incarnation. As man's inner divine life objectified, its effect is no less than human purification; it spiritualizes the race.

"Sombre Figuration," the final canto, promises to restore the loss of original innocence by ensuring the hegemony of "the man below." Beginning with a paean of praise to the Ananke-subman's powers, Stevens next turns to the impending apocalypse his advent heralds. The shape of this future looms in the heavens as a "sprawling portent" revealing "the form / Of a generation that does not know itself" (OP, 68). Thrice insisting on the portent's impalpability to suggest it as the spiritual reality diffused in man and nature, Stevens nevertheless resorts to word picture to paint the intangible subman. What emerges is a gigantic "bulk" in Atlas-like support of the horizon, casting its prodigious shadow over the world's inhabitants, breathing upon them an "immense intent" (OP, 68).

Predictably, the final lines of the poem foresee a future distinguished by the absence of the secondary imagination, a firm and logical conclusion given the assumptions Stevens brings to the nature of man. Insisting that "imagination has an end" (OP, 71), Stevens envisions the "new reality" promised by the reconciliation between man and his Ananke. It is a life of sheer presentness and sensation. Having shed the temporal understanding by which consciousness mediates and orders experience, man is now relieved of history, free to enjoy the "gaudium of being," eternal and timeless:

> To flourish the great cloak we wear
> At night, to turn away from the abominable
> Farewells and, in the darkness, to feel again
> The reconciliation, the rapture of a time
> Without imagination, without past
> And without future, a present time, is that
> The passion, indifferent to the poet's hum,
> That we conceal?

(OP, 71)

Life is purposeless, desultory. Whatever gesture man is capable of is merely a "gesture's whim" (OP, 71) without forethought or intent. Logically, neither the poet nor the statue intrude to disturb this regained paradisal home, for the poet is banished and the statue, having fulfilled its promise, "is not a thing imagined, a stone / That changed in sleep" (OP, 71).[13] Indeed, man no longer needs such supports, having supplanted them with himself, gay "Jocundus," acting out his comic inheritance in what Stevens was later to call an "unspotted imbecile revery" (CP, 172). The promise fulfilled, Ananke restored to his supreme and undisputed status, man returns to the mindlessness of instinctive life, "Night and the imagination being one" (OP, 71).

☾ Chapter 2 ☽

The Transcendental Man

The self of the hero, the solar single,
Man-sun, man-moon, man-earth, man-ocean . . .

Though given to rhetorical excess, "Owl's Clover" outlines a process of spiritual change that Stevens recorded with singleness of purpose, from *Harmonium* to "The Rock." Hence, it is the central poem in Stevens' work, the poet's fullest testament of faith. Critical opinion largely disclaims this view. According to Merle Brown, the poem is "the one major betrayal of his [Stevens'] poetic genius."[1] Joseph Riddel and Louis Martz take the more charitable view that the poem is a transitional piece marking an unfortunate excursion into the ideological arena from which Stevens was to escape both stylistically and conceptually in his following poem, "The Man with the Blue Guitar."[2] That Stevens' poetic idiom changed cannot be gainsaid, but that his subject changed from the "mystique of a universal self" to "the poet singular as earthly leader"[3] is questionable. In the view of this study, "Owl's Clover" not only provides the theoretical justification for the "idea of man" that Stevens was to elaborate in "The Man with the Blue Guitar" and subsequent poems, but also candidly reveals why Stevens gave the imagination such central significance in his work.

The shift in poetic strategy, if not in poetic intention, emerges in the thirties with the appearance of the hero, a figure central to Stevens' thought, not only because he is repeatedly invoked, but because identifying tags such as "abstract man," "central man," and "major man" suggest him as a paradigmatic form—a distillation of the "idea of man" which Stevens sought as substitute for the myth of God. Contrary to the general view that Stevens' hero figure is part of a humanist aesthetic that proposes "our own ideal self, whose definition is its ability to create,"[4] this study suggests that Stevens' hero is the spiritual heir of the Ananke-subman of "Owl's Clover," albeit humanized and stripped of mythological guise.[5] So considered, he remains, to be sure, an image of the imagination, but like the ubiquitous Ananke, humanity's "common god," he represents the "essential

33

imagination," Stevens' instructive effort to distinguish the soteriological imagination from its merely natural, and secondary, counterpart.

☾ ☾ ☾ ☾

We may follow the kinship of Ananke and the hero in several of Stevens' hero poems. The most explicit and obvious link appears in an excised stanza of "Examination of the Hero in a Time of War," a poem of the forties which probes the image of the hero, suggesting him as an alternative form of belief. Though the stanza is brief and the reference oblique, Ananke is invoked as an inexorable principle—"the fatal, / The bold, obedience to Ananke" (OP, 83)—whose appearance concludes a psychic event (the men of the passage "look inwardly" [OP, 83]) marked by "death" and "destruction," allusions which recall the apocalyptic "end of the world" (OP, 49) prophesied in "Mr. Burnshaw and the Statue" (retitled "The Statue at the World's End" in Stevens' revision).[6]

Though Ananke is never again named in connection with the hero, his presence abides in the recurrence of his motifs—those images and themes that define his being in "Owl's Clover." We may discern his features, for example, in "Chocorua to Its Neighbor," a poem included in the 1947 *Transport to Summer.* Generally viewed as Stevens' effort to define the contours of "major man," "fictive man," and the "common man"—rubrics for the figure of the hero—the poem charts a nocturnal colloquy between a "human mountain" (CP, 300) and its "prodigious shadow" (CP, 297), a dyad that recalls the Ananke-subman duo, similarly shrouded in blackness and night. Like the subman, too, the shadow is announced as a "self of selves" (CP, 297) to suggest, it would appear, an underlying psychic stratum somehow purer and finer than the common self in which it lies embedded. Hence, he is at once a creature of darkness and a creature of light; for like the subman, who comes from a "field of lights" (OP, 67), and Ananke, who sits in "ether flamed" (OP, 59), the shadow, too, arises as "fire from an underworld," bathed in radiance and granted the diaphanous quality of spirit:

He was as tall as a tree in the middle of
The night. The substance of his body seemed
Both substance and non-substance, luminous flesh
Or shapely fire: fire from an underworld,
Of less degree than flame and lesser shine.

(CP, 297)

Added parallels suggest themselves: like Ananke, a "fateful" (OP, 59) god; a "lord of prophecy" (OP, 70); a principle of life, the shadow, too, is urged as a "head of fate" (CP, 299); a "fortelleze" (CP, 301) of "a day as yet unseen" (CP, 297); and a "largeness lived and not conceived" (CP, 301). As ubiquitous and eternal as his Ananke counterpart (the shadow is "Without existence, existing everywhere" [CP, 298]), this spirit is joined to images of snow, ice, glass, gold, and silver to emerge as a frozen, immobile, petrified, metallic being—a "new spirit" (CP, 299) who, as befits his intangible presence, is "Hard to perceive and harder still to touch" (CP, 301).

He is, however, made in the image of man—"singular" (CP, 302), to be sure, but nevertheless a distillation of the "common self" (CP, 301). This "common self," moreover, is not entirely autonomous; for deeper relation appears in the form of a "central mind" (CP, 298) that, though posed as a separate entity, is nevertheless indistinguishable from the shadow-soul itself: "a voice / That is my own voice speaking in my ear" (CP, 298). Thus, the shadow, or the spirit residing in the soul, is linked to a corresponding spiritual force; and since, in the portion of the colloquy spoken by the "human mountain" (CP, 300), the shadow is addressed as "bare brother, megalfrere" (CP, 300), we may reasonably conclude that the mountain is the "central mind" that finds its corresponding echo in the soul. Of special interest is the term "megalfrere," for it not only suggests a filial bond between the mountain and its shadow-counterpart, but aggrandizes them both as objects of extraordinary magnitude and power.

Now the concept of "central" and "centre" is important to Stevens, cropping up in both poetry and prose in ways that suggest two meanings. Used with epithetic force in phrases like "central man" (CP, 250); "central mind" (CP, 298); "central heart and mind of minds" (CP, 254), it appears to propose an animate entity, a thing akin to the human. When used as the "centre," however, it conveys the sense of place and location. In this sense, it is variously offered as an antecedent condition of human life—"There was a muddy centre before we breathed" (CP, 383); a place that has been restored—the "return to the subtle centre" (CP, 258); and as the core or "centre of reality" (CP, 205), offered in one poem as the color white whose place in the "centre" of "all circles" imagistically restates and defines something called a "floridest reality" (CP, 366). Here, of course, the image is spiritually resonant, for to join circle, centre, and white—symbols of perfection and purity traditionally associated with the wholeness of divine manifestation—to a "floridest reality" which, by the superlative, manages to suggest a reality that transcends the commonplace, suggests that the poet is offering the "centre" and, indeed, "reality" as spiritual entities.

In this connection, it is well to note that Stevens sometimes uses "central" to qualify the earth, suggesting through this conjunction the spirit of Ananke, similarly named in "Owl's Clover," albeit through his surrogate, the statue. In "Sombre Figuration," for example, the statue (the matrix of regeneration)—interchangeable at this point with the portent-Ananke—is said to ascend ("thudding up" [OP, 70]) from "central earth" (OP, 70) in a form no longer "flesh / In marble" but as something transformed into spirit—"that which is not seen and cannot be" (OP, 70). Similarly, the "celestial paramours," who transform the statue into a living thing and are themselves transformed into the image they have created, are deemed "No longer of air but of the breathing earth" (OP, 52), an image which animates the earth and infuses it with life.

It is well to ponder these images. Ananke, it will be recalled, is not only the initiating spirit of the statue ("He, only, caused the statue to be made" [OP, 60]), but he is also the being into which the statue is transformed, its "pure poetry," in Stevens' phrase. Furthermore, those currently estranged from his being are deemed "pale aliens of the mud," a chthonic image that equally characterizes his emissary, the sculptor-poet—a "Great mud-ancestor" (OP, 64) whose "muddy hand" (OP, 43) shapes forms that evoke "another race, / Above our race, yet of ourselves transformed" (OP, 64). By this token, Ananke, it would seem is a god of the earth—a chthonian deity; and since the statue issues from him and is transformed into his being, its ascension from the "central earth" and its transformation into a "breathing earth" are, in the equivalencies Stevens suggests, equal to its ascension from and transformation into Ananke, its chthonic origin or the earth itself endowed with the property of life and evidently indistinguishable from man himself.

Let us move the argument one step further. The earth, it is commonly granted, is Stevens' abiding concern—his "inamorata"—variously celebrated in the poetry and, at times, identified as "reality," a term most readers have interpreted as roughly equivalent to an objective reality existing outside the self and qualitatively different from the human mind. In view of Ananke's significance, however, it would appear that "reality," in at least one of its senses, means something other than common matter; for if Ananke is the "central earth," it would appear that mankind's "common god" is equally a symbol of reality; indeed, given Stevens' habit of posing equivalencies, if Ananke is the "central earth," he would also appear to be the "centre of reality," an equivalent phrase.

We must also recall, if we are to follow Ananke's importance in the canon, that Stevens offers this chthonic force as the "essential imagination," in this fashion suggesting him as a mental phenomenon. Equally important, he is also a thing which issues from the imagination, as the statue transformed into the life of spirit suggests, so that, in effect, the thing fashioned by the mind becomes in its final form a thing "beyond the mind" or "pure poetry." Above all, as a spiritual force that Stevens designates as *both* the "essential imagination" and the "central earth," he corresponds to the chthonic god within (imagination) and the chthonic god without (reality); or, as Stevens phrases the equation in "The Noble Rider and the Sound of Words," imagination and reality are "equal and inseparable" (NA, 24).

In his guise as the "central earth" of "Owl's Clover" and as the man-mountain of "Chocorua to Its Neighbor," the telluric Ananke is granted the lineaments of the natural world. Hence, when Stevens joins "central" to "man," as he does for the first time in "Asides on the Oboe," the figure offered as a "final belief" (CP, 250) is redefined as a "human globe" (CP, 250), an image that recalls Stevens' idiosyncratic reading of Leibniz' monad, described in "A Collect of Philosophy" as "a man who is not only a man but sea and mountain, too, and . . . a God who is not only all these: man and sea and mountain but a God as well" (OP, 185). It would thus appear that the "central man" of "Asides on the Oboe" bears a family resemblance to the "central earth" of "Owl's Clover"; for if, indeed, he is a "human globe," he encompasses in his very being the earth itself, so that, in effect, "central earth" and "central man" may be reasonably viewed as equivalent—even identical—images. Indeed, so aggrandized, the "central

man" surfaces as the macroanthropos of "Examination of the Hero in a
Time of War" (the poem that invokes Ananke is its excised stanza),
appearing in the superlatives of closure as "The highest man with
nothing higher"—a cosmic figure identified as "Man-sun, man-moon,
man-earth, man-ocean" and swollen to become the omnipresent center
of the universe:

> The highest man with nothing higher
> Than himself, his self, the self that embraces
> The self of the hero, the solar single,
> Man-sun, man-moon, man-earth, man-ocean,
> Makes poems on the syllable *fa* or
> Jumps from the clouds or, from his window,
> Sees the petty gildings on February . . .
> The man-sun being hero rejects that
> False empire . . .
> . . . .
> This is his night and meditation.
>
> (CP, 280)

Though this solar hero is repeatedly attached to images that
suggest the contours of the physical world, he is at the same time
offered as a symbol of the self, internalized in the final line as a non-
physical image encountered in the "night" (a symbol of the "essential
imagination") and in "meditation." It thus appears, if we are to grant
meditation its traditional devotional sense, that the figure who is equal
to the universe is at the same time a spiritual image evidently indigenous to the soul. Indeed, we may press the point a bit further; for if
the hero is the "highest man" embedded in the soul, we may consider
him another version of the shadow "self of selves" of "Chocorua to Its
Neighbor" and the subman "second self" of "Owl's Clover."
Resemblance is further suggested by the nimbus of light that accompanies the hero's being; for like the subman and the shadow-
mountain, this figure, too, is a radiant kaleidoscope of "lights revolving"
(CP, 279), their shimmer reflected in the poet's parallel "hymns"
of "stubborn brightness" (CP, 279). Of equal importance, he, too, is
linked to the "centre," like Ananke (the "central earth") and the
shadow-mountain (a "central mind") considered an "organic centre of
responses" (CP, 279), an image which manages to suggest something
living as well as something inherent or inborn, like Ananke, a
"changeless element" (OP, 59).

The resemblance of the hero of "Examination of the Hero in a
Time of War" to the Ananke of "Owl's Clover" may be further dis-

cerned in the image of a marble statue common to both poems. In "Owl's Clover," it will be recalled, the statue is twice dissolved, once collapsing before the eyes of the Old Woman, and next exorcised by the "celestial paramours." In each instance, however, it is restored or, more accurately, resurrected, in a transformation which animates the frozen image, converting it into a living thing.

Something of the same strategy arises in "Examination of the Hero in a Time of War," where the marble statue, presented this time as an idealized memento of the hero, is conceived as an "allegory" (CP, 279) expressing the "pinchings of an idea" (CP, 276), by which Stevens intends a spiritual force embedded in the graven image but not synonymous with it. For this reason, the poet dissociates his universal Ananke-spirit from the specific heroic form he happens to inhabit—"The hero is not a person" (CP, 276); "It [the hero] is not an image" (CP, 278)—and offers him instead as "a white abstraction only" (CP, 276), available in this immaterial shape to the "Pure eye" (CP, 279) that responds empathetically to the statue's inner meaning. So discerned beneath his outer facade, the hero-spirit, it would appear, inspires a metamorphosis; for, in effect, the percipient eye which appropriates the statue's inner presence becomes itself the abstraction it perceives, in this fashion, granting the statue life in the form of its own being. Hence, as Stevens characterizes the exchange, "Instead of allegory, / We have and are the man," meaning by this that the Ananke-spirit extracted from the statue not only transforms the human soul into its image but that by virtue of his presence in the aesthetic "allegory," the art which he inspirits is itself an instrument of change:

> The hero is a feeling, a man seen
> As if the eye was an emotion,
> As if in seeing we saw our feeling
> In the object seen and saved that mystic
> Against the sight, the penetrating,
> Pure eye. Instead of allegory,
> We have and are the man, capable
> Of his brave quickenings, the human
> Accelerations that seem inhuman.
>
> (CP, 278–79)

The primordial images that crop up in Stevens' portrait of the hero afford added evidence that Ananke is the prototype of his later equivalent. It will be recalled that the telluric god of "Owl's Clover" presides over "The Greenest Continent," so hued to suggest the revivication of man's instictive life for which Ananke is both author and end. The meaning Stevens intends by this life is defined by Ananke's feral subjects, composite creature described as "lion-men" and "jaguar-men" and "serpent-kin," in accord with the universal macroanthropos of "Examination of the Hero in a Time of War" who incorporates in his being all earthly elements, organic and inorganic alike. Since, by this token, the macroanthropos is less akin to ordinary man than to the human form apotheosized and transformed into the cosmos itself, the poet describes him as not only superhuman—he stands "taller than a person stands"—but as a primitive colossus whose music, it would seem, is the melody of the muse compelling the poet's parallel song:

> If the hero is not a person, the emblem
> Of him, even if Xenophon, seems
> To stand taller than a person stands, has
> A wider brow, large and less human
> Eyes and bruted ears: the man-like body
> Of a primitive. He walks with a defter
> And lither stride. His arms are heavy
> And his breast is greatness. All his speeches
> Are prodigies in longer phrases.
> His thoughts begotten at clear sources,
> Apparently in air, fall from him
> Like chantering from an abundant
> Poet, as if he thought gladly, being
> Compelled thereto by an innate music.
>
> (CP, 277)

That Ananke is a universal deity common to humanity seems to be implied in Stevens' conviction that he is mankind's "common god." That he is equally a soteriological figure summoning humanity to an altered condition of spiritual life also appears to mark his presence; for as Stevens announces in the forthright declaratives of "Sombre Figuration," the Ananke-subman (in his guise as the portent) comes as a "lord of prophecy" whose fiery "orb" illuminates the heavens, reminding humanity that within its vestigial "memory" of his erstwhile hegemony lies the divine shape of "time to come":

> The portent may itself be memory;
> And memory may itself be time to come
> And must be, when the portent, changed, takes on
> A mask up-gathered brilliantly from the dirt,
> And memory's lord is the lord of prophecy
> And steps forth, priestly in severity,
> Yet lord, a mask of flame, the sprawling form
> A wandering orb upon a path grown clear.
>
> (OP, 70)

Though Stevens was to temper this kind of evangelical rhetoric in his various definitions of the hero, he was not to forswear its evangelical intent. We may, for example, follow the sense of Ananke as *salvator* in "Montrachet-le-Jardin," a hero poem of the early forties. Arranged as a colloquy between an unnamed persona and the hero, who arises as a "shadow in the mind" (CP, 260), the poem again employs the strategy of the second self. To this purer self the poet offers his love, acknowledging in his tender apostrophe the promise of eternal life he proffers; for without the love that twins the soul to its mate, "Chome! clicks the clock, if there be nothing more" (CP, 260). Hence, the hero is a proper object of devotion to whom the poet offers "amens," the endorsement of prayer.

That this divine self is an image of transcendence promising release from human limitation is affirmed in the subsequent images of captivity and liberation. The poet's mind, it appears, binds and limits him: he is a "prisoner" (CP, 261) confined to an "accustomed cell" (CP, 260). Nevertheless, release is promised by "the hero's being" (CP, 261)—a "deliverer / Delivering the prisoner by his words" (CP, 261) to "an heroic world beyond the cell" (CP, 261). (Since the "cell" would seem to denote the human mind, we can only conclude that a deliverance "beyond the cell" implies a transcendence of the human mind as it is now constituted.) Hence, in a shift to the third person singular, Stevens' customary way of suggesting the coincidence of personal and communal vision, the poem sweeps into futurity, envisioning the redemptive journey to a new "hero-land" revived by "inner miracle":

> Since in the hero-land to which we go,
> A little nearer by each multitude,
> To which we come as into bezeled plain,
>
> The poison in the blood will have been purged,
> An inner miracle and sun-sacrament,
> One of the major miracles, that fall
>
> As apples fall, without astronomy,
> One of the sacraments between two breaths,
> Magical only for the change they make.
>
> (CP, 262)

The "sun-sacrament" Stevens invokes requires no outward rite as sign of God's invisible grace; here, as always, redemption is purely an inner event. Nevertheless, spiritual autonomy is, to a degree, circumscribed; for it depends for its effectiveness on two corresponding forces, personified as "hero" and "prisoner"—the "deliverer" and the delivered—and described as a transaction between "two breaths." The transaction is, moreover, conceived as a rite of purification: some noxious element that defiles man's current constitution is somehow to be "purged," as a result of which the human form will be transformed. It is well to note that Stevens' word for this transformation is "change," since change, it is generally agreed, is fundamental to his thought.

The prospect of deliverance, so prominent in this passage, surfaces with even greater insistency in the militant second stanza of "Examination of the Hero in a Time of War"—uncharacteristic to be sure, but of considerable interest in assessing Stevens' spiritual intent. Seemingly unqualified by what precedes and follows, the passage describes an unnamed warrior-god reminiscent of the minatory Ananke and grants him an arsenal of weapons with which to "deliver" the collective from an unnamed enemy:

> The Got whome we serve is able to deliver
> Us. Good chemistry, good common man, what
> Of that angelic sword? Creature of
> Ten times ten times dynamite, convulsive
> Angel, convulsive shatterer, gun,
> Click, click, the Got whom we serve is able,
> Still, still to deliver us, still magic,
> Still moving yet motionless in smoke, still
> One with us, in the heaved-up noise, still
> Captain, the man of skill, the expert
> Leader, the creator of bursting color

And rainbow sortilege, the savage weapon
Against enemies, against the prester,
Presto, whose whispers prickle the spirit.

(CP, 273–74)

Since this god appears in a poem that celebrates the hero, we can only assume that he is a variant of the hero; indeed, the phrase "common man," which appears as descriptive restatement, is similarly used to name the hero in a later portion of the poem. (He is, moreover, renamed as "Captain," a frequent—and positive—symbol for the masculine principle in Stevens' work.) Evidently an ancient god (note the faintly archaic diction) of force and power, fallen into desuetude but nevertheless capable of revival, as the incremental repetition of the adverbial *still* reminds us, he appears to be mankind's common possession—indeed, is humanity's very self. He is, however, resisted by another force which we gave good reason to assume is some psychic element that refuses proper obeisance. Deliverance requires, therefore, that this recalcitrant enemy be vanquished or "purged." Hence, the martial spirit and apocalyptic tone.

In support of purification, the poet uses two images of considerable interest. The first is "Good chemistry," used to define the anonymous "Got," the second, the image of the deliverer as a mobile figure who yet sits inert, "motionless in smoke." That Stevens should identify his "Got" with chemistry is fitting; chemistry, after all, is the physical science that deals with the conversion of substances into new and altered forms. As such, it is a precise analogue for Stevens' internal spiritual being, similarly an instrument of transmutation. The correspondence is strengthened by the image of the "Got" as a creature of smoke, suggesting not only the heat of an internal fire but, when linked to the earlier image of chemistry, conjuring up a picture of the self as a furnace-laboratory in which some sort of purification and distillation is taking place.

The allusions to chemistry and smoke have more than passing interest. Let us recall that Stevens' hero, whom I have urged as a variation of his Ananke-subman, is at once a psychic force (imagination) and a telluric spirit of nature (reality); that though shrouded in darkness, he is a creature of light, often equated with the sun; that he is projected as a deliverer who will restore mankind to a future "heroland"; and that in his final transfiguration, he is conceived as a macroanthropos, his dominion all of nature. When, in such a spiritual constellation, Stevens embeds images of chemistry and smoke to propose the hero as an agent of inner purification, we can only assume that this figure, elsewhere labelled an "impossible possible philosophers' man" (CP, 250) is not at all a prototype of ordinary humanity but is rather a recreation of the central mystery of spiritual alchemy—the *homo maximus* or divine "Son of the Philosophers," more popularly known as the "philosophers' stone."

For reasons I shall later explore, Stevens refused, for the most part, to acknowledge his true subject directly, preferring instead to put forward his chthonic god and the process of spiritual change he represents as a "Disguised pronunciamento" (CP, 45). One, perhaps inadvertent, comment does, however, casually reveal the view of man that Stevens held. Responding to a query from his Italian translator as to whether the word *dirt* in poem xxi of "The Man with the Blue Guitar" could be translated as *dust*, Stevens notes: "It means the physical earth; the very ground. The anthropomorphic can only yield in the end to anthropos: God must in the end, in the life of the mind, yield to man."[7]

The poet's allegiance to the "physical earth" suggests of course an adamant naturalism, especially in view of his subsequent rejection of an anthropomorphic God. (Stevens repeatedly suggests that images of the divine are merely projections of man himself, meaning thereby that man has mistakenly objectified his own godhead.) When, however, Stevens offers the "anthropos" as surrogate for this rejected God and subsequently links him to man, the poet's allegiance to the physical earth takes on another cast; for the "anthropos" is a traditional image of the Great World, encompassing in his being the "very ground" that Stevens claims for the physical earth. An archetypal figure, he is not man in the ordinary sense but divine man—the androgynous giant considered in many religious systems the mother-father creator of mankind. The mythologies of both East and West record instances of this cosmic figure to whom mankind is thought to be related. In India, he is Purusha, which signifies man; in Persia, he is Gayomart, thought to be descended from a marvelous plant. In the

Zohar, the central book of the Hebrew Kabbalah, he is Adam Kadmon, who is identical to the cosmos itself. In China, he appears in the Taoist myth of P'an Ku, a primordial figure identified with the earth. In his Western form, the androgynous giant appears in Plato's *Symposium*, in Gnosticism, and in the Orphic mysteries.[8] More important to our purpose, he is, above all, the central figure in spiritual alchemy, proposed as the divine soul immanent in the world and in man and invoked as the author and end of a spiritual metamorphosis designed to transform the soul of the believer into his image. This spiritual change, I suggest, is the subject of Stevens' poetry, documented with a fecund inventiveness unparalleled in the tradition which, though it has had its poetic interpreters, has never before been so fully described in the spiritual autobiography of one man.

The strategies Stevens used to describe this vision are, however, oblique, as he evidently desired, acknowledging in a review of his early work that he wished "to be as obscure as possible until I have perfected an authentic and fluent speech for myself" (L, 231). Chief among the poetic elements that have offered difficulty is a dense symbolic system, usually drawn from the natural world and usually perceived by most readers as a system of self-reference serving "to relate the self to its world, not to any greater self or any transcendent world."[9] Indeed, the putative autonomy of Stevens' sign language has led R. P. Blackmur, an astute student of Stevens' verbal patterns, to charge him with a privatism "which no wedge of knowledge brought from outside the body of Mr. Stevens' own poetry can help much to split."[10] In response to what are assuredly common assumptions, I shall urge that not only is Stevens' symbolic world informed by a view of spiritual correspondence fundamental to Hermetic thought, but that it is, in many instances, a received system drawn intact from a coherent and codified symbolic tradition. The justice of my demur must, of course, await explication. I shall therefore turn to the alchemical tradition itself to sketch its spiritual assumptions and analogic code, for only as these are clarified may we appreciate how closely Stevens observed and recorded its vision of the transcendental Man.

PART TWO

The Poetic
Shape of
Metamorphosis

Chapter 3

The Hermetic Vision

Metamorphosis

It is customary among investigators of alchemy to note two distinguishable traditions: exoteric or physical alchemy, which sought to transmute base metals into gold by freeing them of their impurities — in the process developing laboratory equipment and refining techniques inherited by modern chemistry; and esoteric or spiritual alchemy, a mystical process of self-regeneration performed in the mind and designed to bring about the purification of the soul.[1] It is no easy matter to distinguish between the two: although alchemical recipes refer to recognizable mineral substances such as nitre, sulphur, mercury, salt, etc., they employ an analogical and sacred symbolism — often deliberately cryptic — that links chemical changes in matter to transformations effected in the human soul. As F. Sherwood Taylor describes it, the alchemists consistently personified their laboratory work, seeing "the combination of two bodies . . . as *marriage*, the loss of their characteristic activity as *death*, the production of something new, as a *birth*, the rising up of vapors, as a *spirit leaving the corpse*, the formation of a volatile solid, as the making of a *spiritual body*."[2]

So insistent is the analogy that some students of alchemy, adepts and historians alike, conclude that the alchemist was himself the subject of the Work, taking "on the garb of Nature *sub specie interioritatis*."[3] Indeed, one nineteenth-century adept, more candid than is usual among the committed, concludes that alchemy was first and foremost a sacred science whose sole object was the spiritual regeneration of man: "Man then, shall we conclude at length, is the true laboratory of the Hermetic art; his life the subject, the grand distillatory, the thing distilling and the thing distilled, and Self-Knowledge to be at the root of all Alchemical tradition?"[4]

It is this view of alchemy as the "science of God" that shall guide my discussion in these pages, though, to be sure, I shall have occasion to refer to exoteric alchemy, since alchemical theosophy is an allegorical system which requires as gloss the crabbed and allusive symbology

associated with the laboratory Operation. In any case, spiritual alchemy may be described as a doctrine of spiritual regeneration, like
Neoplatonic and gnostic speculation—to which it bears a close
relationship—one that proposes a return to a unified and harmonious
condition of life thought to have been an original human possession.[5]
The major alchemical symbol for this spiritual recovery is the *serpens
mercurii* or Ouroboros, a circular serpent biting its own tail to signify
the principle that "the *opus* proceeds from the one and leads back to
the one."[6] A more overt declaration of the spiritual nostalgia for which
this primary symbol stands is offered by a partisan interpreter of the
tradition:

> . . . the human soul has sustained . . . a "fall"; a declension from
> Super-nature into this world of Nature, a cutting-off—not total,
> but nearly so—from its original environment, allegiance and root
> of being; an arrest of the development it would have experienced
> but for its lapse into an alien state and place of existence. It prom-
> ises that reversion to and re-attainment of its original state are
> alike feasible and desirable.[7]

The yearning to return to an original condition of life has as
presupposition the belief that man descends from a divine hermaphrodite thought to have been the progenitor and paradigm of all creation. In the first treatise of the *Corpus Hermeticum* (the "Poimandres"),
a collection of sacred documents attributed to Hermes Trismegistus,
the reputed father of the alchemical art, the archetypal androgyne appears as the macrocosmic Primal Man "commensurate with . . . physical creation"[8]—the archetype of the human race who is at the same
time the true or essential humanity resident in the human soul. The
Christian alchemist Paracelsus called him "Adech, the 'great man.' "[9]
Elsewhere in alchemical speculation he is known as the *"Deus terrestris,
Salvator*, or *filius macrocosmi*,"[10] an indwelling "harmonia" destined to
be reunited to the soul at the close of the redemptive journey. In
Kabbalistic lore, which was assimilated to Hermetic doctrine in the
syncretistic currents of Renaissance Neoplatonism, he is known as the
bisexual Adam Kadmon, a primordial figure whose body, "as large as
the whole of the heavens,"[11] unites in itself every aspect of the
universe—minerals, plants, animals, and celestial bodies.

Man, it is thought, had once been united to this divine androgyne
who was indistinguishable from the world itself. Unity had, however,
been disrupted by the Fall, with the result that what had previously

been whole, single, harmonious, and perfect, was now divided, multiple, dissonant, and impure. Man had suffered a breach, not only between himself and nature but internally as well; for he was now divided within, estranged from his "original 'Adamic' state."[12] Equally, the nonhuman realm that had once enjoyed the perfection of archetypal life was now infected and tainted, its original purity alloyed and wedded to dross.

The conviction that man descends from a divine protoplastus who had not only created the universe but was himself the universe he had created, leads to the fundamental alchemical assumption that all things, organic and inorganic alike, are interrelated. In this view, man and nature are of one substance; for both had originated in the Great Man who survives in the fallen world as the all-embracing cosmic soul. Man is thus by origin a replica of the cosmos, anatomically akin, as one alchemical text expresses it, to each element of the earth:

> Man is to be esteemed a little world, and in all respects he is to be compared to a world. The bones under his skin are likened to mountains, for by them is the body strengthened, even as the earth is by rocks, and the flesh is taken for earth, and the great blood vessels for great rivers, and the little ones for small streams that pour into the great rivers. The bladder is the sea, wherein the great as well as the small streams congregate. The hair is compared to sprouting herbs, the nails on the hands and feet, and whatever else may be discovered inside and outside a man, all according to its kind is compared to the world.[13]

By virtue of descent, the human soul is equally patterned in the image of its divine ancestor whom Paracelsus calls "the star in us," granting him the lineaments of the natural world: "He is therefore similar to man and consists of the four elements and is an Archeus and is composed of four parts; say then, he is the great Cosmos."[14] Nature similarly participates in the divine Life, its sacred body the abode of an indwelling spiritual principle promising a transcendent mode of being. Paracelsus identifies this hidden power as the Iliaster, claiming that "there is nothing corporeal but has latent within itself a spirit and life, which . . . is none other than a spiritual thing."[15] Its more common designation in alchemical literature is the *prima materia*, the primordial first matter said to be the universal source of life to which all matter would eventually return. Though the alchemists gave this fundamental substance a bewildering number of names, it was repeatedly personified as the hermaphroditic Mercurius and the bisexual Adam, both of whom represented the original macroanthropos.

According to the alchemists, the divine principle of Life that is both the primary substance of the world and the basic substance of the soul is now occulted and hidden, "encrusted with certain alien accretions."[16] It nevertheless survives in a life-germ or vital seed commonly known as the philosophers' stone. Its divine attributes are unmistakable. For Paracelsus, it is the triune principle of godhead immanent in nature and in man and yet transcending both:

> Iliaster. —The hidden power in Nature, by means of which all things grow and multiply; primordial matter; materia prima; A'kâsa. *Iliaster primus*: life; the balsam of Nature. Il. *secundus*: the power of life inherent in matter. Il. *tertius*: the astral power of man.[17]

Its irreducible nature is repeatedly emphasized; it is "the universal substrate of life," the "root life-essence";[18] the *Unum, Unica Res*, and Monad";[19] the "One and All."[20] A self-regenerative principle, it is the "*radix ipsius* (root of itself)"[21] symbolized by the primal serpent whose circularity unites all opposites; a healing agent, it is the "Universal Medicine" or "elixir vitae" destined to restore the fractured cosmos to its original health. Above all, it is continually referred to as a "centre" or "point"—numinous terms designating "the zone of the sacred, the zone of absolute reality."[22] Thus, the *prima materia* is defined as "a mysterious creative centre in nature"[23] and is considered "the point originated by God."[24] In man, one adept writes, "the Centre is God Himself, or the faded image of God."[25] In alchemical iconography, the centre is often pictured as a two-headed hermaphrodite, "the ambisexual philosophic man of the philosophers,"[26] or as a life-giving fountain in the center of a garden. Above all, it appears as a dot enclosed by a circle, a sun symbol that signals the culmination of the Great Work. Indeed, the sun and the "centre" are often used interchangeably in alchemical texts; for light and heat, principles of generation, are the very stuff of the divine substance.

The image of the sun is synonymous with the luminous quality of this divine essence, everywhere defined as the light that irradiates the interior man. For the alchemist Zosimos, this spiritual seed imprisoned in the sensual Adam is an inner man of light whose "universal name is *Phos* (Light); hence, the way of calling men *Photes*."[27] Elsewhere it is personified as the Mercurius Monogene who begets the light that "excels all other lights."[28] Often it is linked to images of fire—Paracelsus calls it "a small spark of the eternal invisible fire"[29]—for like its natural analogue, it is a weapon of destruction which first dissolves the soul in preparation for its ultimate reappearance as the divine archetype, "crowned with his diadem, radiant as the sun, shining like the carbuncle . . . constant in the fire."[30]

The return of the soul to its authentic beginnings in the centre or One is conceived in spiritual alchemy as a series of meditative exercises for which the stages of the physical Operation stand as extrinsic symbols. In conception and form, the process is thoroughly genetic, in keeping with the assumption that the original hermaphrodite had with the Fall divided into sexual contraries which the *opus* proposed to reintegrate. This union of contraries, by which chaos was to be ordered and harmony restored, took the symbolic form of a "chymical marriage," the fruit of which was the "spagyric" embryo incubated and ripened in the alchemical vessel and delivered in the divine birth of the living philosophers' stone.

Two major stages expressed in the adage *solve et coagula* marked this process of rebirth. The first proposed the reduction of matter to its *prima materia* through a process of distillation. The idea that soiled matter could be cleansed and then reduced to original formlessness corresponded on the psychic level to the regression of consciousness to a prenatal, embryonic state equivalent to a symbolic death; for it was thought that the organism had first to be dissolved before it could be regenerated or reborn in its eternal body, considered the second and final stage of the transmutative process (the *coagula*). In brief, the alchemist sought to decrease all determinate forms as a prelude to reconstituting or recreating them as purified forms of the divine Man. "All Animalia, Vegetabilia and Mineralia," writes one adept, "are . . . first putrefied, then separated, rectified and again coagulated and fixed, and regenerated in a glorious pellucid Body."[31]

In laboratory alchemy, this purification took the form of immersing base metals in a mercury bath and subjecting them to intense heat for forty weeks. The metamorphosis that followed, wherein solids became "successively liquid, gaseous, and then solid again," confirmed the alchemical belief that all things, psychic as well as corporeal, possessed a single divine essence "capable of taking on all possible forms and states, without essential alteration."[32] It also supported the notion that through his art the artifex could extract this eternal and immutable essence underlying all transitory forms. Accordingly, the *opus* was

divided into phases (alternatively, four, seven, or twelve), each designated by a color and each recording a stage of the purification process.
The use of chromatic symbols was by no means gratuitous, since color
was regarded as itself a form of the divine *pneuma*: "For the alchemists,
from the outset, colour had a practical significance and was taken at
the same time to reveal the inner nature of the metal and its changes.
Colour was regarded as a form of activity and so as spirit or *pneuma*,
which could be removed from one substance and infused into another."[33]

To grasp the spiritual meaning of the colors, as well as of the
stages of the alchemical Operation, requires special attention to Mercurius (the Roman equivalent of the Greek Hermes), the alchemical
Anthropos who is both the agent and end of metamorphosis and who,
indeed, represents the mystery of the entire Work. By virtue of correspondence, he is at once an inner and outer deity—the internal man
of light as well as the cosmic soul of the world. Because he is a hermaphroditic creature, albeit fractured as a consequence of the Fall, he
represents the soul divided into the sexual contraries that the Operation proposed to reintegrate in a *hieros gamos* (sacred marriage) signalling the restoration of original wholeness. In his feminine half, Mercurius appears variously, known as the "'virgin in the centre of the
earth,'" "Luna," "*puella praegnans*," "Venus"—all synonyms for the
"maternal quality of the prima materia."[34] In this form, too, he assumes various shapes of water—lake, sea, river, spring—symbols of
the *anima* or soul (unconscious) that the alchemists called their *aqua
permanens*—the spiritual waters that simultaneously dissolve and re-
juvenate all forms. Hence water, as Carl Jung remarks, was of special
importance:

> The water that the mother, the unconscious, pours into the basin
> belonging to the anima is an excellent symbol for the living power
> of the psyche. The old alchemists never tired of devising new and
> expressive synonyms for this water. They called it *aqua nostra* . . .
> *succus lunariae*, and so on, by which they meant a living being not
> devoid of substance, as opposed to the rigid immateriality of
> mind in the abstract. The expression *succus lunariae* (sap of the
> moon-plant) refers clearly enough to the nocturnal quality of the
> water . . . [35]

The masculine Mercurius equally assumes various guises, interchangeable with Sol (the sun) whose mate is Luna (the moon); the "red

man" whose feminine counterpart is the "white woman"; the King whose consort is the chaste Queen. Often he is represented by theriomorphic images such as cock, lion, peacock, and eagle, symbols which suggest him as the involuntary and undifferentiated instinctive life that the Operation proposed to restore.

In his more philosophical form, Mercurius is assigned number to designate the multiple significations of the Work.[36] Hence, as the monolith—the One or centre—he represents the *unus mundus*, the original procreative principle of creation. As the divine androgyne who unites and is united in the sexual contraries, he is *Mercurius duplex*, at once "husband and wife, bridegroom and bride, or lover and beloved,"[37] as well as the divine son born of union. When considered triune, he represents mercury (spirit), sulphur (soul) and salt (body), with sulphur acting as mediator, joining together spirit and body, the "two which are antagonistic to each other in themselves."[38] In this role, he often appears as an aerial being and is identified with wind, air, clouds, and vapor, atmospheric elements thought to contain the seminal breath or *pneuma* of the world soul.[39] As the figure who contains the four elements, the four cardinal points, the four seasons, he appears as a *quaternio*. Finally, he is the *quinta essentia* (the quintessence) or the Light of Nature distilled and extracted in the course of the Operation. Indeed, alchemical designations for Mercurius are as protean as his composite being: considered a "supercelestial spirit," he is, according to one text, both hero and "Giant of twofold substance. . . . God by nature, man, hero, etc., who hath the celestial Spirit in him, which quickeneth all things . . . he is the sole and perfect Healer of all imperfect bodies and men, the true and heavenly physician of the soul . . . the triune universal essence, which is called Jehovah."[40]

Mercurius also appears in each stage of the transmutative process. In the *nigredo* (putrefaction), he is portrayed as a headless raven or crow to represent the dissolution of corrupt forms (the soul's shedding of its impure mixture); during the whitening and yellowing stages (the *albedo* and *citrinitas*), he is symbolized in images of purity and solidity that propose his resurrection as an incorruptible "pellucid body," often depicted as congealed water that "flies like solid white snow"[41] in accord with the alchemical tradition that the heart of Mercurius originates at the North Pole, the centre around which everything turns.[42] In these stages, he emerges as the Philosophic gold, described as crystalline and associated with glass and salt, symbols of the "subtle" body of the divine androgyne, "transparent as crystal, fragile as glass."[43]

The condition of transparence is similarly required of the Hermetic vessel, the round glass jar in which the divine Man is hatched and incubated; for the jar is itself the Life which it encloses.

In the final stage—the *rubedo*—Mercurius appears as a *rotundum* of fiery red, a living sun duplicating the solar power of the original primal sphere. Often pictured as crowned and two-headed, he appears with hands outstretched and feet astride the globe—a fourfold *physis* adorned with deep red gems, their hue and hardness signalling the restoration of the indestructible and immutable Life. In this final guise, he is variously known as the "cosmic king," the "elixir," the "red tincture," the "panacea," and, above all, the marvelous "stone of the philosophers." By such enigmatic counters, the alchemist metaphorically imaged the metamorphosis of both soul and cosmos, transformed through a psychological technique known as projection into their original—and unified—state.

The alchemical drama of self-redemption is conducted in the theatre of the mind, its purpose the divine *unio mystica* with ineffable Reality. Though alchemists are inclined to be reticent about this inner experience, we have in Mary Atwood's *Hermetic Philosophy and Alchemy*, originally issued in 1850 as *A Suggestive Inquiry into the Hermetic Mystery*, a relatively candid account, valuable not only because it relies only incidentally on the crabbed symbology of alchemical recipes but also because it draws on the entire esoteric tradition for support. It is as well the work of an initiate who had been "vouchsafed . . . the most advanced and advancing transcendental experience possible on this earth."[44] The work, prefaced in the revised edition by Walter Leslie Wilmhurst's lengthy introduction, may thus help to guide an exploration of some of the psychological and metaphysical assumptions of spiritual alchemy.

According to Atwood (as interpreted by Wilmhurst), alchemical self-redemption is a process of psychic transposition wherein the "unnatural" mind produced by the Fall may be "metamorphosed" into its original "divine principle":

> . . . man's present fallen self . . . can be metamorphosed, re-
> versed, turned as it were inside out and outside in; that divine
> principle which is now internalized and occulted being brought
> forward into consciousness and function, and the natural princi-
> ple now animating him, and exercising in him a usurped self-
> willed control, becoming repressed and put back into subordi-
> nacy and hiddenness.[45]

The psychic element that initiates, sustains, and consummates this reversal is the human imagination, said to be "the star in man, the celestial or supercelestial body"[46] consubstantial with the divine imagination of the cosmic soul. To the alchemist, the imagination signifies the active power of the inner light capable of joining man to cosmic matter, the ultimate Reality; as such, it represents "a concentrated extract of the life forces, both physical and psychic."[47]

The imagination is aided in its work by meditation, in effect, an internal alchemy that proposes "to conjoin the mind to its lost universality and pass the consciousness regressively through its many phases back to that long forgotten life in Reality."[48] In Chinese alchemy, as in Kabbalistic meditation, this return to the "diamond body" is known as "abstract meditation," so called because in its approach to the divine, the soul must first repudiate the sensible world as well as its own soiled and common self, in order thereby to concentrate on the divine center free of quality or attribute. Thus cleansed of images and reduced to a state of nakedness, the soul is prepared to encounter the divine image which is no other than its own true self.

This return to the Divine Idea is often identified in mystical literature as a return to the region of "Nothing"—the absolute Void. In Kabbalistic speculation, it is proposed as the first stage in the manifestation of the *En-Sof*, itself an unknowable divine essence. The highest *Sefirah* in a series of emanations symbolizing God's gradual unfolding, "Nothing" is the *kether*, the divine crown considered by many mystics "infinitely more real than all other reality."[49] Its symbol is the point in the center of the circle, similarly used in alchemical texts to designate the return to the One, the goal of the Operation.

Once purified, the soul, according to Atwood, is granted access to a divine wisdom that reveals "the hidden Forms of manifested Being, and secrets of the Causal Fountain, identically within himself."[50] The conviction reminds us that spiritual alchemy, like all theosophical speculation, proposes a knowledge of divine things accessible through immediate and direct experience and vouchsafing an ontological certainty unamenable to reason or debate. The metaphysical basis for such wisdom can be thought of as Platonic: the divine "nothingness" which absorbs the soul is considered the "Great Archetype"[51] whose undivided unity contains the eternal prototypes of each created thing and whose cosmic memory preserves the full measure of all human events. As the source as well as the totality of all that exists, it combines in itself both psyche and matter, the knower and the known. In its Eastern form, it is the all-pervading and all-embracing Tao of Chinese alchemy, considered the primordial source of every beginning and end. Because all things emanate from the Tao, it is the ultimate metamorphic power, able to transform itself into an infinity of forms, even as it remains the changeless element underlying all appearances.

By virtue of descent, man is consubstantial with this "Great Archetype," containing in his imagination the archetypal forms of each external object. These, when activated through an act of "sympathetic and magnetic attraction,"[52] grant an intuitive knowledge of nature unavailable to the rational mind. Such an attraction is often identified as a "vibration," considered the primordial sound of the original protoplastus echoing from the innermost depths of nature. By hearkening to this divine reverberation, the alchemist unites his soul to the object, thereby linking his imagination to the ultimate reality of the cosmic soul. In effect, he enacts the alchemical belief in the unity of matter through a manipulation of the psyche which transforms the abstract formulations of alchemical metaphysics into the concrete authenticity of human experience. Atwood (according to Wilmhurst) calls this act of mind exploring "the physical world from within it," adding that with this fusion of soul and world the adept is able "to manipulate the metaphysical forces determining its [nature's] normal external guise."[53] According to Walter Pagel, Paracelsus similarly believed that the enlightened soul wielded a "spiritual power" which made it "the equal of nature," able to "achieve what nature effects by means of conception."[54] (In physical alchemy, this view of the magical powers of the human soul is expressed in the final stage known as projection, which assumed that once the red tincture or quintessence had been extracted from its compound it could, when applied to base metals, transmute them into gold, the symbol of perfection.)

Union confers an altered mode of being, allowing the soul to penetrate to the inner life of the object, so that the distinctions formerly imposed by the discursive intellect are erased and one "no longer sees or distinguishes by intellection nor imagines that there are two things, but, consubstantial, becomes herself the ultimate object as she was before the subject in simultaneous accord."[55] In this state of interfusion, perception is radically altered; for to empty the soul of adulterated forms is to prepare it for a new mode of seeing in which the world becomes "transparent," allowing the purged eye access to the sovereign images of eternal forms. Thought is no longer abstract but pictorial, its vehicle the pellucid "subtle" body become a psychospiritual substance that simultaneously reflects and contains every element of the universe. In this state, the soul is relieved of the laws of time and space, functioning like the divine itself "in transcendence of every physical limitation and with a range of vision and a lucidity of perception into the interiors and causes of things, co-extensive with that supra-natural Light with which it had become identified."[56]

Spiritual alchemy considers the soul's assimilation to its universal cosmic center a return to a state of harmony that had prevailed before the disastrous fall into consciousness. Since the concept of harmony is of central interest to this study—indeed, it forms the root of *Harmonium*, the title of Stevens' first volume of poetry—I shall conclude this survey of alchemical speculation with a brief definition of the term as it appears in a manual prepared by relatively modern inheritors of the alchemical tradition (I shall have occasion to return to this group in a later portion of my study):

> *Harmonium*—A state of harmony. . . . As applied to the relation
> ship of the Cosmic to the human soul, it means that state of
> ecstasy where the human becomes conscious of the attunement of
> the natural forces of his being with the Absolute or the source
> from which they emanate.[57]

⟦G⟧ Chapter 4 ⟦Ɔ⟧

The Supreme Fiction

Son only of man and sun of men,
The outer captain, the inner saint . . .

Variously known as the "Life," the "One," the "King of the Earth," the "Great World," the transcendental Man of religious alchemy is an indwelling deity indistinguishable from the human soul as well as from the cosmos he vivifies and animates. Though hidden and reduced to vestigial memory, he is nevertheless the "human form divine" immanent in the imagination and unalterably supreme, superseding all images of deity and systems of belief to which humanity, mistakenly, offers its spiritual allegiance. By this token, man, *in potentia*, is himself a revelation of the divine, requiring for spiritual endorsement not the outer God of traditional belief but a true self-awareness that to the gnostic soul resides in the imagination, itself the image of deity in which the Man is contained and from which he is inseparable.

To this indwelling "common god," Stevens dedicated many of his poems, announcing him as the hero, the "idea of man," "man the abstraction," "man number one," "central man," and "major man" and enjoining his supremacy in frequent disavowals of any godhead distinct from man himself, since in the esoteric tradition to which the Man deity belongs, natural humanity is the true source of spiritual power. To Stevens, the gods were no more than veiled accounts of man's essential qualities — "aesthetic projections" (OP, 209) he once called them, testifying to man's own "fundamental glory" (OP, 209). Indeed, religion was merely an inverted anthropology mirroring the human penchant to create gods in its own image; for as Stevens exults in the "Adagia," man is that "happy creature" who himself "invented the Gods. It is he that put into their mouths the only words they have ever spoken" (OP, 167). Thus, the dissolution of the gods, greeted as "one of the great human experiences" (OP, 206), inspires neither regret nor lament, for to Stevens, the end of obeisance to images of the divine signalled the beginning of spiritual self-sufficiency. Man's validation, he writes in a late poem, requires no outside authority; endorsement is purely an activity of the self:

> . . . only in man's definitions of himself,
> Only encompassed in humanity, is he
> Himself. The author of man's canons is man,
> Not some outer patron and imaginer.

(OP, 109)

This attention to man, as well as Stevens' disdain for traditional forms of belief, has invited the view that Stevens is a humanist—this despite the poet's frequent declarations to the contrary. "Humanism is not enough," he writes in 1945 (L, 489), repeating a distaste expressed five years earlier: "the more I see of humanism the less I like it" (L, 348). Stevens clearly sought an alternative. "The chief defect of humanism," he explains to one correspondent, "is that it concerns human beings. Between humanism and something else, it might be possible to create an acceptable fiction" (L, 449). Embroidering on that "something else," he writes in his gloss to "Notes toward a Supreme Fiction": "The trouble with humanism is that man as God remains man, but there is an extension of man, the leaner being, in fiction, a possibly more than human human, a composite human. The act of recognizing him is the act of this leaner being moving in on us" (L, 434).

The "more than human" figure proposed as a "fiction" and exempted from humanism suggests of course the hero, repeatedly magnified and aggrandized. Indeed, it would appear from Stevens' gloss to "The Man with the Blue Guitar," written sixteen years after the poem's publication, that the "supreme fiction," the "idea of man," and the supra-human hero are interchangeable terms: "If we are to think of a supreme fiction, instead of creating it, as the Greeks did, for example, in the form of a mythology, we might choose to create it in the image of a man: an agreed-on superman" (L, 789).[1]

Stevens' reasons for refusing humanism, as well as for suggesting the equivalence of man, the "supreme fiction," and "superman," are clarified in "A Thought Revolved," a poem published shortly after "Owl's Clover."[2] Located in a new "mystic garden" set in the mundane world, the poem is Stevens' first sustained effort to define the figure of the hero, proposed as the generic "idea of man" and offered as substitute for "the idea of god." In the third section, the poet sets forth the possibility of an "earthly leader":

ROMANESQUE AFFABULATION

He sought an earthly leader who could stand
Without panache, without cockade,
Son only of man and sun of men,
The outer captain, the inner saint,

The pine, the pillar and the priest,
The voice, the book, the hidden well,
The faster's feast and heavy-fruited star,
The father, the beater of the rigid drums,

He that at midnight touches the guitar,
The solitude, the barrier, the Pole
In Paris, celui qui chante et pleure,
Winter devising summer in its breast,

Summer assaulted, thundering, illumed,
Shelter yet thrower of the summer spear,
With all his attributes no god but man
Of men whose heaven is in themselves,

Or else whose hell, foamed with their blood
And the long echo of their dying cry,
A fate intoned, a death before they die,
The race that sings and weeps and knows not why.

(CP, 185–86)

The declaration that the "earthly leader" is the "Son only of man and sun of men" deserves close scrutiny; for in this resonant phrase, Stevens proffers a direct avowal of spiritual intent. In the past, the expression "Son of man," often used by Jesus to characterize his ministry, has traditionally been traced to Jewish apocalyptic literature, where it appears in the vision of Daniel (7:13) to characterize "one like the Son of man" who descends from "the clouds of heaven" to receive "everlasting dominion" over the world. More recent scholarship suggests that its origins lie not in the Jewish tradition but in gnostic Anthropos theology, in turn influenced by the Chaldean mystery tradition widely known in the Hellenistic Orient. According to Carl Kraeling, the Son of Man of the Synoptic Gospels may be traced to ancient Mesopotamia, where he appears in connection with the Iranian Gayomart (life-man), "a mythological celebrity, known as the Great or Upper Man, and said to have been embroiled in a primordial conflict of disastrous results."[3] Syrian gnostics later divided this figure into two Anthropoi named Anthropos and Son of Man to designate respectively the universal Monad, a transcendent totality, and his emanation immanent in the cosmos and considered a representative of ideal or redeemed humanity—"the Perfect Man Within."[4] In Jewish gnosticism this second man was known as the macrocosmic Adam Kadmon, conceived as a material yet spiritual principle indwelling in humanity and in the cosmos. A more metaphysical nomenclature employed in gnostic systems described him as "Soul and Pneuma or Soul and Mind,"[5] in which form he arises as the presiding deity of the *Corpus Hermeticum*, the philosophic and contemplative books of spiritual alchemy. Elsewhere in alchemical speculation, he is known as the "Man of Light," the "second God in man," the scintilla, the point, the centre, the "Son of Man . . . begotten by the philosopher,"[6] and, above all, as the "philosophical stone" extracted from crude and alloyed forms. In the sixteenth century, Carl Jung observes, the effort to assimilate the *lapis* concept to Christ resulted in the formulation that the divine stone was the "*filius macrocosmi*" or "Son of the Great World," as opposed to the "*filius microcosmi*" who was the "son of man."[7]

The punning "sun of men" which follows "Son only of man" is similarly a staple of alchemical symbology, widely used, as I have noted, to represent the inner man of light whom the alchemist sought to resurrect. Like the Philosophic gold from which it is indistinguishable, the alchemical sun is the "foundation of the Art"[8]—an image "of the invisible God"[9] in man, permanent, incorruptible, and "fixed for the length of eternity."[10]

The seemingly exotic title affixed to the passage similarly echoes Stevens' intent. The neologism "Affabulation" descends in its root from the Latin *fabula*, suggesting the poem's didactic intent. The rounded arches characteristic of the "Romanesque," the attributive adjective of the title, present the alchemical *rotundum* or circle, traditionally considered a symbol of psychic totality and wholeness and used interchangeably with gold, stone, and sun to represent the unity of the primal self. Within the stanza, the image proposing the "earthly leader" as "The outer captain, the inner saint" is another version of the Ananke-subman dyad which reaffirms the concept of correspondence fundamental to alchemical thought. That he is a "priest," a "father," a "man / Of men" who is the source of an internal "heaven," further affirms him as the divine Man, at once the "son" (microcosm) and "father" (macrocosm); as do "pine," "pillar" and "pole," traditional images of the sacred center. The reference to the "hidden well" echoes the alchemical belief that the divine image is lodged in the spiritual waters of the soul; while the seasonal alternation—"Winter divising summer in its breast"—is likewise reminiscent of the alchemical Mercurius, who comes from the North to issue in his resurrected form as the fiery sun. And like Mercurius, too, this new Man foretells for his human counterparts a symbolic death—"a death before they die"—which, in the alchemical drama, signals the dissolution of corrupt forms as the prelude to renewal.

The second section of the poem announcing the poet's mission is as spiritually resonant as the section explored above:

> MYSTIC GARDEN AND MIDDLING BEAST
> The poet striding among the cigar stores,
> Ryan's lunch, hatters, insurance and medicines,
> Denies that abstraction is a vice except
> To the fatuous. These are his infernal walls,
> A space of stone, of inexplicable base
> And peaks outsoaring possible adjectives.
> One man, the idea of man, that is the space,
> The true abstract in which he promenades.
> The era of the idea of man, the cloak
> And speech of Virgil dropped, that's where he walks,
> That's where his hymns come crowding, hero-hymns,
> Chorals for mountain voices and the moral chant,
> Happy rather than holy but happy-high,
> Day hymns instead of constellated rhymes,
> Hymns of the struggle of the idea of god
> And the idea of man, the mystic garden and
> The middling beast, the garden of paradise
> And he that created the garden and peopled it.
>
> (CP, 185)

A close scrutiny of the seemingly random images outlining the poet's mundane milieu yields a less than fortuitous arrangement. "Cigar stores" recall the anonymous "Got" of the later poem "Examination of the Hero in a Time of War, associated with "chemistry" (generally thought to have developed from alchemy) and "smoke," both of which recall in turn the alchemical deity—the god of the hearth or stove. (The cigar image, it is well to note, surfaces in "The Greenest Continent," immediately preceding the appearance of Ananke and in the context of "an earth that has no gods" [OP, 58], art and myth having been expelled. As substitute the poet offers a "long cigar" [OP, 58] enjoyed by patrons of a cafe whose proprietor has "a son / In Capricorn" [OP, 58]. In the alchemical system, Capricorn is the tenth sign of the Zodiac associated with Saturn who, in turn, is identical to Mercurius, the "son of the philosophers."[11] Since this deity is the god of the alchemical fire, the cigar image of the passage appears to be emblematic.) "Hatters" is a common symbol for the nimbus or halo accompanying the image of the divine; "insurance" picks up the theme of eternal life traditionally associated with the cosmic Man; and "medicines" appears to be Stevens' oblique reference to the "elixir vitae" or "Universal Medicine," common names for the divine stone.

In this context Stevens announces as the poet's subject the "idea of man" renamed the "One man," recalling in the epithet "One" the "sophic" Man equivalent to the centre or One. His further identification as a "middling beast," both in the title and in the penultimate line, combines in a single image the theriomorphic symbol often used in alchemy to characterize the anima-soul—Sol, the goal of the *opus*, is often called a "great animal"[12]—with the concept of the *"anima media natura,"* a phrase that designates the world-soul immanent in nature and in man and which, as the mediate form standing between spirit and body, is the "glue, holding the world together."[13] An "abstraction" enclosed in the poet's mind in a "space of stone" (a reference, it would seem, to the divine *lapis*, equivalent in alchemical doctrine to the vivifying *pneuma* ["space"]), he is the generative force that has created and peopled the poet's "mystic garden"; hence, he is a proper object of devotion to whom the poet offers "chorals for mountain voices," another image of the divine center represented in alchemical iconography as the cosmic "Mountain of the Adepts"[14] on whose pinnacle stands the resurrected phoenix—a symbol of the liberated soul of the One.

"A Thought Revolved" naturalizes the hero, relying less on the quasi-mythological images of "Owl's Clover" than on a paradigmatic form drawn in man's own image and sufficiently akin to the human to be recognizable as a collective psychic possession. In the image of the hero, Stevens found a suitable substitute for the Ananke-subman, similarly "The outer captain, the inner saint" but, unlike his successor, an Olympian figure incompatible with the exploration of individual experience—the base of Stevens' later meditative mode. The hero, in contrast, allowed Stevens to probe as well as to universalize his own psychic processes, often in an idiom halfway between manifesto and confessional. In this happy conjunction of private vision and social purpose, the poet found a means to celebrate the cosmic One—in Stevens' version, "man number one" (CP, 166)—as the spiritual core of the self, even as he managed to propose him as man-

kind's "common god," celebrated in the poet's song of "A million
people on one string?" (CP, 166).

Perhaps the least ambiguous description of Stevens' Man-hero is
afforded by "Asides on the Oboe," a poem which first appeared in
Parts of a World, Stevens' fifth volume and one in which the Man (the
"World" of Stevens' title) figures prominently in poems like "Exam-
ination of the Hero in a Time of War," "Montrachet-le-Jardin," and
"Idiom of the Hero." (Indeed, so pervasive is his image in this collec-
tion that Stevens originally intended to title the volume "The Man,
That's All One Knows,"[15] a caption which manages to suggest the
Man as the One and All—common names for the Hermetic deity.)
The poem is of special interest because it suggests for the first time the
equivalence of the "central man" and the "fiction"—motifs that Stevens was to treat more fully in "Notes toward a Supreme Fiction"—
and because it served Stevens as a touchstone when, in his gloss to
"Owl's Clover," he sought to explain Ananke as a version of the "fiction" with which he was then preoccupied.

"Asides on the Oboe" opens in the accent of sententiousness
common to Stevens' post-*Harmonium* mode, its brief introductory ter-
cet adjuring a "final belief" in a "fiction" that is to replace the old gods
considered merely "prologues." Exhortation yields next to definition,
as the poet catalogues the features of this "fiction" which, it appears, is
indeed man, but man so modified and altered that, unlike his baser
counterparts, he is sufficient to "stand as god":

> The prologues are over. It is a question, now,
> Of final belief. So, say that final belief
> Must be in a fiction. It is time to choose.

> I

> That obsolete fiction of the wide river in
> An empty land; the gods that Boucher killed;
> And the metal heroes that time granulates—
> The philosophers' man alone still walks in dew,
> Still by the sea-side mutters milky lines
> Concerning an immaculate imagery.
> If you say on the hautboy man is not enough,
> Can never stand as god, is ever wrong
> In the end, however naked, tall, there is still
> The impossible possible philosophers' man,
> The man who has had the time to think enough,
> The central man, the human globe, responsive

> As a mirror with a voice, the man of glass,
> Who in a million diamonds sums us up.
>
> (CP, 250)

The "philosophers' man" whom Stevens twice commends as an alternative object of faith is another common name for the alchemical "son of man," known as the *filius philosophorum*, the "son of the Philosophers."[16] Consequently, Stevens defines his ideal figure in a cluster of images commonly associated in alchemical allegory with the divine protoplastus. Said to walk "in dew," he recalls the "Mercury of the Philosophers," a "Heavenly Dew" exuded by the soul in the purification process;[17] proffered as a "human globe," he parallels the universal "King of the Earth" whose being contains the universe; linked to images of transparence ("glass," "diamonds"), he implies the crystalline "sophic" gold, the pellucid quality of Mercurius resurrect; and, finally, offered as a "mirror with a voice," he suggests the *speculum philosophorum*—The Philosophers' mirror—a common name for the Operation in which, it was said, "the Wise have made a Mirror in which they contemplate all the things of this world, whether it be a concrete reality or a mental reality."[18]

In the penultimate stanza, Stevens links the "central man" to images of death, war, and martyrdom, important alchemical themes which arise repeatedly in the poetry but which must, at this point, be postponed, since they require extensive comment.[19] Less ambiguous is the poem's conclusion; for like the *opus*, which culminates in the Man made resurrect, the final stanza, too, proffers an image of union, emphasizing in the thrice-repeated "one," a common designation of cosmic totality, the reborn "glass man without external reference," Stevens' version of the soul reintegrated, consubstantial at the conclusion of the Operation with the cosmic Life and hence independent of secondary definitions of the divine:

> It was not as if the jasmine ever returned.
> But we and the diamond globe at last were one.
> We had always been partly one. It was as we came
> To see him, that we were wholly one . . .
> . . . .
> The glass man, without external reference.
>
> (CP, 251)

The notion of transparence, implicit in the image of glass from which the "central man" is carved, further affirms the alchemical genealogy of Stevens' "philosophers' man." In section II of the poem, the motif is reaffirmed directly to suggest the soul so assimilated to the external world as to be virtually indistinguishable from it: "He is the transparence of the place in which / He is and in his poems we find peace" (CP, 251). To anticipate a fuller discussion elsewhere, this transcendental fusion of subject and object is contained in the secret of the *lapis*, known for its "hardness, transparency, and rubeous hue"[20]—the qualities of the eternal solar Man. Since he is the immaterial essence inhering in matter, his advent in Hermetic doctrine corresponds to a twinned reveral which at once resurrects the unconscious (the internal *imago Dei*) and dematerializes the phenomenal world, restoring it to its original "subtle" condition—hence, to the world made transparent, revealed as spiritual essence. So seen through a mystical "inner perception," matter becomes a revelation of spirit, affording to the enlightened eye "the reflection of eternal prototypes"[21] that reside equally in the human soul and in nature, so that to see the world "transparent" is to *be* that which is seen, in a "geosophy" which transforms the human soul into the cosmic world itself. For this reason, the "central man" of "Asides on the Oboe" is offered as "the transparence of the place in which / He is"; for he is himself a subtle body of light—the finest gossamer in which the world is contained and through which it is filtered.[22]

We may follow the meaning Stevens attached to transparence in "The Pediment of Appearance," where it is described as a quality sought rather than achieved—the object of a redemptive quest (conducted by an anonymous group of "young men") that seeks to extract the hidden "essential ornament" (CP, 361) from the dross of the sensible world. The hunt for the lost Eden is here confined to the woods, its ostensible object an ornamental pediment whose height, triangularity, and hardness modulate through characteristic sleight of hand into a vague "form," similarly "high," similarly an "essential ornament," and, above all, similarly a stone, its quality of "savage transparence" the real object of the search:

> By its form alone, by being right,
> By being high, is the stone
> For which they are looking:
>
> The savage transparence. They go crying
> The world is myself, life is myself,
> Breathing as if they breathed themselves,
>
> Full of their ugly lord . . .

(CP, 361)

To grasp Stevens' meaning here it is well to recall that the cosmic Man is the Great World whose breath or *pneuma* is at once the vital Life that animates the universe and the divine light hidden in the soul. Hence, the cry that asserts the self as indistinguishable from "world," "life," and "breath" is the cry of correspondence; for to embrace the world and claim it as self is to seek one's own divine being in the belief that the "essential ornament" without is the divine analogue of the "essential ornament" within. Thus, though division between self and world occasions the search for the numinous stone, the premise of rupture lies not in a post-Cartesian dualism, commonly considered the fulcrum of Stevens' thought, but in a vital monism that perceives in all matter a spiritual substance yearning for reintegration.

The ease with which the macrocosmic Man—the outer "essential ornament"—translates into his microcosmic form is apparent in "The Man with the Blue Guitar," where the self is celebrated as a "substitute" for the transcendent gods:

> A substitute for all the gods:
> This self, not that gold self aloft,
> Alone, one's shadow magnified,
> Lord of the body, looking down,
> As now and called most high,
> The shadow of Chocorua
> In an immenser heaven, aloft,
> Alone, lord of the land and lord
> Of the men that live in the land, high lord.
> One's self and the mountains of one's land,
> Without shadows, without magnificence,
> The flesh, the bone, the dirt, the stone.
>
> (CP, 176)

Urged neither as an external "form" nor as the normative "central man," the Anthropos is nevertheless the poem's abiding presence, projected this time in his psychic form as the inner "self" that Stevens elsewhere calls the "essential imagination." Image and theme replicate his form: like him, the aggrandized self swells to cosmic proportions, its place lofty, its dominion all of nature, its honorific "high lord," its symbol the "philosophical" stone. Consistent with the interiority of this sacred "stone," the allusion to the "shadow" of "Chocorua" anticipates the "prodigious shadow" (CP, 297) of "Chocorua to Its Neighbor"—an irradiated "self of selves" (CP, 297) commended to the soul as its "philosopher" (CP, 301) and made synonymous with "The stone" (CP, 300). The "shadow" suggests yet another alchemical theme, embodied in the paradoxical axiom, "The sun and its shadow bring the work to perfection."[23] Though the injunction defies astronomical reality, its figurative meaning corresponds to the alchemical view that the supernal light of the Anthropos is simultaneously its own shadow hidden in the *prima materia*, the soul of matter; hence, the *prima materia* (in its psychic form, the soul) was also known as the shadow.[24] That the self is "without shadows" at the conclusion of the stanza accords with the alchemical belief that in the course of the *opus* the shadow merged with its source to become itself the shadowless principle of divine light, or the marvelous stone that appropriately concludes the final couplet.

The hermaphroditic nature of this shadow is equally useful in mapping Stevens' symbolic geography. As the principle of wholeness, the Anthropos is both masculine and feminine, his autarchic and autonomous nature symbolically summarized in the self-begetting and self-devouring primal serpent. His fall marks the appearance of sexual division, which the alchemist projected onto all of nature, seeing the world as a contrast of sexual opposites to which he ascribed either active (male) or passive (female) qualities, both of which represented the separated parts of the original hermaphrodite. The Anthropos is thus sexually interchangeable, a characteristic that appears in Stevens' frequent use of the feminine archetype to represent his form.[25] The motif of the feminine element of the Man may be discerned in "The Candle a Saint," where the image of light embedded in the title modulates in the body of the poem into its shadow counterpart, personified as a "kindled" (CP, 223) feminine "night" (CP, 223) and celebrated as an "archaic queen" (CP, 223), like her masculine double "abstract" (CP, 223) and like him, too, the seminal source of all images:

> The noble figure, the essential shadow,
>
> Moving and being, the image at its source,
> The abstract, the archaic queen. Green is the night.
> (CP, 223)

That Stevens daubs the night-shadow green may be traced to the synonymity between shadow and sulphur in alchemy's symbolic system. In the physical forms and changeable nature of sulphur, alchemy found a suitable symbol for the spiritual regeneration it sought, at times equating the substance with the "corporal and earthly," at times using it to represent the "occult spiritual principle"[26] inherent in all living things. Its cluster of colors was equally useful, especially green and red, which at times represented the beginning and end of the Work—green standing for the shadow or soul in its occulted form, variously symbolized by the green lion, the green bird, the green son to suggest it as the fecund principle of growth; and red representing the soul made manifest—the "solar sulphur"[27] interchangeable with the stone of "rubeous hue," the sun, the red lion, the red bird, the red man. Green is thus by chromatic synecdoche the incipient seed which ripens in the course of the Operation into its fruit—the homunculus or "philosophical man" whose chromatic mark is red and whose central symbol is the stone.

It is this stone of "rubeous hue" that is the subject of poem iii of "It Must Give Pleasure," the third and final canto of "Notes toward a Supreme Fiction," where, in a series of three-line stanzas[28] marked by a nostalgia for what "might have been," Stevens records the "face of stone" of the red Anthropos—the Hermetic redeemer in his manifest form:

> A lasting visage in a lasting bush,
> A face of stone in an unending red,
> Red-emerald, red-slitted-blue, a face of slate,
>
> An ancient forehead hung with heavy hair,
> The channel slots of rain, the red-rose-red
> And weathered and the ruby-water-worn,
>
> The vines around the throat, the shapeless lips,
> The frowns like serpents basking on the brow,
> The spent feeling leaving nothing of itself,
>
> Red-in-red repetitions never going
> Away, a little rusty, a little rouged,
> A little roughened and ruder, a crown
>
> The eye could not escape, a red renown
> Blowing itself upon the tedious ear.
> An effulgence faded, dull cornelian
>
> Too venerably used. That might have been.
> It might and might have been.
>
> (CP, 400)

In accord with Hermetic pantheosophy, which regards the self as indivisible from the incorporeal spirit of nature, Stevens personifies

the chthonic Man as a recognizably human "visage" which is nevertheless a composite of natural elements—all "lasting" and "ancient" and
"unending," the poet's precise epithets for the incorruptible element
inhering in all matter. With customary honesty (once we read his allegorical system accurately), Stevens compares his stony colossus to a
"deity" answering to the "elementary idea of God" (L, 438); hence, he
reverently continues, "Adoration is a form of face to face" (L, 438),
capturing in this mirror image the sacramental encounter of the soul
with its own true self—the spiritual purpose of the alchemical Work.
Hence, to affirm his devotion to the Man, Stevens employs in his
poetic tribute alchemy's customary counters of godhead to paint a portrait dominated by red, the vibrant hue of revivification which marks
the completion of the Grand Magisterium. In addition to the "sophic"
stone from which the visage is carved, the colossus' symbolic landscape is marked by the spiritual waters (the "sophic" rain); by the
image of the vine attached to the windpipe (signifying the arcane
stone, in one of its many guises known as the cosmic vine in turn
interchangeable with the "breath-soul" or life principle);[29] by the rose,
a symbol of the redeemer's "rose-colored" blood, able, it was thought,
to redeem the world "from its Fall";[30] by the ruby, a frequent
synonym for the *lapis*, known as the stone "of rubeous hue"; by the
crown, used in alchemical iconography to represent the Man's monarchic presence; and finally, by the *serpens mercurii* "basking on the
brow," a common symbol for psychic renewal which Stevens manages
in the term "basking" to associate with the "sophic" fire and its
analogue, the cosmic sun. That this deity, however radiant, has suffered a degree of eclipse—"An effulgence faded, dull cornelian"—is
the sense of Stevens' elegiac lament for what "might have been" had
not the catastrophic Fall intervened.

Stevens concludes the poem by introducing as companion of the
red colossus a "dead shepherd" who issues from hell:

> That might have been.
> It might and might have been. But as it was,
> A dead shepherd brought tremendous chords from hell
>
> And bade the sheep carouse. Or so they said.
> Children in love with them brought early flowers
> And scattered them about, no two alike.
>
> (CP, 400)

In view of Stevens' spiritual assumptions, the association of the "dead shepherd" with "hell" suggests the classical Hermes (the prototype of the alchemical Mercurius),[31] traditionally associated with Arcadia—the land of shepherds—and considered in some mythologic accounts a god of the underworld—a "Hermes of Hades."[32] That Stevens links his subterranean deity to "children" and "early flowers" reminds us that the poet originally intended to caption the first section of "Notes toward a Supreme Fiction" "REFACIMENTO" (L, 431), an Italian noun form meaning remaking or refashioning or restoring, in any of its meanings a Janus-term that gazes in two directions at once—backward to an original model, somehow in disrepair, and forward to the model's resurrection, albeit, perhaps, in altered and modified form. Its temporal modulations encompass a completed past and an incomplete present, representing an on-going effort (necessarily implying futurity) to restore an antecedent, once whole and complete. Thus, though renascence is implicit in its range of meanings, the revival suggested is intimately bound to an antecedent form.

The backward and forward movement suggested in this original title accurately reflects the section's movement as a whole, which begins with the "first idea" (CP, 381), elaborated in irreducible terms that suggest it as a primordial *Urgrund*, and concludes with a Chaplinesque figure, properly dressed in primordial garb (an "old coat" [CP, 389]) and engaged in a quest of retrieval: "Looking for what was, where it used to be?" (CP, 389). It thus appears, given the poem's propositional form, that to seek, which implies futurity, is, in fact, to restore or retrieve a lost but original possession located in the past.[33] This is the sense of an excised couplet intended for "The Man with the Blue Guitar": "Subversive poet, this is most rare. / Forward into tomorrow's past!" (L, 360). It is as well the import of the apocalyptic Ananke-portent of "Owl's Clover," which prophesies a future recapitulating a past that survives in the collective memory of the race:

> The future must bear within it every past,
> Not least the pasts destroyed, ...
> ....
> The portent may itself be memory;
> And memory may itself be time to come ...
>
> (OP, 70)

Now, to retrieve the "first idea" is to restore something at once archaic and juvenescent; for it suggests not only the primordial past but a timeless conditon of spiritual infancy—what Eric Neumann calls the "dawn state" of human consciousness.[34] To remake or refashion the "first idea" is thus to return to youthful origins, as the passage in question suggests. The red Anthropos represents the eternal beginning in iconographic form; he is "what might have been" had not the Fall intervened. With the Fall, however, he has suffered occultation—reduced to a "dead shepherd" hidden in "hell." But because he is the wellspring of man's spiritual life, it is to him that "children" offer "young flowers," though, to be sure, these flowers are now diverse—"no two alike." In short, what we here encounter in the person of the "dead shepherd" is a version of the Ananke "essential imagination"—that "fateful" spark of deity lodged in the soul which continues to compel infinite, though mistaken, spiritual variations— all testifying to man's yearning to return to his primordial source when he was himself indistinguishable from deity.

The "dead shepherd" Stevens notes in his gloss, is an "improvisation" made necessary by "what preceded it in the poem. . . . What the spirit wants it creates, even if it has to do so in a fiction" (L, 438). Since the "dead shepherd" is preceded by the red Anthropos; and since both, it appears, are equivalent to a "fiction," as Stevens' note suggests, we may reasonably conclude that they, like the "central man" of "Asides on the Oboe," similarly labelled a "fiction," are the subject of "Notes toward a Supreme Fiction," the poem that bears their euphemism in its title, suitably prefaced by an image of magnitude to suggest it as the apogee of deity. It is therefore fitting that the poet apostrophize this "supreme fiction" in the tender dedicatory poem, addressing him in the accent of devotion as the "wisest man . . . hidden in me day and night," the "light" in which he is encountered a "vivid transparence" that, in the mutuality of correspondence, irradiates "the central of our being" (CP, 380).[35]

Chapter 5

Cosmic Reality

To find the spiritual in reality . . .

If, as seems likely, the "supreme fiction" is a rubric for the Hermetic Man, there is a good reason to believe that Stevens' thought is governed by assumptions considerably different from those customarily proposed by his critics. Chief among these is the common view that the "supreme fiction" is "broadly poetry itself"[1] or, in Bernard Heringman's more pointed observation, a moment when subject (imagination) and object (reality) meet in a "fictive synthesis."[2] There is of course considerable evidence for this view: Stevens does speak of the world as itself poetry ("There is . . . a world of poetry indistinguishable from the world in which we live" [NA, 31]) and repeatedly refers to the integration of reality and imagination—the "incessant conjunctioning between things as they are and things imagined."[3] Moreover, his consistent refusal to acknowledge traditional notions of the divine has suggested to his critics that concepts such as imagination, reality, and poetry—major elements of his thought—are naturalistically intended—that, indeed, as Louis Martz remarks, Stevens "lives in a world from which the elemental, the supernatural, and the mythical have been drained."[4] Notwithstanding the apparent justice of these arguments, the appearance of the Hermetic Man in a poem evidently dedicated to him invites skepticism of such critical estimates; for if the stony colossus represents a version of the "supreme fiction," it seems reasonable to assume that the imagination / reality dyad which gives rise to his presence equally springs from Hermetic assumptions. And, indeed, Hermetic thought perpetually revolves around this two-fold aspect of the Man, proposing him equally as the interior *imago Dei* lodged in the human imagination and the exterior *anima mundi*—the life-stuff of the universe. Their reintegration—the goal of Hermetic metamorphosis—represents a synthesis (a *unio mentalis*) marked by the color red and rendered iconographically by the resurrected androgyne. In view of Stevens' portrait of the red colossus, it would seem that if, indeed, the "supreme fiction" represents a synthesis between imagination and reality, the synthesis achieved is not poetry in its usual sense but the revival of the Man—what Stevens chose to call "pure poetry."

Perhaps the clearest account of Stevens' assumptions regarding the nature of poetry is afforded by "Large Red Man Reading," which not only describes the Man in the context of "life" and "reality," his traditional attributes, but also boldly asserts his presence in the title, suitably qualified by his customary hue and magnitude:

> There were ghosts that returned to earth to hear his phrases,
> As he sat there reading, aloud, the great blue tabulae.
> They were those from the wilderness of stars that had expected
>   more.
>
> There were those that returned to hear him read from the
>   poem of life,
> Of the pans above the stove, the pots on the table, the tulips
>   among them.
> They were those that would have wept to step barefoot into
>   reality,
>
> That would have wept and been happy, have shivered in the
>   frost
> And cried out to feel it again, have run fingers over leaves
> And against the most coiled thorn, have seized on what was
>   ugly
>
> And laughed, as he sat there reading, from out of the purple
>   tabulae,
> The outlines of being and its expressings, the syllables of its
>   law:
> *Poesis, poesis*, the literal characters, the vatic lines,
>
> Which in those ears and in those thin, those spended hearts,
> Took on color, took on shape and the size of things as they are
> And spoke the feeling for them, which was what they had
>   lacked.
>
>   (CP, 423–24)

That the "poem of life" to which the Large Red Man summons his auditors is indistinguishable from the Hermetic Life is the sense of Stevens' cooking images ("the pans above the stove, the pots on the table") designed to announce the Hermetic god of the hearth—the patron of the redemptive fire.[5] The tulips scattered among these utensils are similarly appropriate, since flowers play the part of the *prima materia* in Hermetic meditation.[6] Hence, in view of Stevens' numinous setting, we may reasonably conclude that poetry in its ordinary meaning is not here intended, though, to be sure, the poem as it is commonly understood is of considerable importance.

To prepare for metamorphosis, the Large Red Man reads from an ostensible text, instructing thereby a group of "ghosts" (the Anglo-Saxon word for spirit or soul) returned to hear his catechism. Since of course he is himself the "poem of life" in which he instructs his auditors, he properly inspires them to transcend the text or, as Stevens phrases it, to "step barefoot into reality," an image of divestment common to the poetry and intended to symbolize the shedding of the profane self as well as its aesthetic devisings. En route, the souls to be redeemed are envisioned (the grammar shifts to the past conditional, which manages to suggest futurity) as shivering in the "frost" (the Man in his congealed form) while touching a "coiled thorn" (the Man in his guise as the *serpens mercurii*) which is "ugly," a common description of the Hermetic Man.[7] Their sacramental journey prepares for the penultimate stanza, which foresees for them a *"poesis"* of "being" predictably "literal" rather than figurative, since the "poem" to which it alludes represents an ontological condition of "life" qualitatively different from the static trope which merely adumbrates its possibility.

"Large Red Man Reading" is of unusual interest, not only because it affords another portrait of the Man but because it once again affirms Stevens' concern with two poetries: "the poem of the idea within the poem of the words" (OP, 174). "Owl's Clover," as we have seen, expressed this doubleness in the image of the statue, transformed in the course of the poem from an inert thing containing the divine idea of the Man (in this case, the mythic Ananke) to a living being, or the idea actualized—transformed into "pure poetry." Here, too, a similar possibility is entertained, guided equally by the assumption that the poetic text prefigures the poetic "life"—that, indeed, the text is the element from which "life" springs. By this token, the Large Red Man is himself a poem, but a poem distilled from an aesthetic object and made equivalent in Stevens' account with "being," which, in Hermetic terms, is another name for the spiritual metamorphosis undertaken in the imagination and culminating in the revivification of the Man. It would thus appear, if we grant the equivalence of the red colossus and the Large Red Man, that Stevens means the "supreme fiction" to represent a transcendental condition of life.

It seems equally likely that Stevens regarded this transformation as a higher form of poetry, which he consistently sought to distinguish from its "lesser" model by attaching to it qualifying epithets such as "supreme," "pure," "ultimate," "larger," "central," and "grand." Indeed, in view of this arbitrary conjunction of the Hermetic Man with a peerless "poetry," there is good reason to believe that Stevens' initial decision to title his first collection of poetry "THE GRAND POEM: PRELIMINARY MINUTIAE" (L, 237) reflects an early preoccupation with the Man; for the title not only suggests the cosmic One in the epithet of magnitude Stevens consistently used to distinguish him *qua* poem from the ordinary poem, but manages to strike a note of the anticipatory as well as of the incomplete to announce, it would seem, the aesthetic object as a form "preliminary" to the advent of the Man. Even more suggestive of the importance Stevens attached to the Man is his desire to caption his *Collected Poems* "THE WHOLE OF HARMONIUM" (L, 831); for if the "THE GRAND POEM" and *Harmonium* are interchangeable, as Stevens appears to have thought, and if, to restate the argument, "THE GRAND POEM" is another euphemism for the Man, it would follow that "THE WHOLE OF HARMONIUM" is equally a rubric for the One, who is equivalent in Hermetic thought to the "whole" which heralds the restored *unus mundus*. It would thus appear that the Man is Stevens' major, if not sole, concern, as he himself proposed (albeit with usual indirection) when, in a brief autobiographical comment, he acknowledged the "supreme fiction" as his "central theme" (L, 820).

Stevens' essays afford additional instances of his desire to propose the Man in the guise of a "supreme" poetry. In "The Relations between Poetry and Painting," for example, a variation of "THE GRAND POEM" arises in the poet's reference to an aesthetic order subsuming all its "manifestations" (NA, 160)—a "universal poetry that is reflected in everything" (NA, 160). Later in the same essay, it is entertained as a "mystical aesthetic" (NA, 173) which establishes that "all things, whether below or above appearance, are one" (NA, 174), a locution which echoes the Hermetic doctrine of correspondence: "What is below is like that which is above, and what is above is like that which is below, to accomplish the miracles of one thing."[8] "A Collect of Philosophy" proposes the Man as a "cosmic poetry" that generates the exchange of a "lesser life for a greater one" (OP, 189) much like a "transmutation of poetry" (OP, 189), suggesting in the reference to the "one" and to "transmutation," the alchemical word for the transformation of matter, the "pure poetry" of the Man (the "greater one") extracted from the "lesser" poem.[9] In "Imagination as Value," the *anima mundi* appears as the "universal mind" which the imagination seeks to "satisfy," thereby to compose a "fundamental poetry even older than the ancient world" (NA, 145). Finally, "The Figure of the Youth as Virile Poet" suggests the universal soul as a "mystical *vis* or *noeud vital*" (NA, 49) that is a "center of poetry" (NA, 44). Later in the same essay, it emerges as "the center of a physical poetry" (NA, 65) that, for all its physicality, is a metaphysical "non-geography" corresponding, in typical Hermetic fashion, to man's "own thoughts and . . . feelings" (NA, 66).

ⓖ ⓖ ⓓ ⓓ

In pursuing further the implications of Stevens' Hermetic Man for the poetry as a whole, it is useful to note that the Large Red Man is associated with "reality," a term usually understood by Stevens' readers in the context of Cartesian dualism. We may perhaps probe this assumption by exploring the opening stanza of "An Ordinary Evening in New Haven," which begins by questioning phenomenal reality ("The eye's plain version" [CP, 465]), introduces next the "never-ending meditation" (CP, 465), the mode of Hermetic metamorphosis, continues with the shedding of the profane self ("a second giant kills the first" [CP, 465]), and concludes with the Man as cosmic poem—"A larger poem for a larger audience"—described equally as "A recent imagining of reality":

> A recent imagining of reality,
> Much like a new resemblance of the sun,
> Down-pouring, up-springing and inevitable,
> A larger poem for a larger audience,
> As if the crude collops came together as one,
> A mythological form, a festival sphere,
> A great bosom, beard and being, alive with age.
>
> (CP, 465–66)

Using the device of a cumulative catalogue which allows for multiple equivalencies,[10] Stevens here compares the Man to "sun" and "sphere," his traditional symbols; proposes him as "being," alive and venerable; intimates in "inevitable" the inexorable law he represents (a version of the "fateful" Ananke); associates him with the "sophic" waters ("down-pouring"); charts in "down-pouring" and "up-springing" the *descensus* (distillation) and *ascensus* (sublimation) that mark the stages of alchemical purification; and suggests the joyous beatitude of union ("festival"). Above all, the strategy of cumulative epithets permits Stevens to link the Man-poem to an image of cooking, described as the preparation of "crude collops" (a dish cooked over coal) which, when subjected to the "sophic" fire, assimilate one to the other to produce the cosmic "one." It would thus appear, if we are to grant Stevens' culinary metaphor its apparent intent, that the Man-poem is a being distilled from a secondary "crude" substance; and since Stevens persistently associates him with poetry, we can only assume that the base form from which he arises is the "lesser" poem that Stevens created to project his being. Of interest, too, is that Stevens considers the Man synonymous with reality, but this reality, it would seem, is an "imagining"—a thing created by the mind and apparently distinguishable from the sensible world. And, indeed, this view of reality is reaffirmed in section v of the poem—again in connection with a thing "seen by the mind," but this time associated with "water," "glass," and "mirror," common Hermetic symbols of the "sophic" Man:

> Reality as a thing seen by the mind,
> Not that which is but that which is apprehended,
> A mirror, a lake of reflections in a room,
> A glassy ocean lying at the door . . .
>
> (CP, 468)

From this account, it appears that if, indeed, the Man-poem is equivalent to reality, the real he represents is something cultivated and fashioned in the imagination, a view consistent with Hermetic meditation, as I shall shortly note. First, however, it is well to point out that Louis Martz has affirmed the importance of meditation in Stevens' poetry. Though persuaded of Stevens' naturalism, Martz sees a resemblance between Stevens' meditative mode and the formal religious meditations of Donne, Herbert, and Hopkins, suggesting that Stevens adopted a religious form to forge a secular "poetic self"[11] as a substitute for the loss of religious belief. The analogy is suggestive, if somewhat puzzling; and we might well ask, as has Adalaide Kirby Morris, why it is that "a modern poet vastly different in knowledge and belief from the seventeenth-century meditative poets" should find meditation "congenial."[12] The answer, it may be, is to be sought in the title of Stevens' late poem "The World as Meditation," which takes as its meditative subject the cosmic Great World of Hermetic thought. And, indeed, Stevens clarifies this important connection between the Man and meditation in his description of the macroanthropos of "Examination of the Hero in a Time of War," painted as "Man-sun, man-moon, man-earth, man-ocean" and accorded the rite of contemplation: "This is his night and meditation" (CP, 280). Equally, his appearance as "the larger poem" and "mythological form" of "An Ordinary Evening in New Haven" prompts an avowal of "perpetual meditation, point / Of the enduring, visionary love" (CP, 466). From these suggestive allusions, it would seem that Stevens' kinship to seventeenth-century meditative poets is perhaps closer than Martz had thought; for the religious element inherent in the meditative mode appears to be common to both.

Since I have elsewhere chronicled the stages of Hermetic meditation, I shall focus here on its metaphysical and epistemological assumptions. According to Hermetic doctrine, the rebirth of the divine androgyne effected in the imagination connotes a spiritual denouement which qualitatively alters both soul and world, substituting for the workaday world of ordinary matter the metaphysical terrain of the absolute Real. Known in Hermetic lore as an intermediate realm midway between pure spirit and gross matter (the "*anima media natura*"), this interworld is similar to the world of Platonic Forms. But whereas Platonic metaphysics presupposes the absolute separation of Ideas and matter, Hermetic metaphysics embeds the universal Forms in the physical world and grants them phenomenological substance reputedly "seen" by the purged and irradiated eye. According to Henry Corbin, a student of ancient Zoroastrianism and its revival in Iranian Shaikhism—an Islamic interpretation of the alchemical tradition—these archetypes are generated in the imagination and are projected outward, calling into being their corresponding image residing in the natural object. Accordingly, the earth so perceived is experienced as a spiritual extension of the self, affording the soul the existential truth of the unity of matter, alchemy's fundamental premise and the spiritual goal of the Operation:

> Essentially this mode of perception implies an intellectual faculty that is not limited to the sole use of conceptual abstraction nor to the sensory perception of physical data. . . . [It is] essentially a

psychic event which can "take place" neither in the world of im-
personal abstract concepts nor on the plane of mere sensory data.
The Earth has to be perceived not by the senses, but through a
primordial Image and, inasmuch as this Image carries the features
of a personal figure, it will prove to "symbolize with" the very
Image of itself which the soul carries in its innermost depths.[13]

The perception of a radically altered reality—what Stevens calls
"pure reality" (CP, 471) or, more precisely, "the reality / Of the other
eye" (CP, 448)—is of course a familiar feature of Stevens' thought,
arising in the "Adagia" in the poet's ruminations on the sacramental
suggestiveness of the sensible world seen by the intuitive eye: "The
thing seen becomes the thing unseen" (OP, 167); "The poet is the
priest of the invisible" (OP, 169); "What we see in the mind is as real
to us as what we see by the eye" (OP, 162). Realism, as it is commonly understood, is consequently dismissed as "a corruption of reality" (OP, 166); for as Stevens notes to a correspondent, "The mind
with metaphysical affinities has a dash when it deals with reality that
the purely realistic mind never has because the purely realistic mind
never experiences any passion for reality" (L, 597). In "The Irrational
Element in Poetry," the poet's task is described as "the transposition of
an objective reality to a subjective reality" (OP, 217), for only by so
perceiving the outer world in its spiritual guise can the poet approach,
Stevens elsewhere notes, "a reality of or within or beneath the surface
of reality" (OP, 213). Hence, since reality is the impalpable seed of
Life common to both the inner and outer world, Stevens can claim,
without the least contradiction, that "Reality is the spirit's true center"
(OP, 177) and can reverently invoke a spiritual reality consubstantial
with the world itself: "Feed my lambs (on the bread of living) . . . The
glory of god is the glory of the world . . . To find the spiritual in
reality . . . To be concerned with reality" (OP, 178).

The transcendental Real born in the Hermetic soul is the spiritual
entity that Stevens proffered in the name of aesthetics, proposing it,
variously, as the "supreme fiction," "pure poetry," the "ultimate

poem," the "poem of pure reality." Though the conjunction is no
doubt arbitrary, if not deliberately misleading, Stevens did attempt to
clarify his meaning in "Owl's Clover" and continued to do so repeatedly in his susbsequent work. One such poem, clearer than most
in its assumptions and structure, is "A Primitive Like an Orb," titled
to represent the Man—always pictured as spherical in accord with the
cosmic World he represents. Like many of Stevens' poems, it is
shaped by the requirements of Hermetic correspondence,[14] moving in
centrifugal fashion from the interior Man lodged in the imagination to
the outer cosmic Life, personified in the concluding stanzas as a "prodigious" giant. The introduction, an exordium of sorts, states the
poem's premise in a series of encomiastic equivalencies which celebrate the Hermetic "essential gold" (CP, 440), the Man in his guise as
the perfected substance of the alchemical art. (In Hermetism "essential" signifies the spiritual or "subtle" body of the archetype.)[15] The
poet next turns to the difficult question of proof. Since the divine Man
is a metaphysical entity unamenable to empirical verification, his
form, it appears, may be experienced in art, the "lesser" poem that
inspires a psychic resonance in the soul confirming the Man's ineffable
presence:

> We do not prove the existence of the poem.
> It is something seen and known in lesser poems.
> It is the huge, high harmony that sounds
> A little and a little, suddenly,
> By means of a separate sense. It is and it
> Is not and, therefore, is. In the instant of speech,
> The breadth of an accelerando moves,
> Captives the being, widens—and was there.
>
> (CP, 440)

The poem struggles to record the mystery of the beatific vision
common to the mystical tradition to which Hermetism belongs.
Fragmentary, transient, yet, withal, bringing to the soul so irradiated
"a valid and ineffable apprehension of the Real,"[16] the sacramental
encounter with the divine image constitutes the supreme moment of
revelation. Though joy is its invariable accompaniment, as Stevens' *O
altitudo!* testifies, it is, according to mystical testimony, intractable to
language; hence, to transcribe it as recollection, Stevens notes, is "always too heavy for the sense / To seize, the obscurest as, the distant
was" (CP, 441). Effort is consequently abandoned, as the poet resorts

to characteristic superlative, proposing that for "clairvoyant men that need no proof" (CP, 441), the "central poem" is simply a plenum—a "fulfillment of fulfillments" (CP, 441).

The proof of the intuitive eye yields next to a description of metamorphosis, urged in the accent of hypothesis to imply futurity—the condition of Life accessible but as yet unrealized. Typically, transmutative possibility follows the alchemical pattern of divestment and acquisition, urged first as the need for earth, sky, tree, and cloud to "lose" their "old uses" (CP, 441) (read the shedding of their material disguise) in order that the "central poem" (the immaterial Man) may be perceived in its equivalence to the cosmic "world." Typically, too, palingenesis takes the shape of the "chymical marriage" which unites "poem" and "summer" to create the "one" immanent in world and self and not, the poet reminds us, a "light apart, up-hill":

> It is
> As if the central poem became the world,
> And the world the central poem, each one the mate
> Of the other, as if summer was a spouse,
> Espoused each morning, each long afternoon,
> And the mate of summer: her mirror and her look,
> Her only place and person, a self of her
> That speaks, denouncing separate selves, both one.
> The essential poem begets the others. The light
> Of it is not a light apart, up-hill.
>
> (CP, 441)

With inexorable logic, the motif of cosmic assimilation leads next to a panegyric to the "poem of the whole" (CP, 442), the Hermetic *unus mundus* appropriately personified as a spherical power—"The roundness that pulls tight the final ring" (CP, 442)—and considered, once again, the prototype of its secondary manifestations—"the miraculous multiplex of lesser poems" (CP, 442). A more philosophical formulation follows, offering the *vis Mercurii* in terms of light, height, force, kinship, order and rest, his traditional attributes, and proposing him as the object of meditation:

> And that which in an altitude would soar,
> A vis, a principle or, it may be,
> The meditation of a principle,
> Or else an inherent order active to be

> Itself, a nature to its natives all
> Beneficence, a repose, utmost repose,
> The muscles of a magnet aptly felt,
> A giant, on the horizon, glistening . . .
>
> (CP, 442)

The appearance of the "glistening" giant prompts the customary catalogue of nimbus images—the "bright excellence" (CP, 442), "familiar fire" (CP, 442), "scintillant sizzlings" (CP, 442) appropriate to the god of the "sophic" fire. To this, the poet adds the equally customary images of inflation—the giant is "prodigious" (CP, 443), "large" (CP, 443), "massive" (CP, 443), of "parental magnitude" (CP, 443), a "majesty" (CP, 442)—locates the Man in the sacred "centre on the horizon" (CP, 443)[17] and reaffirms his immaterial presence in the mind—"an abstraction given head" (CP, 443). A final "definition" paints him as "the skeleton of the ether" (CP, 443) ("ether," in alchemical parlance, in another name for the diaphanous and incorruptible quintessence), as well as the exemplification of "nothingness," a common designation in the esoteric tradition for the immaterial realm of spirit subsuming the phenomenal world. So conceived, he arises in the peroration as the archetypal patron of all art and myth—secondary expressions of his being:

> That's it. The lover writes, the believer hears,
> The poet mumbles and the painter sees,
> Each one, his fated eccentricity,
> As a part, but part, but tenacious particle,
> Of the skeleton of the ether, the total
> Of letters, prophecies, perceptions, clods
> Of colors, the giant of nothingness, each one
> And the giant ever changing, living in change.
>
> (CP, 443)[18]

Chapter 6

The Hermetic Dyad

. . . a law of inherent opposites,
Of essential unity, is as pleasant as port . . .

"'The search / For reality,'" Stevens has Professor Eucalyptus say in "An Ordinary Evening in New Haven," "'is as momentous as / The search for god'":

> It is the philosopher's search
>
> For an interior made exterior
> And the poet's search for the same exterior made
> Interior . . .
>
> (CP, 481)

If, as seems likely, the "philosopher" to whom Stevens alludes is the "philosopher" of Hermetic thought, the passage affords a succinct account of a spiritual quest that perceives deity as at once the inner core of the self and the outer core of the world. Far from being common matter alien to human sentiency, the "real" in this religious view is the "subtle" world of spirit—what the Hermetist sought to disengage from its coarse and mortal mixture in the course of meditation. Accordingly, Professor Eucalyptus' "'search for reality'" can be justly regarded as "'The search for god,'" as Stevens avers; for the Hermetic Man is himself the "subtle" real, spawned, nurtured, and delivered in the imagination. In short, he is a god who is both "interior" and "exterior," in Stevens' accurate description.

Such spiritual assumptions suggest, perhaps, that Stevens is not the unsystematic thinker he is commonly thought to be. For when he celebrates the imagination's metamorphic powers, at the same time as he seemingly reverses himself by urging the mind's effacement before reality, he is not, if we grant him the premises I have urged, engaged in an unresolved dialectic marked by "division" and "contradiction," as J. Hillis Miller concludes,[1] but is attending to the various stages of a spiritual metamorphosis which originates in the imagination and culminates in a mystical perception of the Real—the metaphysical essence thought to be indistinguishable from the self. Such an act, as Harold Watts rightly observes, implies "man emptied," for it results from a psychological reversal that restores the hegemony of the unconscious, bare of the "institutions, codes, history" that are the legacy of estrangement.[2] To divest the soul of its "unnatural" ideas is, however, to prepare it for the universal—or, in Stevens' terms, the "first"—idea, boundless, formless, eternal, its image, created in the mind and projected outward, an act of perception that Stevens properly considers an "act of grace" (OP, 39). By this standard, what has generally been taken as Stevens' thoroughgoing nominalism, relieved of "the oppressive distortion of ideas,"[3] is, in fact, a thoroughgoing realism, which not only proposes the world as a purely subjective conception, but so welds it to mind that it is transformed into mind itself. Following the logic of these spiritual assumptions, Stevens could properly alternate between imagination and reality, claiming each as "the only genius" (OP, 177; 179) without contradiction, for both imply and involve each other; neither has an existence apart from its correlative.

The metamorphosis of self and matter constitutes the core of Hermetic monism, which regards man and nature as one substance—a view reflected in Stevens' conviction that "Life and Nature are one" (L, 533). The view is often reaffirmed in the poetry: "It is the earth itself that is humanity," Stevens writes in one poem, completing the affirmation of Hermetic monism with images of the Man's masculine and feminine elements—the "inhuman son" and the "fateful mother, whom he does not know" (CP, 454). Elsewhere, the conviction is stated in an idiom reminiscent of propositional form: "The soul . . . is composed / Of the external world" (CP, 51); "I am what is around me" (CP, 86); "Nota: his soil is man's intelligence" (CP, 36); "The world is myself. Life is myself" (OP, 172). Similarly, Stevens often roots his characters in the cosmic soil, granting them names such as "Johannisberger Hans," "Mrs. Alfred Uruguay," "Mr. Homburg," "Redwood Roamer," "Professor Eucalyptus," to announce their affinity to the celestial earth.

Though the conviction of unity guides the purpose of Hermetic metamorphosis, Hermetism combines in its ethos the common gnostic sense of division and unity, separation and integration, estrangement and return. Hence, the metamorphic process undertaken to restore the divine androgyne is rooted initially in fracture, at times intimated in the doctrine of correspondence, which proposed that though divided the world soul (macrocosm) and individual soul (microcosm) had formerly been one (the *unus mundus*), at times painted in alchemical iconography in images of the separated masculine and feminine contraries which the Work proposed to join. Reintegration at the culmination of religious contemplation constituted "a restoration of the original state of the cosmos,"[4] or the moment of synthesis when the soul joined its "divine unconsciousness" to the analogous substance of its cosmic counterpart.

In Stevens' work, the tonal modalities of exile and reintegration range from a despair which "anatomizes a stale and withered life" to an "ecstatic idiom" which "proclaims . . . the pure good of being"— Helen Vendler's useful description of Stevens' shifting moods.[5] The alternation may be ascribed to the Hermetic dyad, at times described as divided, at times affirmed as reintegrated in the guise of poetry *extraordinaire*. These putative antinomies Stevens faithfully formulates as "a law of inherent opposites, / Of essential unity" (CP, 215), repeatedly affirming their interrelatedness in images of paired coordinates essential to a vision that perceives deity as a divided, though ultimately single, force.

In its least inventive and obviously derivative guise, the Hermetic dyad arises in images of rock, mountain, air, and circle, traditional alchemical symbols of the *prima materia* (the Man) common to man, earth, and the over-arching cosmic spirit. Thus, it is proffered in "The Rock" (titled to represent the *lapis*) as halves of the numinous "stone," at once the "gray particular of man's life" (CP, 528) and "the stern particular of the air" (CP, 528), the last characteristically swelling to become a cosmic "mirror of the planets" (CP, 528). "Credences of Summer" expresses the parallels between earth and heaven in the image of the cosmic mountain "half way green" (CP, 375), while its counterpart, "The other immeasurable half" (CP, 375), dissolves into spirit, "such rock / As placid air becomes" (CP, 375). In "Repetitions of a Young Captain," the Perfect Man assumes the shape of a circle, halved to represent, on the one hand, the chthonic element—a "half-arc in mid-earth" (CP, 309)—and, on the other, the pneumatic element, a "half-arc hanging in mid-air" (CP, 309). "Dezembrum" states the division of the Hermetic Great World without recourse to symbol:

> Over and over again you have said,
> This great world, it divides itself in two,
> One part is man, the other god:
> Imagined man, the monkish mask, the face.   (CP, 218)

More opaque but decidedly ingenious is Stevens' personification of the macrocosm/microcosm duo in poem xxx of "The Man with the Blue Guitar." Here the macrocosm is represented by an "old fantoche," while the microcosm takes the form of the community of "Oxidia"—its name deriving from "Oxide" (L, 790) to suggest the divine *pneuma* embedded in the base compound:

> From this I shall evolve a man.
> This is his essence: the old fantoche
> Hanging his shawl upon the wind,
> Like something on the stage, puffed out,
>
> His strutting studied through centuries.
> At last, in spite of his manner, his eye
>
> A-cock at the cross-piece on a pole
> Supporting heavy cables, slung
>
> Through Oxidia, banal suburb,
> One-half of all its installments paid.
>
> Dew-dapper clapper-traps, blazing
> From crusty stacks above machines.
>
> Ecce, Oxidia is the seed
> Dropped out of this amber-ember pod,
>
> Oxidia is the soot of fire,
> Oxidia is Olympia.
>
> (CP, 181–82)

The poem divides into two parts, half a description of the "old fantoche," French for marionette or puppet, half a description of a seemingly ordinary community—a "banal suburb." The two are, however, appropriately joined in the image of "cables" (a symbol of light and of Hermetic interrelatedness) borne by the "old fantoche" and "slung" across to his constituency. In this fashion, the "old fantoche" assumes the double role of the Man, at once the active transformer of the soul (the slinger of cables) and the passive soul transformed (a mechanical puppet or artifice created by the imagination). Hence, the Man is described as pneumatic—an "essence" and "wind . . . puffed out"—and assumes the form of a *quaternio*—an "eye / A-cock at the cross-piece on a pole"—which manages as well to suggest in "cock" the soul made resurrect.

Since the "old fantoche" is the transmutative agent, the community to which he is attached is properly regenerated in the pattern of the Operation. Transformation begins in "Oxidia," the base element considered in Stevens' allegory "the typical industrial suburb, stained and grim" (L, 790). To suggest the preliminary stage, Oxidia is made a suburb to propose its origin in the mind (the prefix "sub") as well as its distance from the divine center. The allusion to installments but half-paid similarly signifies the condition of scission, the state that gives rise to the contraries. Thus, Stevens notes, Oxidia and Olympia "are opposites. Oxidia is the antipodes of Olympia" (L, 790).

The initiation of the Work is signalled by the Philosophic fire emerging from "dew-dapper clapper traps," "not a modern piece of equipment," Stevens notes, but one that emits "a white heat" (L, 791). (In Stevens' sketch drawn in the margin of his note, the contraption assumes the shape of a smokestack with a lid on top.)[6] From this "sophic" furnace there next drops a "seed" (a common term for the divine *filius*) from an "amber-ember pod," its fiery yellow interchangeable in alchemy's chromatic spectrum with white, the symbol of purification. The process culminates in "Ecce," the heraldic call announcing the new-born Man extracted from the "soot of fire" and made synonymous with "Olympia," the cosmic mountain. To outline the fundamental alchemical notion that the *filius* is both the embryo *and* its life-sustaining vessel, Stevens explains that Oxidia "is both the seed and the amber-ember pod from which the seed of Olympia drops. The dingier the life, the more lustrous the paradise. But, if the only paradise must be here and now, Oxidia is Olympia" (L, 789).

It is well to note that Stevens' gloss to this poem affirms the "old fantoche" (the Man) as the subject of meditation and proposes him as mankind's "abstract . . . ancestor"—an unreal but of course luminous figure who, in the whimsy of sustained allegory, turns out to be currently employed by the "Oxidia Electric Light & Power Company":

> Man, when regarded for a sufficient length of time, as an object of study, assumes the appearance of a property, as that word is used in the theatre or in a studio. He becomes, in short, one of the fantoccini of meditation or, as I have called him, "the old fantouche." . . . As we think about him, he tends to become abstract. We cannot think of him as originating in Oxidia. We go back to an ancestor who is abstract and being abstract, that is to say, unreal, finds it a simple matter to hang his coat upon the wind, like an actor who has been strutting and seeking to increase his importance through centuries, whom we find, suddenly and at last, actually and presently, to be an employe of the Oxidia Electric Light & Power Company. (L, 791)

That Stevens considers the "old fantoche" an "abstract" image recalls the figure of "major man," announced at the conclusion of "It Must Be Abstract" (the first section of "Notes toward a Supreme Fiction") as "The major abstraction" (CP, 388). The significance of this conjunction, which evokes an ostensible human form only to deny it particularity, can be best grasped, perhaps, in the image of the "old fantoche," equally a figure patterned in the image of man but one which is quickly internalized and proposed as an apparition ("fantoccini") encountered in the mind in the course of "meditation." So interiorized, he becomes a nonsensible or, more precisely, suprasensible entity for whom the epithet "abstract," in the sense of impalpable, may be properly applied. Since he is a purely mental conception or image, he may be said to be an "idea"; indeed, in Hermetic metaphysics, he is the archetypal Idea—the model and source of all life. Hence he is the patriarch without peer who, because he is the prototype of humanity (mankind's "ancestor," as Stevens puts it), may with justice and consistency be deemed the "idea of man" who is equally the "first idea"—a concept repeatedly explored in the opening stanzas of "It Must Be Abstract" and reaffirmed in the appearance of "major man," its personified form and a version of the supreme "abstraction" encountered in Hermetic meditation.

Since "major man," like the red colossus, represents the final stage of Hermetic meditation, his appearance in "It Must Be Abstract" is preceded by a version of the contraries—an earlier stage and one Stevens often uses to presage reintegration:

> We say: At night an Arabian in my room,
> With his damned hoobla-hoobla-hoobla-how,
> Inscribes a primitive astronomy
> Across the unscrawled fores the future casts
> And throws his stars around the floor. By day
> The wood-dove used to chant his hoobla-hoo
> And still the grossest iridescence of ocean
> Howls hoo and rises and howls hoo and falls.
> Life's nonsense pierces us with strange relation.
>
> (CP, 383)

The opposites are here proffered in the guise of an Arabian (the "moon" [L, 433]), chanting a "primitive" text of the "future" in the "night" of the imagination, while his external counterpart, the wood-dove, chants the same text in the "day" as "he used to," expressing in the grammar of past action the primordial Life in its original unitary form. The "hoo" chant common to both acts as the vocalic tie which echoes in the irradiated "sophic" waters of the soul; but because the divine "ocean" has yet to be distilled from its gross mixture, Stevens appropriately qualifies it as "grossest," only to suggest its purification in the rise (sublimation) and fall (distillation) of the shared chant. The allusion to the "Life"—the Man who produces the "strange relation" between the imagination and its external counterpart—reaffirms the concept of correspondence and reintegration that governs both structure and theme.

The putative "nonsense" syllables uttered by both Arabian and wood-dove are of special interest; for the word "hoo" is an Arabic term that in its calligraphic form looks like the number four. Hence, in Sufism, the Islamic counterpart of Western alchemy, the word is regarded as a quaternity symbol chanted in Sufic liturgy "to produce ecstatic states."[7] Stevens seems to have had a particular interest in the word; for it appears in one of its mutations as the name "Hoon" accorded a majestic figure who dominates the early lyric "Tea at the Palaz of Hoon" (CP, 65). This figure Stevens glosses as "the expanse of sky and space" and as the "son of old man Hoon" (L, 871) to suggest the familial correspondence between father (macrocosm) and son (microcosm).[8] Elsewhere the word surfaces in the early "Bantams in Pine-Woods" to characterize a sound uttered by a "universal cock" (CP, 75) whose "henna" hue, in combination with the iterated syllable "tan," Chinese for the divine "elixir," suggest him as yet another version of the cosmic Man.[9] In "Sea Surface Full of Clouds," the syllable characterizes the sound of "gongs" issuing from the "sophic" waters and heard just after the poet apostrophizes the Man as "*mon frère du ciel, ma vie, mon or*" (CP, 100). "Mozart, 1935" invokes the word as part of an adjurative recipe—addressed ostensibly to the poet—advising him to extract the sound of "hoo" from the piano (the poet's verses). Subsequently, it takes on its customary primordial and prophetic resonance, described as a "lucid souvenir of the past" (CP, 132), as well as an "airy dream of the future" (CP, 132).

Stevens' use of a vocable to designate the Heavenly Man reflects the importance accorded music and sound in Hermetic thought. The notion that both the universe and man are constructed on the same harmonic proportions homologous to music is a common theme in alchemy, deriving perhaps from the Pythagorean conception that the numerical relationships between the notes of the musical scale equally defined the harmonic relations of the cosmos. According to the *Corpus Hermeticum*, the "science of music" corresponds to the order of the universe designed in its musical consonance by the supreme protoplastus—"by nature a musician, and not only works harmony in the universe at large, but also transmits to individuals the rhythm of his own music."[10] In alchemical iconography, the music of the "supreme artist" is reflected in frequent musical motifs, represented, at times, by Hermes, the reputed founder of the Hermetic art and the patron of music, and by allegorical and mythological figures bearing musical instruments, among them the lyre and the lute, instruments akin to the guitar strummed by Stevens' guitarist. Indeed, John Read conjectures that the alchemical belief in musical influences encouraged a musical accompaniment to the Operation:

> . . . in view of the alchemical belief in the beneficent influence of music, it is likely that the processes of the Great Work were sometimes performed to the accompaniment of musical chants or incantations. To the religious mystics among the alchemists, in particular, these processes partook of the nature of a religious ritual, and it would be natural for them to introduce music from one of these closely related activities to the other.[11]

The Hermetic *harmonia mundi* that served to title Stevens' first volume of poetry vibrates like a sacred obbligato throughout the poetry. Indeed, the entire canon may be profitably considered a "musical trope"—John Hollander's apt description of a poetic music which recalls the romantic search for an "authentication of human music as an instance of something transcendent."[12] And, indeed, the parallel may stand, if accommodated to the Hermetic vision which appears to have shaped Stevens' musical image.

In appraising the place of the aural motif in Stevens' attention to the Hermetic coordinates, it is well to note at the outset that just as the poet is committed to the notion of two poetries, so, too, does he propose two versions of music and sound. As always, the paradigmatic gloss for this hierarchy is to be sought in the character of the Ananke-subman of "Owl's Clover." Ananke, it will be recalled, is an estranged god, though, to be sure, he continues to exert his spiritual power in art and myth—the "lesser" forms that express a lapsed condition of consciousness. Hence, his music in the fallen world finds its echo in the surrogate forms of art, or, as Stevens phrases it, "His hymn, his psalm, his cithern song of praise / Is the exile of the disinherited" (OP, 59) that resound in "the perpetual verses in a poet's mind" (OP, 59). For this reason, his subman counterpart directs humanity to pierce the "masks of music," so to penetrate the surface disguise that hides the original music of the primordial Life:

> He turns us into scholars, studying
> The masks of music. We perceive the mask
> To be the musician's own and, thence, become
> An audience to mimics glistening
> With meanings, doubled by the closest sound,
> Mimics that play on instruments discerned
> In the beat of the blood.
>
> (OP, 67)

The estrangement that gives rise to poetry, a mere echo of the original divine music, is similarly the theme of "To the One of Fictive Music," a poem addressed to the feminine element of the One (incorporated in the title). Tenderly apostrophized in the opening stanza, she is the poet's muse, but the music she inspires, it is well to note, arises from the scission "That separates us from the wind and sea" (CP, 87), Stevens' twin symbols for the divine essence and its corresponding analogue in the "sophic" waters of the soul. Hence, the poem concludes on a note of supplication, entreating the divine "musician" to bear on her brow "A band entwining, set with fatal stones" (CP, 88)—the alchemical symbol of redemption—thus to restore the primordial imagination anterior to the birth of "fictive music"—Stevens' phrase for the aesthetic forms that arose with humanity's severance from its primordial source:

Unreal, give back to us what once you gave:
The imagination that we spurned and crave.

(CP, 88)

Since Hermetic doctrine considers the Man the supreme musician, he is himself the principle of music coincident with the human soul, as Stevens acknowledges, urging with customary indirection that "The principle of music would be an addition to humanity if it were not humanity itself, in other than human form, and while this hyperbole is certain to be repulsive to a good many people, still it may stand" (OP, 233). A less expansive version of the same view appears in one of the letters: "In music we hear ourselves most definitely, but most crudely. It is easy enough to look forward to a time when crudely will be less crudely, and then subtler: in the long run, why not subtler than we ourselves?" (L, 350). In this conjunction of music and humanity, though, to be sure, a music heard "crudely" and then made "subtler" (words that recall the alchemical "subtle" body extracted from the "crude" substance), Stevens expresses the common theosophical belief that music is identical to the cosmic spirit—that, indeed, in the phrasing of one initiate, it is, in its fallen form, "essentially a power . . . the faint, much-changed, much-enfeebled, sole relic, and tradition, and reminder of Man's Lost Paradise."[13] In Kabbalistic lore, this original though "enfeebled" music is considered the "inner voice" which echoes "in the innermost depths of all things," its sound an "infinite light which, by refraction in the ether, has been transformed into revelatory, creative and redemptive 'sound.' "[14]

This redemptive voice babbles, murmurs, hums, and buzzes in Stevens' poetry, its music a duet of the pneumatic essence and its corresponding echo in the soul. In "The Woman That Had More Babies Than That," the resonant "humming of the central man" (OP, 82) reverberates in the soul's redemptive waters—the "central humming of the sea" (OP, 82). Hence, in true gnostic fashion, Stevens considers the soul as itself a sacramental "cloister," its interior life a harmonic dyad of innate "remembered sounds" joined to a vocalic mate—"a voice that doubles its own" (OP, 82). In "Evening without Angels," the echoic movement is reversed, appearing first as the outer primordial sound—the "antiquest sounds of air" (CP, 137)—repeated in the human soul "In an accord of repetitions" (CP, 137). The redemptive encounter of "Things of August" is similarly transacted between "the voice of one" which "Meets nakedly another's naked

voice" (CP, 489), their conjunction personified by another image of
the monarchic red Man who instructs humanity to seek his being beyond the symbols of the poet's speech:

> A crown within him of crispest diamonds,
> A reddened garment falling to his feet,
> A hand of light to turn the page,
> A finger with a ring to guide his eye
> From line to line, as we lie on the grass and listen
> To that which has no speech,
> The voluble intentions of the symbols,
> The ghostly celebrations of the picnic,
> The secretions of insight.
>
> (CP, 492)

Possibly the most inventive account of the redemptive sound, this
time used to chart the stages of the Work, is the avial aria of "It Must
Change." The operatic principals are here imaged as a "bird / Of
stone" (CP, 394) (the Man granted a common symbol of spirit) whose
beckoning "bethou me" is opposed to the "ké-ké" song of wren, jay,
and robin. Properly "inimical . . . opposing sounds," as Stevens notes
(L, 438), they represent the import of the transmutative process,
which begins in discord and ends in harmony, so that, in effect, their
counterpoint articulates the metamorphosis or "change" that is the
subject of the section as a whole. For this reason, the quartet takes
place in a "glade," a symbol of metaphysical reality, and is accom-
panied by rain, the purifying "sophic" waters:

> Bethou me, said sparrow, to the crackled blade,
> And you, and you, bethou me as you blow,
> When in my coppice you behold me be.
> Ah, ké! the bloody wren, the felon jay,
> Ké-ké, the jug-throated robin pouring out,
> Bethou, bethou, bethou me in my glade.
>
> (CP, 393–94)

The epithets "bloody" and "felon" that qualify wren and jay respectively represent the conflict of the opposites (Stevens notes that
wrens are "fighters" [L, 435]) which precedes the ritual death that
dissolves the soul in preparation for its resurrection. Hence, the
"minstrelsy" of the avial quartet takes on the quality of mutilation,
which Stevens renders as "clappers going without bells" and which he

glosses as a "change [that] destroys them utterly" (L, 438).[15] But since, the poet continues, "In the face of death life asserts itself" (L, 438) (read the Life made resurrect), the poem concludes with conflict resolved and reintegration achieved. This Stevens manages by blending his images so that, he explains, referring in customary fashion to the One, "a number of faces become one, as all fates become a common fate, as all the bottles blown by a glass blower become one, and as all bishops grow to look alike, etc. . . . there is just one bird, a stone bird" (L, 438):

> One voice repeating, one tireless chorister,
> The phrases of a single phrase, ké-ké,
> A single text, granite monotony,
> One sole face, like a photograph of fate,
> Glass-blower's destiny, bloodless episcopus,
> Eye without lid, mind without any dream—
> These are of minstrels lacking minstrelsy,
> Of an earth in which the first leaf is the tale
> Of leaves, in which the sparrow is a bird
> Of stone, that never changes.
>
> (CP, 394)

The interrelated north/south, winter/summer pairs that crop up repeatedly across the corpus represent another subset of the Hermetic dyad, restated at times by the kindred images of ice, cold, and snow to represent the Great World and by fire and heat to signify the Little World, its microcosmic "mirror." In selecting polar images to stand for the external essence, Stevens is faithful to alchemical precedent, which locates the Mercurius deity in the North Pole and endows him with a heart of fire that was sometimes compared to the northern lights and the Polestar (the North Star).[16] Hence, Stevens perpetually paints him in images of congealment: the Man-hero of "Examination of the Hero in a Time of War," for example, is urged as a figure fashioned of "winter's / Iciest core, a north star, central / In our oblivion" (CP, 275). The anonymous voice of "The Dwarf" similarly adjures the self to spin and weave a "winter web" (CP, 208) divested of "mask" and "garment" (CP, 208)—its flawed disguises—so to fashion itself into a "mirror of cold" (CP, 208) reflecting its cosmic counterpart. "In the Element of Antagonisms" presents the cosmic deity in a cumulative catalogue which includes "The tower, the ancient accent, the wintry size" (CP, 426). The cosmic mountain of "Chocorua to Its Neighbor" is similarly defined in images of congealment as well as in images of air and light:

> He was a shell of dark blue glass, or ice,
> Or air collected in deep essay,
> Or light embodied, or almost, a flash
> On more than muscular shoulders, arms and chest,
> Blue's last transparence as it turned to black . . .
>
> (CP, 297)

The north/winter/ice/snow cluster defines as well the aesthetic object; for when Stevens turns to the statue of "Owl's Clover," its colors are said to come "From snow, and would return again to snow" (OP, 57) to suggest its origin and end in the Ananke-Man. Since "return" in Hermetic metamorphosis is preceded by the dissolution of the profane soul, Mercurius is as well the "universal solvent"—a role Stevens assigns the peerless "poem," forwarding the cosmic Man as "the great poem of winter, the man," (CP, 238), his "manner of thinking, a mode / Of destroying" (CP, 239). In brief, the polar Mercurius represents *both* stages of the alchemical process—the *solve* which dissolves the soul and the *coagula* which congeals the soul—and it is this double quality that Stevens inventively captures in "The Emperor of Ice-Cream," associating his spiritual sovereign not only with an icy substance, at once fluid and solid (the two major stages of the alchemical substance), but with a delicacy that is ingested to suggest the symbolic sense of the alchemical Ouroboros, an autarchic creature that devours and begets its own being.[17]

Like many of Stevens' poems, "The Emperor of Ice-Cream" is constructed as a recipe (the standard form of many alchemical texts) that outlines the stages of the Work. The cook as well as the dish prepared is the Hermetic sovereign, who rolls "big cigars" (CP, 64), an image suggesting the "sophic" fire, and whips "concupiscent curds" (CP, 64), a phrase reminiscent of the alchemical *concupiscentia* used to designate the mating of the masculine and feminine contraries.[18] In Stevens' version, the masculine principle is represented by "boys" who offer "flowers in last month's newspapers" (CP, 64), while the feminine element appears as "wenches" garbed, in the grammar of fused time, "As they are used to wear" (CP, 64).

Since flowers represent the *prima materia* in Hermetic meditation, Stevens explains that the "cast off newspapers" in which the flowers are wrapped "contribute to . . . staleness,"[19] a precise, if whimsical, translation of the divine substance contained in a flawed compound—the premise underlying the initiation of the Work. The flowers must therefore be extracted before the Work can be completed; and this the poet affirms in an adjurative couplet that contrasts the ultimate condition of Being with the imperfect and illusory world of seeming:

> Let be be finale of seem.
> The only emperor is the emperor of ice-cream.
>
> (CP, 64)[20]

The *solve* required in Hermetic metamorphosis is the subject of stanza two; and since this stage—faithful to alchemical allegory—follows the appearance of the contraries in stanza one, Stevens affirms that "The second verse is a little closer to the center,"[21] suggesting thereby the soul's movement towards the One (the "center"). Dissolution is proffered in two images of loss and death—the first a mutilated dresser lacking "three glass knobs" (CP, 64), a disavowal, it would seem, of the Christian trinity; the second, the corpse of a woman, her face covered by a sheet (to signify mystic self-loss) embroidered with "fantails" (CP, 64), a symbol of the ascending spirit often pictured in alchemical iconography in the image of a dove.[22] On the corpse now "cold and dumb" to signify the soul congealed—beyond the verbality of ordinary humanity—the poet adjures, "Let the lamp affix its beam" (CP, 64), so irradiating the soul with divine light—the culmination of the Operation and, accordingly, glossed as "the conclusion or denouement of appearing to be" (L, 341).

At times, Stevens paints the contraries through the nuptial image common to the *coincidentia oppositorum,* the alchemical phrase for the fusion of psyche and earth—the divided halves of the divine androgyne. An especially instructive poem in this mode is the late "Study of Images II," which not only observes the customary pattern of separation and reintegration but joins these to the musical image to suggest the harmonic accord that coincides with the sacrament of assimilation. The contraries here take the form of metaphysical images which inhere in *media mundi,* according to Hermetic spiritism. Divided, these disembodied forms arise, on the one hand, as "pearly women that drop / From heaven and float in air, like animals / Of ether" (CP, 464) and, on the other, (in corresponding theriomorphic form), as "the ice-bear sleeping in ice-month / In his cave" (CP, 464). To propose their fusion, the poet typically shifts to the idiom of hypothesis, announcing their "betrothal" and "espousal" in the sexual imagery common to the "chymical marriage." Immediately, there follows the immaculate "birth of harmony" attended by "burning," the fiery alchemical midwife, and proposed as "the final relation" or the ultimate condition of the unified Life:

> As if, as if, as if the disparate halves
> Of things were waiting in a betrothal known
> To none, awaiting espousal to the sound
>
> Of right joining, a music of ideas, the burning
> And breeding and bearing birth of harmony,
> The final relation, the marriage of the rest.
>
> (CP, 464–65)

Perhaps the best-known descriptions of the alchemical *hieros gamos* are the three "mystic" marriages of "Notes toward a Supreme Fiction." The first of these is especially indebted to the traditional features of the Mercurius deity, whose attributes Carl Jung conveniently summarizes:

> Mercurius stands at the beginning and end of the work: he is the *prima materia,* the *caput corvi,* the *nigredo;* as dragon he devours himself and as dragon he dies, to rise again as the *lapis.* He is the play of colours in the *cauda pavonis* and the division into four elements. He is the hermaphrodite that was in the beginning, that splits into the classical brother-sister duality and is reunited in the *coniunctio,* to appear once again at the end in the radiant form of the *lumen novum,* the stone. He is metallic yet liquid, matter yet spirit, cold yet fiery, poison and yet healing draught—a symbol uniting all opposites.[23]

These features of the bisexual Mercurius Stevens collects (with some modifications) in a catalogue of the opposites: The masculine man / day / winter / morning / North / sun; and the feminine woman / night / spring / afternoon / South / rain. Conceived initially as separate but dependent, they nevertheless announce the "origin of change" (read metamorphosis) which the poet renders as sexual fusion to signify the onset of the *coincidentia oppositorum:*

> Two things of opposite natures seem to depend
> On one another, as a man depends
> On a woman, day on night, the imagined
> On the real. This is the origin of change.
> Winter and spring, cold copulars, embrace
> And forth the particulars of rapture come.
>
> (CP, 392)

So wedded, the opposites rearise as the reborn self, consubstantial with the deity that gave it birth. Hence, the poem concludes with a panegyric to the "one," resurrected in the soul as an amalgam of "captain" and "men"; of "sailor" and "sea"; and, above all, of "sister" and "brother" to signify the restored being of the androgynous Heavenly Man:

> The partaker partakes of that which changes him.
> The child that touches takes character from the thing,
> The body, it touches. The captain and his men
> Are one and the sailor and the sea are one.
> Follow after, O my companion, my fellow, my self,
> Sister and solace, brother and delight.
>
> (CP, 392)

Though still structured by the contraries, the second nuptial scene sounds a more personal note, avowing in its conclusion an organic link between redemptive vision and artistic purpose. In this instance, Stevens personifies his contraries more directly, offering as the feminine element the figure of "Nanzia Nunzio" ("Nanzia" suggests the Old English *nan* from which the modern word *nothing* derives; while "Nunzio," Italian for *messenger*, suggests the alchemical Hermes-Mercurius, traditionally known as the messenger of the gods), engaged in a "trip around the world" (CP, 395), an obvious reference to the Great World; while her masculine consort is represented by "Ozymandias," a name that recalls Shelley's fallen statue and hence

suggests the annihilation of art that lies at the core of Stevens' redemptive vision. Defined by images of burning and divestment and
garbed in the redemptive "stone-studded-belt," the feminine element
beckons the soul to her pure being, offering herself as the divine I AM
(Exodus 3:14) commonly used in the esoteric tradition to signify the
soul's absorption in—indeed, identity with—the universal essence:

> I am the spouse. She took her necklace off
> And laid it in the sand. As I am, I am
> The spouse. She opened her stone-studded belt.
>
> I am the spouse, divested of bright gold,
> The spouse beyond emerald or amethyst,
> Beyond the burning body that I bear.
>
> I am the woman stripped more nakedly
> Than nakedness, standing before an inflexible
> Order, saying I am the contemplated spouse.
>
> (CP, 395–96)

To the poet (Ozymandias), the divine spouse urges the celebra-
tory word appropriate to her holy radiance (a "final filament"). In response, Ozymandias faithfully dedicates his art to her form, promising the "fictive covering" that "weaves always glistening from the
heart and mind":

> Clothe me entire in the final filament,
> So that I tremble with such love so known
> And myself am precious for your perfecting.
>
> Then Ozymandias said the spouse, the bride
> Is never naked. A fictive covering
> Weaves always glistening from the heart and mind.
>
> (CP, 396)

In the final "mystic marriage," (CP, 401) the heavenly duo takes
the form of a "great captain" (CP, 401) associated with the sun—the
Man's traditional symbol; and "Bawda," his corresponding anima-
earth named to represent the alchemical *concupiscentia*. Following alchemical formula, their union is preceded by initial resistance to
suggest the conflict of opposites that initiates the Work:

> This was their ceremonial hymn: Anon
> We loved but would no marriage make. Anon
> The one refused the other one to take,
> Foreswore the sipping of the marriage wine.
>
> (CP, 401)

Resistance is, however, resolved, and the marriage of "The one" and "the other one"—both aspects of the Man, as the repeated "one" advises—takes place in the "ever-hill Catawba" (CP, 401). Since their union corresponds to the Hermetic *unio mentalis* said to resolve the cosmic disorder initiated by scission, the partners are adjured to "stop the whirlwind, balk the elements" (CP, 401); for their fusion initiates the harmony that accrues to the soul's embrace of the Man—"love's characters come face to face" (CP, 401).

Chapter 7

Decreation

Modern reality is a reality of decreation . . .

In an effort to determine the significance of Stevens' "ultimate poem," Roy Harvey Pearce draws attention to Stevens' view that "Modern reality is a reality of decreation" (NA, 175), intended, according to Pearce, to suggest the mind's attempt to abstract the "adventitious" and "contingent" from reality in order that it may appropriate "a reality within reality."[1] Though Pearce is persuaded that Stevens' layered reality is "intranatural" or "infranatural"[2]—a "difficult idea to conceive," as Joseph Riddel comments[3]—his attention to the decreative aspect of Stevens' thought is of considerable importance. Even more, his conviction that Stevens' late poems hover about the idea that "poetry, in being poetry, manifests the existence of a poetry beyond poetry"[4] is equally germane to this study; for as I have urged, the extrapoetic entity that Pearce discerns is equivalent to the "poetry" of the Hermetic Man—Stevens' "reality within reality," to restate Pearce's useful description—synonymous in the poet's arbitrary lexicon with the "ultimate poem."

It is well to note, in assessing the meaning of decreation in Stevens' thought, that the passage in which it appears is preceded by the view (borrowed from Simone Weil) that "decreation is making pass from the created to the uncreated" (NA, 174), a locution which echoes the Hermetic belief in the *increatum* to which the soul aspires in its meditative revery. The resemblance is suggestive; for if the "ultimate poem" represents the culmination of Hermetic meditation, as seems likely, given Stevens' attention to the Hermetic Man (the "supreme fiction"), it seems equally likely that decreation represents an important stage in his resurrection. And, indeed, the annihilative meaning inherent in the term points to the purifying impulse of the Hermetic Work. For at the core of the Hermetic vision lies the soul's rejection of all accustomed forms that veil the profoundly spiritual character of the universe. To pierce this "exoteric envelope," the soul journeys during meditation beyond the things of sense and extent, so to encounter its own true image in the divine and nameless "nothing" that constitutes the veritable Real. This realm Stevens often invokes as the "giant of nothingness" (CP, 443), "An immaculate personage in nothingness" (CP, 434) a "priest of nothingness" (OP, 88), a "lustred nothingness" (CP, 320), a "vermilioned nothingness" (CP, 328)—in each instance attaching to "nothingness" epithets of magnitude or purity or light or redness—all attributes of the Man.

The return to "nothingness" is preceded in alchemical allegory by the *solve*, which dissolves and annihilates the sensible soul (and, by extension, the phenomenal world), purifying it of the historical past and its accumulated traditions and images. This return to the "un-created" arises in Stevens' work in the perpetual refrain of denudation and cleansing—the yearning to shear, to wash, to strip, to doff, so to restore a condition of "ignorance," "nakedness," "poverty," and "bare-ness." "The integrations of the past," Stevens writes in his prophetic strain, "are like / A *Museo Olimpico*, so much / So little, our affair, which is the affair / Of the possible: seemings that are to be, / Seemings that it is possible may be" (CP, 342). Characteristically proposed in the language of futurity, these "seemings" are Stevens' spiritual concern, prefigured, to be sure, in the Olympian postures of frozen forms, but ultimately to be discarded in the soul's ascent to the divine.

In terms of poetic practice, Stevens' effort to paint the soul's retreat from the sensible world required extraordinary tact, since the logic of being, if one can so categorize a mystical state that dissolves distinctions imposed by the discursive reason, transcends artifactual shape and dispenses with the images of the secondary imagination, whereas the logic of aesthetics requires that the secondary image be arranged in a linguistic system possessing the coherence of art. Nevertheless, the artifact is indispensable since, in the dialectics of vision, it contains the image of the divine Man; hence it is an instrument of spiritual renewal. For this reason, Stevens both exalts and excoriates the artist and his artifact, simultaneously elevating the shaping influence of art and denigrating its metamorphic powers. On the one hand, art is a necessary aid to human renewal, promising the restored vigor of Being. On the other, however, art represents a deterioration of man's former life, at best a surrogate for the paradisal home, at worst, a barrier, since it provides an outlet for a sense of divinity that man seems content to objectify rather than experience. When the transformative effect of art is uppermost, Stevens assigns the poet extraordinary powers and accords his fictions a high priority in human life. "The power of literature," he writes in this vein, "is that in describing the world it creates what it describes" (L, 495), meaning that literature creates the image of the Man, always the "world" in Stevens' symbolic geography—and thereby acts as the catalyst of transformation. When, however, he wished to paint the attractions of the "new reality," he grew impatient with poetry, demanding the "thing itself" freed from the "evasions" of metaphor, or he insisted on "a land beyond the mind," a "bare reality," and, eventually, on the "ultimate poem." "Reality [read the Man] is the great *fond*," he writes when nostalgia is uppermost, "and it is because it is that the purely literary amounts to so little" (L, 505). Such views suggest the annihilation of art; the divine reality Stevens sought could be satisfied only by dissolving the distinction between life and art, subject and object. Absorbed in universal Being—the divine abstraction—man was himself to be the "ultimate poem," supplanting the cultural object with unmediated, spontaneous experience. Thus, like the guitarist who is "The maker of a thing yet to be made" (CP, 169), it was Stevens' fate to create the fiction that would ultimately serve in its own annihilation.

Stevens' recourse to poetry to project the image of the Man involved him in the classic paradox of the mystic, forced to express through language, which implies temporal and spatial distinctions, that which is ultimately unamenable to determinate form. Stevens frankly acknowledged the difficulty in "The Man with the Blue Guitar," typically lamenting the inadequacy of poetry to "bring a world quite round," an allusion to the cosmic sphere merely prefigured in the poet's song:

> I cannot bring a world quite round,
> Although I patch it as I can.
>
> I sing a hero's head, large eye
> And bearded bronze, but not a man,
>
> Although I patch him as I can
> And reach through him almost to man.
>
> (CP, 165)

Nevertheless, the poet remained confident of the spiritual efficacy of art, employing his genius in forms that perpetually argued their opposite. These annihilative themes Stevens proposed in a number of ways: by repeatedly dramatizing the alchemical rite of purfication that requires for its consummation the disintegration of flawed forms; by denying the very image he had himself created to personify the Man; by questioning the validity of the aesthetic object; and by addressing—indeed, celebrating—the initiatory death that heralds the advent of the resurrected Life.

◖ ◖ ◗ ◗

A useful clarification of the meaning Stevens attached to decreation arises in his description of MacCullough, a character introduced in the opening canto of "Notes toward a Supreme Fiction." Like many of Stevens' names, MacCullough's too invites comparison to the Hermetic Man: the prefix (son of) proposes the alchemical *filius*, while the root, descended from the Latin *colligere*—in its two senses meaning to gather and to tie or bind—suggests the interrelated father and son of Hermetic correspondence. Since he would thus appear to be another version of the divine Man, the poet accords him the emphatic rite of enumerative catalogue, naming him variously as "The first idea" (CP, 387); an "imagined thing" (CP, 387); a "pensive giant prone in violet space" (CP, 387); "major man" (CP, 387); and the divine "Logos" (CP, 387), the last recalling the alchemical Hermes-Mercurius, similarly conceived as the divine Word immanent in creation.[5]

Despite his resemblance to the Man, however, MacCullough is carefully distinguished from the Man himself, since he is but a surrogate—a poetic image—whereas the Man is the soul's godhead actualized. Hence, the poet offers him as an "expedient" (CP, 387), and a "crystal hypothesis" (CP, 387) to suggest his mediate function in the metamorphic process. To illustrate more precisely how the Man as poem may be transformed into the Man as Being, Stevens next involves MacCullough in Hermetic purification, typically using the idiom of hypothesis to forward the possibility of spiritual completion.

The redemptive landscape is the sea—the "sophic" waters that dissolve the soul, returning it to its fluid, primordial state. In these cleansing waters—a variation of the mercury bath of laboratory alchemy—MacCullough is figuratively "drowned" (CP, 387) and washed in preparation for the encounter with the divine soul—here proposed as a "leaner being" (CP, 387) and commended as the healing agent of the fractured self. Since by this redemptive rite of self-annihilation MacCullough is freed of the aesthetic image, Stevens turns in the following poem to the question of art, dismissing the frozen image as merely "declaimed clairvoyance" (CP, 387) that while appropriate to "apotheosis" (CP, 387) is not of itself the "origin of the major man" (CP, 387). The true "major man," the poet muses, is a nameless "foundling" who arises in the "midnight" (CP, 388) of the soul to inspire the poet's "accurate songs" (CP, 388):

> He is and may be but oh! he is, he is,
> This foundling of the infected past, so bright,
> So moving in the manner of his hand.
> Yet look not at his colored eyes. Give him
> No names. Dismiss him from your images.
> The hot of him is purest in the heart.
>
> (CP, 388)

That Stevens considers the apparition of "major man" a nameless "foundling" recalls the alchemical view of the *lapis*, of which it was said, "This Orphan stone has no proper name."[6] The precept may be traced to Anthropos theology: according to Carl Kraeling, the anonymity of the cosmic Primal Man (the alchemical stone) has its origins in the Iranian Gayomart, a mythological figure fashioned from Spendermad, the Angel of the Earth; and from the primordial fire of the sun. Considered the father of mankind, he originally bore a generic name meaning "Life-Man" or "Mortal Life." Only in later gnostic thought, Kraeling notes, did the Anthropos assume his proper name:

> Among the designations applied to our figure, only Anthropos, Adam and Adamas can be called proper names. These, however, represent a late development. The earliest terminology applied to the Anthropos is entirely descriptive, as for instance "Upper Man," "Great, Most Glorious and Perfect Man" and, perhaps, even "Primal Man." In the strict sense of the word the Anthropos is then originally nameless.[7]

This tradition of archetypal anonymity arises repeatedly in Stevens' poetry, used not only to suggest the Man as the generic protoplastus but to divest him of formal substance, so to commend him as the nonsensible being to which the soul is assimilated in the course of Hermetic meditation. The hero, for example, is proffered as an

"anonymous" (CP, 279) "one" (CP, 279) whose image the poet perpetually denies in an effort to separate his concrete figuration in the
poem from his true being—immaterial, mental, and abstract. Thus,
"To meditate the highest man" (CP, 280), the poet counsels, is to dissolve particularity; for the hero is "not a person" (CP, 277); "not an
image" (CP, 278); he cannot be "conceived, being real" (CP, 279). The
shadow of "Chocorua to Its Neighbor" is similarly an incorporeal
"image, / But not the person" (CP, 299); a "thought, / But not the
thinker" (CP, 299). Impalpable, he is "Hard to perceive and harder
still to touch" (CP, 301)—an "eminence, / But of nothing" (CP, 300);
"substance and non-substance" (CP, 297). And because the poet
means him to represent Being actualized and free of the discursive
reason as well as its aesthetic forms, he is properly, "A largeness lived
and not conceived" (CP, 301).

Elsewhere, the desire to divorce image from form is variously—
indeed, obsessively—adjured, dramatized, and expounded. The
guitarist, for example, exhorts the dissolution of acquired forms—the
"definitions" (CP, 183), "names" (CP, 183), and "shapes" (CP, 183)
that circumscribe and qualify—urging in their stead the soul's retreat
to the "madness of space" (CP, 183), there to conceive its "jocular
procreations" (CP, 183), a phrase suggesting the begetting of the *filius*.
(The motif of procreation arises in Stevens' notation "Dessins d'un
[Embryo] pour un beau monde à venir,"[8] which appears to link the
divine *filius* born in Hermetic meditation to a future condition of life
merely adumbrated in written forms.) For the anonymous voice of
"The Man on the Dump," the dump is the repository of the invidious
image—the "trash" (CP, 202) that "One rejects" (CP, 202), so to feel
the "purifying change" (CP, 202) that may herald the birth of "*stanza
my stone* (CP, 203; Stevens' emphasis), the divine issue of a "philosopher's honeymoon" (CP, 203). In "The Latest Freed Man" the static
image is proscribed by contrast to the newly-risen cosmic sun ("the
strong man vaguely seen" [CP, 204]), compared in its divine nothingness to "a man without a doctrine" (CP, 205) and ultimately transformed into a cosmic ox, its "organic boomings" (CP, 205) signalling
the soul's return to "the centre of reality" (CP, 205). The proscribed
image of "An Ordinary Evening in New Haven" takes the shape of a
"statue of Jove" (CP, 482) but a statue dissolved, blown up, like the
collapsed statue of "Owl's Clover" a token of Stevens' repeated effort
to banish mistaken forms of the divine. To compensate for what has
been lost, the poet advises that "The consolations of space are name-

less things" (CP, 482), supporting the solacing words with the promise of the divine conjunction between "space and the self" (CP, 483).

"The Ultimate Poem Is Abstract" proposes dissolution of the flawed image by challenging the constructive effort of the human mind—the "intellect" that questions "This Beautiful World Of Ours" (CP, 429), a suitably capitalized euphemism for the divine cosmos. To so perceive the cosmic planet, the preceptor of the poem advises, is to be removed from the cosmic center "Helplessly at the edge" (CP, 430). Alternative arises, however, in the image of a cosmic intellect "present / Everywhere in space at once" (CP, 430), its polestar the sacred "middle" (CP, 430). Similarly, Mr. Homburg of the late poem "Looking across the Fields and Watching the Birds Fly" nostalgically compares the mindlessness of the cosmic sun to the metaphoric inclinations of the human mind, conjecturing in his ruminations the "discovery" (CP, 518) of a "pensive nature" (CP, 517) somewhat like man's but liberated from "his literature and without his gods" (CP, 518)—a random vacuity free of "imagery or belief" (CP, 518).[9]

A more expansive account of the alchemical *solve* that Stevens called decreation arises in "The Auroras of Autumn," prefigured in the opening poem in the image of the serpent—alchemy's major symbol for the "sophic" Man. The serpent image, it is worth noting briefly, extends across the canon. An early version appears in "The Comedian as the Letter C" in Crispin's interior voyage to a "land of snakes" (CP, 31) where he discovers his familial bond to "serpent-kin" (CP, 32). In the 1935 "Like Decorations in a Nigger Cemetery," the serpent image appears in conjunction with Ananke, described in the icy images of the polar Man:

> The sense of the serpent in you, Ananke,
> And your averted stride
> Add nothing to the horror of the frost
> That glistens on your face and hair.
>
> (CP, 152)

One year later in "The Greenest Continent," the cosmic serpent is envisaged as a hypothetical "god" (OP, 54), its coils drawn across the statue in a gesture of death. In "The Bagatelles the Madrigals" (1942), it is addressed as the chthonic deity slumbering in an icy "crevice of earth" (CP, 213), its "image" arising from the "dominance" of one mind formed "Out of all the minds" (CP, 213). "Notes toward a Supreme Fiction" assigns the serpent to its exact counterpart—the red colossus who bears it on his brow. In "Saint John and the Back-Ache," it plays a prophetic role, foreseen as a spirit residing in the "invisible" cosmic tree, its "venom" and its "wisdom" promising restored totality, the cosmic "one":

> The possible nest in the invisible tree,
> Which in a composite season, now unknown,
> Denied, dismissed, may hold a serpent, loud
> In our captious hymns, erect and sinuous,
> Whose venom and whose wisdom will be one.
>
> (CP, 437)

Equally a "means of prophecy" (CP, 503) the serpent of "One of the Inhabitants of the West" assumes the shape of the Medusa invoked by a "reader without a body" (CP, 503) (the immaterial Man) who foretells the fall of darkness on all of Europe:

> "Horrid figures of Medusa,
> These accents explicate
> The sparkling fall of night
> On Europe, to the last Alp,
> And the sheeted Atlantic. . . ."
>
> (CP, 504)

In sense and function the cosmic serpent of "The Auroras of Autumn" corresponds to its symbolic function elsewhere. Like the serpent of "Saint John and the Back-Ache," it is the anticipated transcendent, foreseen in one of Stevens' perpetual modulations of futurity as the nocturnal Man:

> These lights may finally attain a pole
> In the midmost midnight and find the serpent there,
> In another nest, the master of the maze . . .
>
> (CP, 411)

The association of the serpent with "midnight" recalls Stevens' many nocturnal figures, variations, for the most part, of the "sophic" Man hidden in the human imagination. Prototypical is the subman of "Sombre Figuration," "Steeped in night's opium" (OP, 66), but equally the features of this occulted god may be discerned in the shadow of "Chocorua to Its Neighbor," "tall as a tree in the middle of / The night" (CP, 297); in the irradiated Man-hero of "Examination of the Hero in a Time of War," "Approaching in the dark approaches" (CP, 279); in the creature of "Pieces," announced as "a person at night, / A member of the family, a tie / An ethereal cousin, another milleman" (CP, 352); and, above all, in the "hero of midnight" of "An Ordinary Evening in New Haven" to whom the poet offers obeisance from a "hill of stones":

> The point of vision and desire are the same.
> It is to the hero of midnight that we pray
> On a hill of stones to make beau mont thereof.
>
> (CP, 466)

Though this figure is clearly a symbol of the "generic self," as Frank Doggett accurately observes,[10] his association with the "sophic" stone as well as a subsequent apostrophe claiming him as an "ancientest saint ablaze with ancientest truth" (CP, 467) mark him as yet another personification of the Man, like the irradiated serpent of "The Auroras of Autumn" an image of the redemptive light, and like the serpent, too, hidden in the "midnight" of the "essential imagination."

In keeping with the metamorphic structure of Hermetic meditation, the cosmic serpent of "The Auroras of Autumn" is a "changeable' creature, living, in Helen Vendler's happy description, "in present participles, gulping, wriggling, flashing, and emerging"[11] that suggest him as the cosmic egg, his struggle for birth the simultaneous death knell of existing forms:

> This is form gulping after formlessness,
> Skin flashing to wished-for disappearances
> And the serpent body flashing without the skin.
>
> (CP, 411)

The three poems that follow outline early stages of transformation, each prefaced by the elegiac "Farewell to an idea" to suggest the soul's return to the *increatum* —the poem's "ancestral theme" (CP,

412). The first of these proffers the onset of vacancy in the image of a deserted cabin (the mind emptied), located on the "beach" (the "sophic" waters) and adorned with "flowers" (the *prima materia*)—all distinguished by white, the chromatic hue of purification and the symbol of the "subtle" body of the earth made "visible" to the visionary eye:

> Here, being visible is being white,
> Is being of the solid of white, the accomplishment
> Of an extremist in an exercise . . .
>
> (CP, 412)

With the signal "The season changes" (CP, 412), the redemptive process begins, bringing in its initial stage a "cold wind" (CP, 412) from the "north" (CP, 412), brilliant, icy, and fiery, its "enkindlings" (CP, 413) signalling the advent of the polar Man smelted and forged in the "sophic" fire:

> With its frigid brilliances, its blue-red sweeps
> And gusts of great enkindlings, its polar green,
> The color of ice and fire and solitude.
>
> (CP, 413)

Poems iii and iv restate the metamorphic process in terms of the contraries, personified as the cosmic mother envisaged in a "room" (CP, 413) (the imagination), and the cosmic father seated in "space," his monarchic form the principle of duration as well as of multiplicity and change:

> Master O master seated by the fire
> And yet in space and motionless and yet
> Of motion the ever-brightening origin,
> Profound, and yet the king and yet the crown . . .
>
> (CP, 414-15)

The image of the mother occasions another account of the alchemical *solve*, described once again as the dissolution of the aesthetic object. Thus, though the poet acknowledges the "mother's face" as "The purpose of the poem" (CP, 413), he nevertheless advises that she is but "half dissolved" (CP, 413); for the poem, as Stevens appears to have believed, stands only midway in the redemptive process. To suggest the total dissolution that gives rise to Being, the poet tenderly apostrophizes his muse, at the same time as he rejects her allegorical image, disdained as a "carving not a kiss." Forthwith, she, too, is "dissolved" and "destroyed" in the "sophic" fire, which swells with apocalyptic force to consume the poet's own creations as well as the written record of mankind's accumulated wisdom:

> And yet she too is dissolved, she is destroyed.
> She gives transparence. But she has grown old.
> The necklace is a carving not a kiss.
>
> The soft hands are a motion not a touch.
> The house will crumble and the books will burn.
> They are at ease in a shelter of the mind
>
> And the house is of the mind and they and time,
> Together, all together.
>
> (CP, 413)[12]

With decreation complete, the poet turns to the theme of Hermetic rebirth (recreation), extended to humanity and offered as the "instinctive poem" (CP, 415). Thus, joined in domesticity, the Hermetic mother and father invite the commonal to share in a collective *coincidentia oppositorum* enacted by dancing "negresses" (CP, 415) (the inner Man) and by "blocks of wood" summoned "out of air" (CP, 415) (the outer Man). To initiate the redemptive dance, the father instructs the chord of the "instinctive poem" for which "There is no play" (CP, 416), since the actors are themselves the divine image, or as Stevens phrases it, managing to suggest the cosmic One, "the persons act one ["the instinctive poem"] merely by being here" (CP, 416).

In the coda to "Notes toward a Supreme Fiction," Stevens addresses the Man as "soldier," acknowledging him as his comrade in the "war between the mind / And sky" (CP, 407) and according him spiritual fealty in a catalogue of correspondence: "The two are one. / They are a plural, a right and left, a pair, / Two parallels that meet" (CP, 407). The martial imagery of the passage is by no means aberrant, surfacing across the canon not only in poems like "Gigantomachia" and "Examination of the Hero in a Time of War," which address specific features of the Man-hero, but in poems that appear to be only marginally concerned with the hero, if at all. Indeed, the note of conflict is a recurrent motif in Stevens' work, stretching from the early "Phases" to the relatively late "Dutch Graves in Bucks County." The thematic center of these poems dealing with war, armies, soldiering, and death has of course little to do with actual political and social reality; rather, war and warlike activity are metaphors for the psychic battle waged by the soul for the restoration of its true self, a clash symbolically rendered in alchemical texts in the symbol of Mars, the war god whose sword opens the *opus* under the sign of Aries, the ram.[13]

In its least ambiguous guise, the spiritual purpose of the war poems is discernible in "Belgian Farm, October, 1914" included in "Phases," a sequence of war poems that Stevens submitted to Harriet Monroe under the pseudonym Peter Parasol. The assumed name is of course instructive; for "Peter" derives from the Greek *petros*, meaning rock or stone; while "Parasol" suggests the alchemical first matter, a metaphysical substance gained by virtue of the soul's retreat from sensible forms.[14] The continuity of Stevens' spiritual concerns is suggested further in the binary images of "Belgian Farm," which picture the Man as an "Old Man of the Chimney" and an "Old Man" of the "breeze"—an early version of the coordinates Stevens habitually used to personify the Little World and the Great World, though here the poet's recourse to the "sophic" furnace relies less on characteristic whimsy and wit than on the deliberate exploitation of received symbol:[15]

> The vaguest line of smoke (a year ago)
> Wavered in evening air, above the roof,
> As if some Old Man of the Chimney, sick
> Of summer and that unused hearth below,
>
> Stretched out a shadowy arm to feel the night.
> The children heard him in their chilly beds,
> Mumbling and musing of the silent farm.
> They heard his mumble in the morning light.
>
> Now, soldiers, hear me: mark this very breeze,
> That blows about in such a hopeless way,
> Mumbling and musing like the most forlorn.
> It is that Old Man, lost among the trees.

(OP, 5)

The struggle to retrieve the "lost" Old Man to which the poet summons unredeemed humanity (addressed as "soldiers") accords with the alchemical view of deity as lost and sleeping in matter. It is marked in the alchemical system by the ritual death, apostrophized in another poem in the "Phases" sequence:

> Death's nobility again
> Beautified the simplest men.
> Fallen Winkle felt the pride
> Of Agamemnon
> When he died.
> What could London's
> Work and waste
> Give him—
> To that salty, sacrificial taste?
> What could London's
> Sorrow bring—
> To that short, triumphant sting?
>
> (OP, 4)

The view of death here proposed—ennobling and beautifying, endured as sacrifice and savored as the taste of salt, a synonym for the *prima materia*[16]—is a death fundamentally different from death as natural process, commonly considered Stevens' recurrent theme. If, indeed, "Death is the mother of beauty, mystical" (CP, 69), as "Sunday Morning" proposes, it is so because in the Hermetic drama of regeneration "mystical" death initiates the birth and revelation of the inner Man. The distinction is clarified in "A Thought Revolved," which urges for mankind "a death before they die" (CP, 186). Similarly, "Burghers of Petty Death" describes symbolic dissolution as a "devastation" (CP, 362) of "great height / And depth" (CP, 362) (the celestial and terrestrial attributes of the Man) that qualitatively alters the soul, "Filling the mind" (CP, 362).

The clearest account of the Hermetic death is afforded by "The Owl in the Sarcophagus." Titled to suggest the Man as the font of wisdom—the *sapientia Dei* entombed in the soul—the poem treats three images of death as they appear in the meditative revery of an anonymous persona. The first considered is "high sleep" (CP, 431), named to signify the soul's dying-away to its profane self and considered, in the logic of reversal, the "ultimate intellect" (CP, 433), affording the *gnosis* of things divine. Next arises "peace after death" (CP,

434) who appears "flourishing the world" (CP, 434) to suggest cosmic reintegration—a radiant figure of "holy doom and end" (CP, 434) in whom the "nothingness" of Being stands allied to the redemptive "stone":

> Adorned with cryptic stones and sliding shines,
> An immaculate personage in nothingness,
> With the whole spirit sparkling in its cloth,
> . . . .
> Peace stood with our last blood adorned, last mind,
> Damasked in the originals of green,
> A thousand begettings of the broken bold.
>
> This is that figure stationed at our end,
> Always, in brilliance, fatal, final, formed
> Out of our lives to keep us in our death . . .
>
> (CP, 434)[17]

The final figure to appear is the feminine cosmic earth—the "mother of us all" (CP, 432)—who directs the return to first matter with "backward gestures of her hand" (CP, 435) and who stands "tall in self not symbol" (CP, 435) to signify her release from the aesthetic form that merely presages her being. The poem concludes with an image of filial correspondence, attributing the mind's phantasms to "pure perfections of parental space" (CP, 436), their offspring the divine Hermetic child whose lullaby induces the redemptive sleep:

> It is a child that sings itself to sleep,
> The mind, among the creatures that it makes,
> The people, those by which it lives and dies.
>
> (CP, 436)

Among its various uses, the Hermetic sacrificial death suggests an eschatological sense. The militant voice of "Dutch Graves in Bucks County," for example, foresees an "end of evil" (CP, 291). Evil is similarly the adversary of the hangman-hero of "Examination of the Hero in a Time of War," engaged in a "war" that pits the "common man against evil" (OP, 84). "Sombre Figuration" introduces the death of evil in the course of self-questioning: "Which counts for most, the anger borne / In anger; or the fear that from the death / Of evil, evil springs" (OP, 69). In "Extracts from Addresses to the Academy of Fine Ideas," the poet links the concept of evil to two deaths—an evil and a good—the last approved because it destroys the first; "It is a good death / That puts an end to evil death and dies" (CP, 253).

The significance Stevens attached to the death of evil may be pieced together from several fragmentary references in the poetry. In "Five Grotesque Pieces," for example, the concept of evil surfaces in the poem's final section entitled "Outside of Wedlock" (OP, 76) to suggest the unconsummated marriage—a traditional Hermetic metaphor for the soul's alienation from its source. The poem itself links the notion of estrangement to poetic motive, suggesting that the poet's music is inspired by a sense of cosmic disorder—of "hard times, / In a world forever without a plan" (OP, 76)—that awakens the soul to a "sense of evil" (OP, 76). Subsequently, estrangement is reaffirmed in an allusion to the ancestral androgyne, the *"père* Benjamin, the *mère* Blandenah" whom "we have forgot" (OP, 77). In this context, it would appear, evil refers to the cosmic wrench which severed the soul, leaving in its wake "the dumbfoundering abyss / Between us and the object" (CP, 437) lamented in "Saint John and the Back-Ache."

Stevens' brief treatment of the Fall in this poem suggests corruption as a mental event coincident with the dethroned sovereignty of the divine unconscious. Bifurcation thus characterizes the mind in its current state of estrangement, a view expressed in the "Adagia" in terms of psychic struggle: "The poet represents the mind in the act of defending us against itself" (OP, 174). A similar phrasing suggesting the mind as a battleground occurs in "Saint John and the Back-Ache":

> The mind is the terriblest force in the world, father,
> Because, in chief, it, only, can defend
> Against itself.
>
> (CP, 436)

In these observations, the mind is aggrandized, presented as an instrument of power and force analogous to the "central mind" of the cosmic Life. So conceived, mind is for Stevens "the most powerful thing in the world" (OP, 162), like the divine light to which it is compared in "The Figure of the Youth as Virile Poet," a cosmic force which "colors, increases, brings to a beginning and end, invents languages, crushes men, and, for that matter, gods in its hands" (NA, 62). Mind is not, however, uniformly celebrated, as may be expected in a vision that proposes spiritual corruption in terms of psychic duality. For when Stevens considers the mind as a fallen entity—a mixture from which the divine Mind must be disengaged—he aches to transcend its limitations, proposing in the accent of nostalgia a realm "beyond the mind" (CP, 252) or, more precisely, the end of mind itself. It is in this second sense—mind conceived as a fallen substance—that we may seek the meaning Stevens assigned to the death of evil.

"Esthétique du Mal," as its title suggests, affords a useful introduction to this important motif:

> The genius of misfortune
> Is not a sentimentalist. He is
> That evil, that evil in the self, from which
> In desperate hallow, rugged gesture, fault
> Falls out on everything: the genius of
> The mind, which is our being, wrong and wrong,
> The genius of the body, which is our world,
> Spent in the false engagements of the mind.
>
> (CP, 316–17)

Evil is here personified as a "genius of misfortune" whose arena is the self and who, in keeping with the sense of his appellation, is a dire being from whom "fault / Falls out on everything," an observation that manages in its word play to suggest the cosmic fissure. In the course of the stanza, this "genius of misfortune" is made coordinate with the "genius of the mind," equally disdained as irremediably mistaken and pejoratively opposed to its opposite, the "genius of the body," to which Stevens attaches as coordinate the "world," an equivalence which in effect identifies the body as the "subtle" or "glorified body" of the cosmic Great World. By this token, the term "body" shifts from its ordinary meaning as something merely natural to that which is infused with spirit, still physical, to be sure, but physical in a sense that transcends the commonsensical notion of materiality.

This spiritual sense of "body" is discernible in the concluding stanza of the poem:

> The adventurer
> In humanity has not conceived of a race
> Completely physical in a physical world.
> The green corn gleams and the metaphysicals
> Lie sprawling in majors of the August heat,
> The rotund emotions, paradise unknown.
>
> (CP, 325)

Though Stevens twice invokes the word "physical," once in relation to "humanity" and again in relation to the "world" to suggest the alchemical unity of matter, he immediately restates the concept in terms of vaguely personified "metaphysicals" associated with the heavenly light ("gleams"), the "sophic" fire ("heat"), the *rotundum* ("rotund"), and with spiritual restoration ("paradise")—all prefaced by the verb "conceived" to suggest the divine embryo engendered in the imagination. We may thus conclude that when in the earlier passage Stevens celebrates "the genius of the body," opposing it to the "false engagements of the mind," he is not alluding to the ordinary phenomenal world but rather to the transfigured "body" of the Hermetic mystery—a "body" that may indeed be claimed as physical since, in the logic of spiritual vision, it has been purified of its opposite and adversary—the fallen and tainted mind.

Since Stevens is a methodical poet, this culminating announcement of purification is prefigured in poem xiii where evil, personified as an "assassin," assumes degree and hierarchy:

> Evil in evil is
> Comparative. The assassin discloses himself,
> The force that destroys us is disclosed, within
> This maximum, an adventure to be endured
> With the politest helplessness. Ay-mi!
> One feels its action moving in the blood.
>
> (CP, 324)

That Stevens considers the "assassin" evil, though less so than the evil he destroys, recalls the diabolical aspects of the alchemical Mercurius, depicted in the initial stages of the Work as a loathsome and poisonous serpent that devours itself, thereby bringing itself to life. Accordingly, Hermetic thought considers good and evil two sides of the same coin, or, more precisely, evil is part of a metamorphic process that "begins with evil and ends with good."[18] The view is clarified in Stevens' description of the "central man" of "Asides on the Oboe," whom the poet considers *both* a "central evil" and a "central good" (CP, 251), confirming the kinship of the two in the image of "bloody martyrdoms" (CP, 251)—an allusion to the Hermetic figurative death, often depicted in alchemical texts in images that parallel the martyrdom of Christ.[19]

The fullest account of the transposition of evil into good is afforded by "Extracts from Addresses to the Academy of Fine Ideas," which not only offers the clearest expression of Stevens' eschatological hopes but orders them repeatedly in the Hermetic metamorphic pattern, so that, in effect, poetic structure and metamorphic structure are single and indistinguishable. The lengthy title anticipates Stevens purpose: "Extracts," recalling the *spiritus mundi* extracted from the base compound, suggests Stevens' intention to consider the divine quintessence; "Addresses," etymologically akin to the Latin *directaire* (to direct), suggests preparatory instructions; the "Academy," which recalls Plato's school founded in the groves of Akademos, anticipates the metaphysical nature of the poet's concern, subsequently confirmed by a reference to Plato in the text; and "Fine Ideas" suggests through the epithet *fine*, a variant of pure, the pristine quality of the abstraction that Stevens considers the "first idea," thus returning in typical circularity to the initial "Extracts" of the title.[20]

Since the divine *lapis* is extracted from a heterogeneous element, the poem opens in parallel vein, as the poet seeks to separate the natural quintessence—"the silent rose of the sun"—from the "paper" rose or the aesthetic object with which it is intertwined. The distinction urged is between the immortal life of the Man and ordinary mortal death; hence, in his guise as a "blood-rose," the redeemer assumes the shape of life—a thing "living in its smell"—whereas the "false roses" are dismissed as merely "dust." The stanza's spiritual sense is tersely captured in the preceptorial "That states the point"; for in the alchemical metaphorical table, the "point" is the equal of the extracted quintessence:[21]

> A crinkled paper makes a brilliant sound.
> The wrinkled roses tinkle, the paper ones,
> And the ear is glass, in which the noises pelt,
> The false roses—Compare the silent rose of the sun
> And rain, the blood-rose living in its smell,
> With this paper, this dust. That states the point.
>
> (CP, 252)

To propose the distillation of Life from the frozen poem is necessarily to abjure the fallen mind from which the poem issues. Hence, in a shift of tonal accent, the poem modulates from sententiousness to nostalgia, from assertion to quest, seeking through the self-confirming rhetorical question a "land beyond the mind" where the soul, free of the distinctions imposed by reason, may exist "as part / Of reality, beyond the knowledge of what / Is real" (CP, 252). Transcendence is perforce extended to the phenomenal world as well; for not only must the mind be purged in its quest of the mystical Real, but so, too, must nature, dismissed in its gross, sensuous form as "only an eye, . . . no better than paper things" (CP, 252–53).

The metaphysical nature of renewal outlined, the poet next considers the annihilative act that in the ritual of rebirth reverses the evil endured by the Fall. Since this annihilation is the task of the redeemer, it is to him, in his guise as a suitably capitalized "Secretary for Porcelain" (the chthonic deity represents the mystical earth perceived as translucent, the quality of "porcelain") that the poet addresses his words:

> Let the Secretary for Porcelain observe
> That evil made magic, as in catastrophe,
> If neatly glazed, becomes the same as the fruit
> Of an emperor, the egg-plant of a prince.
> The good is evil's last invention. Thus
> The maker of catastrophe invents the eye
> And through the eye equates ten thousand deaths
> With a single well-tempered apricot, or, say,
> An egg-plant of good air.
>
> (CP, 253)

The twice-repeated allusion to "catastrophe" conveys the sense of the lesson urged; for in its sense of an overturning or overthrowing, the term precisely captures the alchemical transposition that reverses corruption, returning the soul to original first matter. In this task, the Man plays a dual role, at once the evil of the death-dealing serpent, and the good of the heavenly *lapis*. He is therefore, in Stevens' accurate description, an "evil made magic," suitably located in the "eye/I" of the soul, suitably "glazed" (transparent), suitably offered as "the fruit / Of an emperor" (the soul transformed into his kingly image), and suitably made equivalent to "An egg-plant of good air" (an allusion to the cosmic egg). Though evil may bring death, the poet consoles, "It is good death / That puts an end to evil death and dies" (CP, 253), meaning in this power accorded to "good death" its ability to destroy the usurping reason ("evil death") so to usher in the "divine unconsciousness," whereby the awareness of death is dissolved. Added consolation follows in a numinous pentad that binds star, bird, and flower—all symbols of the redeemer—to the words of the "philosophers" (CP, 253) and "Plato" (CP, 253), suggesting in this conjunction the Platonic universal Forms that alchemy adapted to its spiritual purpose.

In customary fashion, Stevens turns in poem iii to collective humanity, summoning it to the true revelation of the god within. Contrasting the "old world" and the "new," the poet dismisses the church as an instance of the first, suggesting in its place a future race of autonomous men preaching the message of human godhead. To these possible "priests," the poet issues the call of unity, proposing as the focus of their heretofore inchoate and diverse spiritual strivings, a catalogue of the *imago Dei* residing in their own souls—the "central heart," the "mind of minds," the androgynous "King" and "Queen," the "One man"—all epithets for the Man and all offered as the sacramental "bread" and "wine" that lies in the mind itself:[22]

> The lean cats of the arches of the churches,
> That's the old world. In the new, all men are priests.
> They preach and they are preaching in a land
> To be described. They are preaching in a time
> To be described. Evangelists of what?
> If they could gather their theses into one,
> Collect their thoughts together into one,
> Into a single thought, thus: into a queen,
> An intercessor by innate rapport,
> Or into a dark-blue king, *un roi tonnerre*,
> Whose merely being was his valiance,
> Panjandrum and central heart and mind of minds—
> . . . .
> One man, their bread and their remembered wine?
>
> (CP, 254)

The evangelical call for collective transmutation is matched in poem iv by the transmutative experience of the single self, Stevens' oft-used means of universalizing his personal faith. The occasion is a Sunday in April to suggest through day and season the revivification of the Man; the place, a landscape of "winter hills" (CP, 254) (the external *anima mundi*) matched by the "water in the lake" (CP, 254) (the internal *imago Dei*), its iciness "melted" (CP, 255) to signify the onset of the redemptive process. The image of correspondence is completed by the "winter wind" (CP, 255) (the divine *pneuma*) that through modulation of article takes on a double character, blowing equally in "an empty place" (CP, 255)—the unspecified "nothing"—and in "the empty place" (CP, 255), signifying in the altered determiner its location in the particular soul.

With the announcement "It was time to be himself again" (CP, 255), the poet charts the redemptive process rendered metaphorically through a description of the natural landscape. Putrefaction and mortification (the initial stages) arise in the image of fiercely lashing black waters swirling around "dead rocks" (CP, 255), not yet, the poet reminds us, "live rocks" (CP, 255); sublimation follows in water that sprays upward, joining the divine air in a fusion marked by the color white. Next follows an escape from the enthralling "abstraction"—the petrified image—succeeded immediately by the animate Life, its restored vitality throbbing with the participles of Being:

> If,
> When he looked, the water ran up the air or grew white
> Against the edge of the ice, the abstraction would
> Be broken and winter would be broken and done,
> And being would be being himself again,
> Being, becoming seeing and feeling and self,
> Black water breaking into reality.
>
> (CP, 255)

Poem v recapitulates the transmutative vision through the motif of "chaos," a concept that has two meanings in alchemical doctrine. On the one hand, it represents the *"massa confusa"* or the initial disordered state that the artifex gradually reduced to order by his Operation.[23] It signifies as well the condition of original matter "before the separation of the opposites and hence before the advent of consciousness."[24] Its sense thus expresses both the lapse from, and the return to, perfection; or to phrase its dual meaning in the terms Stevens selects, chaos stands for the disintegration of the One into the many,

each an amalgam of base and pure elements; and the reintegration of
the many into the One. These two significations, governed as always
by the law of spiritual progression, structure the section which,
through Stevens' habitual equivalencies, introduces "chaos" as the
"one" embedded in plurality and diversity and equivalent to humanity
itself, shifts next to a version of the *solve* in which chaos is personified
as "philosophic assassins" who destroy one another, except for the
"one" who "remains"; and culminates finally in the celebration of
"chaos," now transformed into the single "pure idea" or the distilled
quintessence—another version, in short, of the "Extracts" of the title:

> The law of chaos is the law of ideas,
> Of improvisations and seasons of belief.
> Ideas are men. The mass of meaning and
> The mass of men are one. Chaos is not
> The mass of meaning. It is three or four
> Ideas or, say, five men or, possibly, six.
> In the end, these philosophic assassins pull
> Revolvers and shoot each other. One remains.
> The mass of meaning becomes composed again.
> He that remains plays on an instrument
> A good agreement between himself and night,
> A chord between the mass of men and himself,
>
> . . . .
> This warmth in the blood-world for the pure idea . . .
>   (CP, 255-56)

The apostrophe to the "pure idea" leads in Stevens' usual structured fashion to the mind—the cradle of the Man—though, as may
be expected, there are two minds in Stevens' vision, the one dismissed
as "systematic thinking" (CP, 256), the other endorsed as "the ultimate
poem" (CP, 256), the source of "life." Their mixture in the fallen
world inspires the lament of scission—a "half earth, half mind; / Half
sun, half thinking of the sun" (CP, 257)—that nevertheless culminates
in a vision of cosmic reintegration celebrated as the union of soul and
"weather":

>   What
> One believes is what matters. Ecstatic identities
> Between one's self and the weather and the things
> Of the weather are the belief in one's element,
> The casual reunions, the long-pondered
> Surrenders . . .
>   (CP, 258)

The catharsis required of union arises next in a hypothetical journey to the moon, where the soul is immolated in the divine *pneuma* —"drowned in the air of difference" (CP, 258)—and returned to the earth "naked" and "in poverty" (CP, 258), its restoration to the original Life depicted as an "inhalation" that marks the "return to the subtle centre" (CP, 258).

In the final poem, Stevens returns to the question of death and evil, proposing in a series of quasi-propositions the power of the cosmic earth to dissolve evil. The argument rests on two alternative but unacceptable versions of mortality and immortality that prepare for a third, espoused view. In the first argument, Stevens advances the notion of a "total" death as prelude to immortality in this life, but it is an immortality that permits the body to sustain and suffer pain without hope of respite. This, the poet asserts, is an evil that is unacceptable. To die a mortal death is therefore preferable, but to die and lie entombed in an earth considered evil is likewise unacceptable. Hence, in a logic tenuous by standards other than those that rest on vision, the poet arrives at a third and final view, reasoning that if immortality in this life is evil if it permits pain; and if mortality is equally evil if, upon death, we return to an evil earth, then the only solution is to consider the earth an element of good that "dissolves" (CP, 259) evil upon death. Once we accept this proposition, the poet urges, we may accept the equivalent proposition that the earth (by this time personified as an active agent to suggest its transmutative power) can dissolve evil "while / We live" (CP, 259). In this circuitous fashion, the prospect of immortality in this life advanced in the earlier proposition comes to rest in the chthonic deity, equally a "total" death but one that eradicates the evil of pain, since pain is a purely human response unknown to archetypal, transconscious Reality.

Recreation

The infinite of the actual perceived
A freedom revealed, a realization touched,
The real made more acute by an unreal.

Writing in 1951 of "philosophic ideas that are inherently poetic" (OP, 190), Stevens declares that "poetry is to a large extent an art of perception" (OP, 191). The view raises the expectation that the poet will address the interchange between the perceiving eye and the sensory object, commonly considered his major subject. It appears, however, that the physical world is not Stevens' concern; for he appends as illustration of the "art of perception" a world entirely created in the mind:

> The material world, for all the assurances of the eye, has become immaterial. It has become an image in the mind. The solid earth disappears and the whole atmosphere is subtilized not by the arrival of some venerable beam of light from an almost hypothetical star but by a breach of reality. What we see is not an external world but an image of it and hence an internal world. (OP, 191)

The passage suggests of course the metamorphic powers of the human imagination; and, indeed, Stevens often speaks of the mind's transformations of the physical world—"The difference that we make in what we see" (CP, 344). Equally, however, he can and does disdain the imagination, urging instead fidelity to the thing itself, "Without evasion by a single metaphor" (CP, 373). When Stevens writes in this vein, he encourages the view that he is committed to the phenomenal world—that, in fact, as John Malcolm Brinnin remarks, he is "a poet [who] transmutes his thinking faculties into the dumb feeling of natural phenomena."[1] The apparent contradiction has puzzled his readers; and, indeed, Sister Bernetta Quinn, an astute critic of Stevens' idealist strain, finds his "devotion to things as they are . . . hard to reconcile with his wish to remold them to what they should be."[2]

The difficulty, it may be, springs from the common view that Stevens' thought is "secular and earth-bound,"[3] bereft of the least transcendental sanction. But as I have argued in the pages of this study, there is considerable evidence that Stevens' interest in the interchange between imagination and reality is inspired by his commitment to Hermetism, a natural religion which seeks not to transcend matter but to transform it into spiritual presence. The mystery of this transformation is contained in the Hermetic doctrine of transcendental perception, to which I shall now turn in the hope that a review of its assumptions will help to resolve the supposed contradiction in Stevens' thought.

As I have noted elsewhere, spiritual alchemy or Hermetism holds that within the dross of common matter lies hidden the living and original seed of creation (the *prima materia*, equivalent, in turn, to the Anthropos, the divine androgyne). To extract this seed—the goal of the Operation—is to transform the earth (and man) into the original "subtle" body—the condition, it was thought, of the universe before the birth of consciousness. In laboratory alchemy, this return to the "glorified body" is allegorized as the extraction of gold from a base substance. In spiritual alchemy, it takes place in the human imagination during meditation, in the course of which the profane secondary soul is dissolved and the original primary soul resurrected, its restored purity vouchsafed by its ability to perceive the supranatural archetype inhabiting the sensible world and corresponding to the soul itself. In short, spiritual alchemy transmutes the phenomenal world by inviting the soul to cultivate a new way of seeing.

This power of the imagination to remold reality into the image of the Man is known in Hermetic "science" as the return of the soul to "things that are,"[4] a familiar phrase in Stevens' work, slightly revised as "things as they are" (CP, 165). According to Henry Corbin, this remarkable mental feat constitutes the culmination of Hermetic meditation, arising in the "active imagination" as an archetypal "*Imago Animae*" (the soul's primordial image of itself) that the soul "projects into beings and things," thereby actualizing the archetypal "*Imago Terrae*" residing in the object and apprehended through a special faculty of perception.[5] Accordingly, the imagination is the "organ of metamorphoses" that dematerializes matter, transmuting "sensory data . . . into the purity of the subtle world":[6]

> This Imagination does not *construct* something unreal, but *unveils* the hidden reality; its action is . . . the spiritual exegesis practised by all the Spirituals of Islam, whose special quality is that of

alchemical meditation: to occultate the apparent, to manifest the hidden. It is in this intermediary world that those known as the *'urafā'*, the mystical gnostics, have meditated tirelessly, *gnosis* here being taken to mean that perception which grasps the object not in its objectivity, but as a sign, an intimation, an announcement that is finally the soul's annunciation to itself.[7]

Since the apparitions apprehended through visionary sight are actualized and "seen" as real things, the speculative theosophy of Islamic alchemy holds that they reside in *media mundi*, an intermediate realm that participates in corporeal matter "because it possesses shape, dimensions, and extent," at the same time as it represents incorporeal "intelligible substance, because it is essentially made of light."[8] In a word, the archetypal world of spirit is both "immaterial matter and the incorporeal corporealized"[9]—or the earth itself relieved of its sensible dross and restored to its divine purity through an act of mental sight. So perceived, the earth is transformed into its feminine "Angel of the Earth"[10] whose image is "the very image of the soul, the image through which the soul contemplates itself,"[11] since both issue from the "resurrection body" of the archetypal Man.

The Mazdean "Angel of the Earth" recalls Stevens' "necessary angel of earth" (CP, 496), which the poet renames "a man / Of the mind" (CP, 497) to reaffirm the Hermetic belief in the reciprocity between celestial matter and celestial imagination. Their conjunction in the course of meditation awakens the perception of the Hermetic "first matter"—a purified reality to which Stevens obsessively returns, celebrating it as a "birth," a "revelation," a "clarity." The "Adagia" records this ascesis in terms of the One: "Perhaps there is a degree of perception at which what is real and what is imagined are one: a state of clairvoyant observation, accessible or possibly accessible to the poet or, say, the acutest poet" (OP, 166).

In its poetic guise, the transmuted reality of Hermetic meditation if proffered as "The poem of pure reality" (CP, 471), appearing after the metaphysical encounter—"a conversation between / Two bodies disembodied in their talk" (CP, 471)—and exhorted as a direct spiritual transaction between subject and object, unmediated "By trope or deviation" (CP, 471)—the halfway measures of art. Elsewhere, it is described as a moment of awakening when the spirit, sinking into an object of perception, becomes identical to it, inspiring the rapture that accrues to absorption:

A waking, as in images we awake,
Within the very object that we seek,
Participants of its being. It is, we are.
He is, we are. Ah, bella! He is, we are . . .

(CP, 463)

Though less rhapsodic, the moment of purified perception recurs in "Notes toward a Supreme Fiction," this time, however, associated with the word "artificial"—a term of some importance in Hermetic thought:

A bench was his catalepsy, Theatre
Of Trope. He sat in the park. The water of
The lake was full of artificial things . . .

(CP, 397)

The allusion to "catalepsy" suggests the onset of psychic withdrawal, a motif restated in the reference to "Theatre / Of Trope," which proposes the illusion ("Theatre") and the mental reversal ("Trope," literally a turning) that accompany Hermetic transcendental vision. With the return to first matter, as always aided by the "sophic" "water of / The lake," there arise "artificial things," subsequently restated as "changing essences" (CP, 397) to designate their apparitional character. These, in one of Stevens' characteristic catalogues of resemblance, take on particularity of form, but the forms are abstract, composed of diaphanous entities that resist precise sensible shape: they are "Like a page of music, like an upper air, / Like a momentary color, in which swans / Were seraphs, were saints" (CP, 397). They are meant, in short, to represent archetypal and suprasensible images that the soul actually sees in the psychic transposition of self and world.

Now these forms are labelled "artificial," a word whose semantic resonance embraces both the means and end of Hermetic metamorphosis. In its root meaning of skill or way or method, the initial particle (the Latin–*ars*) has a reflexive sense, pointing not to the thing created but to the means or agency by which it is made—in short, to the artist himself who possesses the art or skill to create. The root –*fic* similarly suggests the maker, its origin the Latin *facere* (to make, do) and *fingere* (to shape, fashion, form, mold), the last assuming the metaphoric sense of a mental fashioning that represents the process of conceiving or imagining. This metaphoric sense of the verb is akin, in turn, to the nominative *fictor*, meaning an image-maker or molder; and *fictiō*, the feigned thing created. Thus, in its total semantic range, "artificial," like the word "fiction," a cognate form, embraces the multiple roles of the "sophic" Man, who represents the act of imagining, the imaginer, and the thing imagined of Hermetic metamorphosis.

In yet another sense, Stevens' view of the Man as an "artificial" thing created in the mind by the artist's own hand follows alchemical precedent. Alchemy is known as the "royal art," not alone for its association with the making of gold, the traditional royal metal, but because its practitioner, known as an artifex or artist, deliberately molds his own soul, transforming it into the shape of the kingly Man. To do this requires that he reverse his psychic resources, an act of extraordinary concentration and will, often designated *contra naturam* (contrary to nature), as opposed to the supposedly "natural" psychic hierarchy in which consciousness functions as the sovereign of the soul. The process is thus necessarily "artificial," as opposed to "natural"; for it does not arise spontaneously but must be assiduously cultivated by an "act of the mind." The "fiction" that arises from this self-transformation is similarly "artificial," since it presents itself to the soul as an archetypal idea without analogue in natural forms.

In alchemical allegory, the artificial nature of metamorphosis is represented by the *vas Hermeticum*, a round bottle or jar in which the divine *filius* is incubated and hatched. Carl Jung explains its symbolic meaning:

> The bottle is an artificial human product and thus signifies the intellectual purposefulness and artificiality of the procedure, whose obvious aim is to isolate the spirit from the surrounding medium. As the *vas Hermeticum* of alchemy, it was "hermetically" sealed (i.e., sealed with the sign of Hermes); it had to be made of glass, and had also to be as round as possible, since it was meant to represent the cosmos in which the earth was created. Transparent glass is something like solidified water or air, both of which are synonyms for spirit. The alchemical retort is therefore equivalent to the *anima mundi*, which according to an old alchemical conception surrounds the cosmos.[12]

In this account of the alchemical retort, an artificial thing created by the human mind and meant to represent the cosmic Man, we may discern the intent of Stevens' much-discussed "Anecdote of the Jar," which uses as its central symbol a round artifact fashioned of glass.

Clearly a principle of order, unity, and harmony, as well as a well-spring of authority, the jar arranges and pacifies a slovenly and feral wilderness in what has generally been taken as a repudiation of nature's indigenous forms:

> I placed a jar in Tennessee,
> And round it was, upon a hill.
> It made the slovenly wilderness
> Surround that hill.
>
> The wilderness rose up to it,
> And sprawled around, no longer wild.
> The jar was round upon the ground
> And tall and of a port in air.
>
> It took dominion everywhere.
> The jar was gray and bare.
> It did not give of bird or bush,
> Like nothing else in Tennessee.
>
> (CP, 76)

On the surface, the jar suggests an unresolved conflict between a thing created by the human imagination and the natural world on which it is imposed and to which it appears alien. On closer view, however, Stevens' putative irresolution yields to the consistency of vision; for through the phonological cluster that joins the twice-repeated "round"—the shape of the jar—to "surround," "around," and "ground," words that compel when articulated a labial pursing, the jar assumes cosmic shape, in sense and sound a symbol of the circle of perfection, the unfailing attribute of the Heavenly Man. To the phonology of the Man Stevens adds his cosmic stature (the jar is "tall") and universal totality, arranging the jar in both "ground" and "air" to signify, in a version of the Hermetic dyad, its rule of earth and heaven. So granted dominion over nature, it is the metamorphic agent that transforms the sensible world into celestial matter—bare, to be sure, of "bird" and "bush," nature's ordinary forms, but for all that the plenum of the mystical "nothing" accessible to irradiated vision as the "see" of "Tennessee" suggests.[13] In this fashion, the artifice (the jar or *vas Hermeticum*) created in and by the mind alters both self and world, transmuting them to the Hermetic "first matter."

A more overt attention to the artificial nature of the Hermetic Operation arises in "Someone Puts a Pineapple Together," a poem appended to the prose piece, "The Realm of Resemblance." Structured like many of Stevens' poems to reflect the stages of Hermetic meditation, the poem begins with the premise of correspondence, a spiritual event engendered in the imagination and signalled by an invocation to "juventes" and "filii" (NA, 83)—the activated archetypes contained in the *filius*, the "son of the philosophers." Evoked in contemplation, these apparitions correspond to the archetypal essence artificially created in the mind; hence, Stevens considers them "A wholly artificial nature, in which / The profusion of metaphor has been increased" (NA, 83).

The allusion to "metaphor" requires a brief excursus, since Stevens ascribes to it a hierarchical sense—a "gradus ad Metaphoram" (NA, 81) as he calls it in "Three Academic Pieces." At the pinnacle of metaphor stands the "metaphysical" Man, who bears it as honorific in "Chocorua to Its Neighbor":

> Not father, but bare brother, megalfrere,
> Or by whatever boorish name a man
> Might call the common self, interior fons.
> And fond, the total man of glubbal glub,
> Political tramp with an heraldic air
> Cloud-casual, metaphysical metaphor . . .
> (CP, 300–301)

Though the use of "metaphor" in this context appears arbitrary, it may be reasonably justified if viewed in the context of Hermetic correspondence. The voice of the passage is Chocorua, the *anima mundi* here represented as a mountain. He is speaking of the "prodigious shadow," his microcosmic counterpart. Though described as separate entities, they are aspects of the One—"metaphysical" because impalpable, a metaphor because analogous, their correspondence constituting the resemblance implied in the metaphoric equation. Below them stands the secondary metaphor, the poem, which Stevens consistently upholds as an artifact composed of "two poetries" to suggest it as an amalgam of abstract spirit and concerete form. Thus, the poem contains metaphor's two principal elements: an implied analogy between two items thought to have a modicum of resemblance; and a transference whereby one element takes on the characteristics of the other.[14]

Since the apparitions Stevens calls forth are aspects of the Man, it is likely that in this instance "metaphor" is meant to represent

Hermetic correspondence. And, indeed, to emphasize this relationship, Stevens has the perceiving eye move outward to its archetypal
counterpart—the Man in the form of a pineapple, suitably round,
suitably the fruit of nature, and suitably emerald to signify the per-
durable stone. The Hermetic belief that nature and man are one inspires the poet's conviction that the pineapple is "seen" as an extension
of the perceiver, who is himself "the irreducible X / At the bottom of
imagined artifice" (NA, 83).

   The premise of correspondence established, the poet turns next
to decreation, illustrating his meaning in another version of the Operation. The image proffered is the "jar" or *vas Hermeticum* in which lies
the gestating divine son—"the shoots of an infant country, green /
And bright" (NA, 83). Next follows the *solve / coagula* pattern, transforming the jar into an "urn," its "ashes" revived as "A green that is
the ash of what green is" (NA, 83) and made equivalent in its cosmic
rebirth to "planetary orginals" (NA, 84). In customary fashion, the
recreation of the Man prompts attention to the secondary metaphor of
the poem, opposed as "The metaphor that murders metaphor" (NA,
84). To the imperfect metaphor, Stevens opposes the true metaphor of
the "subtle" Man, variously named "a second of the self, / Made subtle" (NA, 84); "the true light of the truest sun" (NA, 84); "sound's
substance" (NA, 84); and the pineapple—the last occasioning a lament for the lost Eden, "an age / When a pineapple on the table was
enough" (NA, 85). Though denied its original supremacy, the poet
muses, the cosmic image nevertheless remains one of "the incredible
subjects of poetry" (NA, 85) granting the solace of faith, "a purpose to
believe" (NA, 85).

   The recreation of the Man leads next to the purification of "reality," typically stripped "Of its propriety" (NA, 86) to suggest its
spiritualization and arranged in a "third planet" (NA, 86), Stevens'
version of the *anima media natura*. A surreal vision of twelve numbered
lines[15] next outlines the primordial origins of this realm ("yesterday's
volcano" [NA, 86]); its cosmic totality, ("the coconut and cockerel in
one" [NA, 86]); and, finally, its sublimation (the "sea . . . spouting
upward out of rocks" [NA, 86]). These, the poet declares, are
"sprigs / Of Capricorn" (NA, 86), an image that invokes the tenth sign
of the Zodiac, associated in the alchemical system with Saturn-
Mercurius.[16] To illustrate the spiritual nature of this deity, Stevens
describes an ascent "Up the pineapple" (NA, 87), which now becomes
the cosmic mountain "distilled" from "molten mixings of related

things" (NA, 87) (the alchemical terminology is exact), its final form the artificial Man equivalent to the "total artifice" made equal, in turn, to the celestial earth—the "total reality" (NA, 87).

"Of Ideal Time and Choice," the poem that follows, presents the "ideal" Man as a *quaternio* associated with the *lapis* and with "day," the temporal symbol of Hermetic resurrection:

> this is the day
> That we desired, a day of blank, blue wheels,
> Involving the four corners of the sky,
> Lapised and lacqued and freely emeraldine
> In the space it fills, the silent motioner
> There, of clear, revolving crystalline . . .
>
> (NA, 88)

It is this form, the poet declares, that is "the center of resemblance" (read correspondence); hence, it is offered to mankind as a "heroic nature" that is "we ourselves" (NA, 89).

The artificial reality recreated by the Hermetic soul following its de-creation of sensible soul and phenomenal world constitutes the unity of subject and object, known in Hermetic thought as the resurrected *unus mundus*. As with all other stages of Hermetic metamorphosis, this one, too, arises in Stevens' poetry, characterized by what John Malcolm Brinnin sees as Stevens' yearning to "unite [himself] with unthinking objects . . . thereby to realize something of primal being-ness."[17] The spiritual premises of this stage are outlined in many poems but none, perhaps, affords the clarity of "The Bouquet." In this poem the relationship between purged sight and the natural object centers on a bouquet of red clover ("farouche")—in sense and hue a symbol of the red Man—arranged in a "jar" (the *vas Hermeticum*) and redefined as "metaphor" to suggest the concept of correspondence Stevens seems to have attributed to the term. To suggest its making in the mind, Stevens describes it as an "inner world" (CP, 448) arising from "the place of the duck" (CP, 450) (the "sophic" waters) and offered as a primordial thing, "centi-colored and mille-flored" (CP, 450). Hence, it represents the metaphysical "reality / Of the other eye" (CP, 448) that the poet "enters, entering home" (CP, 448) to signify the return of the soul to its original habitation.

To return to spiritual reality, the poet continues, is to encounter a transcendental world of "meta-men" (CP, 449) who reign as "transparent magistrates" (CP, 449) in "a land / Without a god" (CP, 449), for according to Hermetic thought, the soul assimilated to the cosmic earth is itself consubstantial with the Man. So graced, the soul perceives the world of objects as incorporeal "para-things" (CP, 449) that materialize by virtue of a mental conjunction described as "a consciousness of red and white as one" (CP, 450). (The phrase recalls the "chymical" marriage of the *mulier candida* [white woman] and *vir rubeus* [red man], which equally gives rise to the "one.")[18] In terms of the epistemology of vision, the conjunction testifies to the union of subject and object, or, as Stevens phrases a fusion which dissolves the distinction between thought and thing, "The meta-man behold the idea as part / Of the image" (CP, 449).

This hierophany of the earth, Stevens elsewhere declares, places "God in the object itself" (CP, 475), for the object so perceived through transcendental vision is the composite soul of the Man—the "True nothing" (CP, 449)—revealed as the "infinite of the actual perceived" (CP, 451). So seen, the object exists "unversed" (CP, 452), its release from the frozen image "growing / In glue" (CP, 449) yielding to the unfixed and fluid—a thing "dithering" in a "torrent's wave" (CP, 452) and experienced in the timelessness of eternal duration, "Neither remembered nor forgotten, nor old, / Nor new, nor in the sense of memory" (CP, 451). In support of this view of existential Being, the poem concludes with an image of the soldier, who enters an empty room (the soul denuded of sensible forms) and topples the bouquet (the poetic image), sending it "over the edge" and onto "the floor" (CP, 453) in a version of the alchemical *descensus* that in the final stages of the Operation, returns the soul to its habitation in "central earth."

Though "The Bouquet" outlines the cosmic dimensions of "true nothing," it does so in a *post hoc* discursive idiom foreign to the ontological condition it is meant to describe. In a word, the contradiction between theme and form inherent in "The Bouquet" is the contradiction common to the corpus as a whole; for Stevens' effort to describe the ineffable invites disjunction between the thing as it is, undifferentiated and unsusceptible to the ordinary categories of reason, and the thing arranged by the discursive intellect—a dilemma argued in the memorable caveat, "The poem is the cry of its occasion, / Part of the res itself and not about it" (CP, 473). Nevertheless, Stevens perpetually argued an extralinguistic vision in the very medium it was designed to supplant. That he did, in measure, resolve this problem is demonstrated by "The Snow Man," assuredly the poet's most successful effort to describe the psychic vacancy of the enlightened mind absorbed in the ineffable "nothing."

To explain that the poem is intended to outline the reintegration of man and nature—the goal of Hermetic meditation—Stevens writes that "The Snow Man [is] an example of the necessity of identifying oneself with reality in order to understand and enjoy it" (L, 464). Fusion is imaged in the marvelously apt "snow man," like the "ice cream" image of "The Emperor of Ice-Cream," a man-made object symbolizing the *imago Dei* artificially dissolved and congealed in the "sophic" waters and reborn as the cosmic One, properly the first word of the poem. The snow man is thus granted a "mind of winter," signifying in this fusion of inner and outer elements the two halves of the cosmic Man. These are further attached to the image of the overarching cosmic wind—the three together recalling the body, soul, and spirit of the triune stone:

> One must have a mind of winter
> To regard the frost and the boughs
> Of the pine-trees crusted with snow;
>
> And have been cold a long time
> To behold the junipers shagged with ice,
> The spruces rough in the distant glitter
>
> Of the January sun; and not to think
> Of any misery in the sound of the wind,
> In the sound of a few leaves,
>
> Which is the sound of the land
> Full of the same wind
> That is blowing in the same bare place
>
> For the listener, who listens in the snow,
> And, nothing himself, beholds
> Nothing that is not there and the nothing that is.
> (CP, 9–10)[19]

Though the poem outlines the condition of transcendental perception, it does so provisionally, resorting to the idiom of hypothesis to paint a vision only proximate in its iconic form. In support of incipiency, the perceiving eye is figured in the grammar of future-like infinitives, echoing in their intimations of absence the "distant glitter" of the cosmic sun. The multiple negations of the final line similarly affirm the poem's mediate function, typically distinguishing between two nothings—the base "nothing" given formal utterance in the poem and hence a "Nothing that is not there"—and the pure "nothing" of Being—the "nothing that is"—which represents the consummate moment discerned by thought alone in the spiritual loneliness of personal encounter.

Despite these rhetorical disclaimers, "The Snow Man" urges a vision of paradise restored that governs every element of its densely webbed and textured surface. Since for Stevens artistic form is determined by the requirements of vision, "The Snow Man" is a single sentence, arguing in its organic syntax the being of the One to which it is committed in theme. Equally, the poem's predominant monosyllables, a lexical echo of pure, elemental mind, are chosen with an eye to their aural suggestiveness, replicating in the assonance of "sound," "cold," "blowing," "boughs," and "snow"; as well as in the "eye-I" sound of "time," "ice," "pine," and "mind," the image of the alchemical sphere and its corresponding echo in the transcendental eye of the soul. Cosmic interrelatedness is equally implied in the poem's alliterative pattern, a binding strategy that Stevens consummately uses to place the "January sun" in the very center of the poem, evoking its cosmic harmony in a torrent of sibilants indistinguishable from the heavenly music from which they derive and so cunningly arranged in the words "snow" and "is" that conclude the initial and final stanzas as to suggest the beginning and end of Hermetic metamorphosis. Indeed, the cohesion that collapses spirit, word, sound, and structure into a single thing transforms the poem into numen, throbbing with the Life that informs its verbal facade.

The bare, elemental landscape of "The Snow Man" recalls the Hermetic view of mystical consciousness, described in the *Corpus Hermeticum* as "deep silence," the "suppression of all the senses," and the cessation of "all bodily movements"[20]—elements, in short, that imply the mystic's conversion to an embryonic condition, a metaphor for the divine beginning. Though this transmutative drama testifies to the power of the transcendental self to enact its own salvation, it is nevertheless bent on transcending the mind, or at least that portion of the psyche wedded to the sensible and the corporeal. Hence, the mind that achieves union with the divine principle is at the same time the mind that dissolves its own imperfect being, gaining in its stead the undifferentiated, universal source—what Stevens called a "land beyond the mind."

"Of Mere Being," a late lyric typical of what Helen Vendler calls the "great and remote poetry of Stevens' old age,"[21] records this self-transcendence through the double prism of negation and affirmation, employing as symbols of the "end of the mind" the palm tree and a "gold-feathered bird," both traditional symbols for the *opus* and its consummation:[22]

> The palm at the end of the mind,
> Beyond the last thought, rises
> In the bronze distance,
>
> A gold-feathered bird
> Sings in the palm, without human meaning,
> Without human feeling, a foreign song.
>
> You know then that it is not the reason
> That makes us happy or unhappy.
> The bird sings. Its feathers shine.
>
> The palm stands on the edge of space.
> The wind moves slowly in the branches.
> The bird's fire-fangled feathers dangle down.
>
> (OP, 117–18)

To signify a condition of Life only incipient in the aesthetic object, Stevens affixes to the poem a truncated title grammatically akin to the fragmentary nature of the formal image. In the body of the poem, the wide-angled perspective similarly functions in the service of spiritual prefiguration, removing the bird to the panoramic "distance" and arranging the palm at "the edge of space" to suggest the remote, albeit accessible, vision embedded in the image though not synonymous with it. Despite these caveats, however, the poem manages to outline the prospect of psychic transposition, offered on the one hand in the universal music of the bird, sufficiently removed from ordinary consciousness to sound a "foreign song," alien and "without human meaning"; and, on the other, in a bare, reductive syntax as elemental grammatically as the state of Being it records. The beckoning to an altered mode of life is implied in the final image, which foresees the resurrection of the chthonic god in the bird's "fire-fangled feathers" arranged to point "down" to signal the descent of the soul into the central creative source.

ᘓ ᘓ ᘒ ᘒ

"One thing about life," Stevens writes in his gloss to "The Man with the Blue Guitar," "is that the mind of one man, if strong enough, can become the master of all the life in the world" (L, 360). Though the comment includes the usual references to the Life and the One, of greater interest is its suggestion of human aggrandizement—even, perhaps, of apotheosis. And, indeed, Stevens' observation recalls the Hermetic view that the soul reborn in Mind is itself consubstantial with the cosmic soul. According to the *Corpus Hermeticum*, he who has got knowledge "is already divine,"[23] being "by that birth . . . another; he is a god, and son of God."[24] So redeemed, the soul may "grow to a like expanse with that greatness which is beyond all measure," able in its aggrandizement to "rise above all time, and become eternal," to be "everywhere at once, on land, at sea, in heaven," so to "grasp . . . all times and places, all substances and qualities and magnitudes together."[25]

There is some evidence that Stevens may have held a similar belief in human apotheosis. The strident declaratives of "The Sail of Ulysses," for example, foretell in apocalyptic accent the appearance of a "final order" (OP, 101) in which "the genealogy / Of gods and men" (OP, 102) will have been "destroyed" (OP, 102) in the "sophic" "fire" (OP, 102). Once delivered from "The ancient symbols . . . To that which they symbolized" (OP, 102) (a reference, it would seem, to the bondage of the recorded word), man, it appears, will have access to the "knowledge" that "is the only life" (OP, 100) (evidently *gnosis*, associated in Hermetic teachings with the cosmic Life). So reborn, man is viewed as "Master of the world," vouchsafed by his mental recreation of the Man ("the world"):

> Master of the world and of himself,
> He came to this by knowledge or
> Will come. His mind presents the world
> And in his mind the world revolves.

(OP, 102)

More obliquely, "A Rabbit as King of the Ghosts" describes cosmic afflatus in images of light, stone, night, and space, Stevens' recurrent symbols for the Man. Like the nocturnal One interred in the soul "black as stone," the "rabbit-light" of the poem swells to become the suzerain of nature, its ultimate abode, cosmic "space":

> the grass is full
> And full of yourself. The trees around are for you,
> The whole of the wideness of night is for you,
> A self that touches all edges,
> You become a self that fills the four corners of night.
> The red cat hides away in the fur-light
> And there you are humped high, humped up,
> You are humped higher and higher, black as stone—
> You sit with your head like a carving in space
> And the little green cat is a bug in the grass.
>
> (CP, 209–10)

Finally, there is "Life on a Battleship"—perhaps the most re-markable expression of Stevens' soteriological hopes. Though the poem has bemused Stevens' critics,[26] its title suggests that it is in-tended as yet another account of the cosmic Life, personified as an omnipotent "captain" (a variation of the Hermetic "Son . . . of man" of "A Thought Revolved," similarly described as a "captain") who in three soliloquies drafts "rules" for a *Regulae mundi* (OP, 80). To as-sert his unconditioned power, he advances first his major weapon—a "single ship" (OP, 78) which swells into a mighty "divinity of steel" (OP, 78) located in "the center of the world" and made coequal to the self, similarly "the center of / The divinity, the divinity's mind, the mind / Of the world." So armed and aggrandized, the captain com-mands at will the human race, garbing it in "stone masks" (the Hermetic symbol of redemption) and compelling it to fall "backward" with the force of his divine breath, so restoring to humanity its "natu-ral" origins in the Life:

> "Given what I intend,
> The ship would become the center of the world.
> My cabin as the center of the ship and I
> As the center of the cabin, the center of
> The divinity, the divinity's mind, the mind
> Of the world would have only to ring and ft!
> It would be done. If, only to please myself,

I said that men should wear stone masks and, to make
The word respected, fired ten thousand guns
In mid-Atlantic, bellowing, to command,
It would be done. And once the thing was done,
Once the assassins wore stone masks and did
As I wished, once they fell backward when my breath
Blew against them or bowed from the hips, when I turned
My head, the sorrow of the world, except
As man is natural, would be at an end."

(OP, 78)

In the two soliloquies that follow, the captain drafts rules for the world in propositions of correspondence, asserting that the whole is the sum of its parts and, conversely, that the part is the "equal of / The whole." Since such a view confirms the divinity of each man, the captain foresees the demise of the social polity, considered in the dialectics of vision as merely a "phase" from which there is to evolve "a society / Without a society":

". . . But society
Is a phase. We approach a society
Without a society, the politicians
Gone, as in Calypso's isle or in Citare,
Where I or one or the part is the equal of
The whole. . . ."

(OP, 79)

Prophecy yields to the lament that in the fallen world, where the artifact substitutes for the divine "whole," "The sound of a dozen orchestras / May rush to extinguish the theme" (OP, 79). Nevertheless, the captain muses, the vision survives in the promise of "this pushing life," renamed the "vine of Key West," Stevens' abiding metaphor for the fecund chthonic Life pulsating in all creation:

"On *The Masculine* one asserts and fires the guns.
But one lives to think of this growing, this pushing life,
The vine, at the roots, this vine of Key West, splurging,
Covered one morning with blue, one morning with white,
Coming from the East, forcing itself to the West,
The jungle of tropical part and tropical whole."

(OP, 80)

In the final stanza, the poet responds to the captain's two "*Regulae mundi*" with his own "Third" rule—"The whole cannot exist without

/ The parts"—confirming himself thereby as a "gunman" whose art becomes the means of dissolving the "commune" in the struggle for celestial restoration:

> The first and second rules are reconciled
> In a Third: The whole cannot exist without
> The parts. Thus: Out of the number of his thoughts
> The thinker knows. The gunman of the commune
> Kills the commune.
>
> (OP, 80)

Acknowledging that his "rhapsodic strophes" (OP, 81) are not the equal of the captain's "guns"—that, in short, his "grand / Simplifications approach but do not touch / The ultimate one" (OP, 80), he nevertheless claims their urgent mediate nature; for "Without them it [the "ultimate one"] could not exist" (OP, 80).

The passage concludes with a remarkable apostrophe to the soteriological imagination, given form in a numinous "sceptre" stained with the blood "Of martyrs" (OP, 81) and transmitted "Through prophets and succeeding prophets, whose prophecies / Grow large and larger" (OP, 81). To what is evidently a continuing evangelical tradition, the poet dedicates his "rhapsodic strophes" (OP, 81), their purpose it appears the declaration of human autonomy ("Our fate is our own" [OP, 81]) which forthwith is restored to the Man—the divine "center of a circle" (OP, 81).

PART THREE

The Rosicrucians of Pennsylvania

Chapter 9

Crispin and the Hermits of the Wissahickon

The katy-dids at Ephrata return . . .

The critic who would probe the origins of Stevens' spiritual commitment faces a formidable task, dictated in part by the nature of the Hermetic vision, traditionally known as an *"operatio secreta artis,"* in part by Stevens' habitual reticence and indirection.[1] Above all, critical exegesis is hampered by the absence of biographical detail that would supplement our meager knowledge of Stevens' formative years. We have, to be sure, something of a record of the years 1898–1912 in the poet's journal as well as in his letters to Elsie Moll, who was later to become his wife, but these, dismayingly, are less than satisfactory, bearing in both instances the mark of careful editing and excision.[2] Thus, the effort to reconstruct Stevens' spiritual education, as well as to suggest the means by which he came to know the Hermetic vision, must, ultimately, remain speculative. Notwithstanding, the task is not futile; for as I have noted in the pages of this study, Stevens was uncommonly frank about spiritual matters traditionally shrouded in secrecy.[3] In view of his willingness to reveal, however ambiguously, the intimate details of Hermetic arcana, we may reasonably expect that he was equally willing to acknowledge his spiritual mentors, if only with customary obliqueness.

Perhaps the most useful, if preliminary, means of tracing Stevens' spiritual indebtedness is his long autobiographical narrative "The Comedian as the Letter C," which first appeared in *Harmonium* when Stevens was forty-four years old.[4] Partly a reenactment of the sacramental journey of redemption, partly a confession of the aesthetic dilemma spiritual rejuvenation entailed, the poem sets forth the experience of the fictive Crispin embarked on a symbolic odyssey which takes him from east to west and from south to north, the geography of Mercurius *quadratus*,[5] whose being Crispin represents. The name Crispin further marks Stevens' persona as a personification of the Man; for Crispin, descended from the Latin *crispus* (curly-headed) suggests the arcane substance (*prima materia*), known in one of its many guises as the *capilli*, a form of the Latin *capillus*, meaning the hair of the head or of the beard.[6] In alchemical lore, a variation of the term arises in the mysterious Aelia-Laelia-Crispis Inscription, an allegedly ancient epitaph said to have been found in Bologna and claimed by the alchemists as the words of "an artificer of old to the honour of God and in praise of the chymic art."[7] According to alchemical interpretation, the names Aelia-Laelia stand for the contraries of sun and moon respectively, while Crispis represents their unity as the arcane substance which is " 'obvoluta, intricata,' therefore curly."[8] This sense of Crispin's symbolic meaning Stevens captures in Crispin's progeny, dubbed "And Daughters with Curls" (CP, 43) (the title of the final section) and proffered as a group of four to identify their cosmic parentage.

The "Comedian" of the title reminds us that Stevens renamed "man the abstraction" of "Like Decorations in a Nigger Cemetery" "the comic sum," (CP, 156), suggesting thereby that he considered the abstract Hermetic Man equivalent in some fashion to the comic or comedy.[9] The equivalence is reaffirmed elsewhere in the same poem, this time in connection with Jack and Jill, another version of the masculine and feminine contraries. These, the poet joins to the redeemer's music and graces with the chromatic symbols of purple and red, the regal colors of the Man:

> The comedy of hollow sounds derives
> From truth and not from satire on our lives.
> Clog, therefore, purple Jack and crimson Jill.
>
> (CP, 154)

The "Letter C" which completes the title appears to have been chosen for its phonological resonance; indeed, Stevens was at pains to emphasize the aural suggestiveness of his whimsical rubric, thrice commenting that the euphony of the letter was a special feature of the poem and thrice offering the line "Exchequering from piebald fiscs unkeyed" (CP, 43) as example (L, 294; 352; 778). Noting that he intended the various sounds of the letter to have "a comic aspect" (L, 294), he explains that "the letter C is a comedian" (L, 294), an observation that manages to collapse Crispin, "Comedian," and the "Letter C" into one. Such fusion suggests, perhaps, that Stevens considered the soft *C* a homophonic echo of purged perception, the equivalent of "see" as it arises, for example, in the punning "Tennessee" of "Anecdote of the Jar" or in the notation "A few pages of C Major."[10] The import of the hard *C* is suggested in another brief jotting, "the *c*adets of *c*igarette Road"[11] (Stevens' emphasis), where the sound arises in the context of smoke. The association reminds us that *K* is the meteorological symbol for smoke, a motif Stevens often uses in conjunction with the "sophic" fire. In view of Crispin's genealogy, it may be, too, that the sound of the hard *C* is related to the Greek *chemeia*, the name for the alchemical art (the prefix *–al* was later added by Arabic interpreters of the tradition) which, in turn, may owe its etymological origin to the coptic *chem*, which means black and which signified Egypt as the "Land of the Black or Fertile soil."[12] Egypt is often proposed as the birthplace of the alchemical art.

"The Comedian as the Letter C" is Stevens most direct declaration of spiritual intention, unveiled under the guise of aesthetics and intertwined with the poet's problematic relationship to his art. The rebirth of the soul—the poem's major subject— is allegorized in a contrastive symmetry which takes Crispin on a metaphorical journey from the old world to the new; from sea to land; and from imagination to reality. The quest for reintegration is matched by the poem's division into two major sections (of three cantos each), each headed by an instructive epigram which announces on the one hand, man as the suzerain of the cosmic soil ("Nota: man is the intelligence of his soil" [CP, 27]), and, on the other—in reversed predication—the cosmic soil as the source of man's dominion ("Nota: his soil is man's intelligence" [CP, 36]). Since the second announces the fruit of transmutation that Crispin undergoes in the course of the poem, Stevens introduces his hero on a note of mockery, deriding him as a "nincompated pedagogue" (CP, 27), unfit because as yet unredeemed to act as "the Socrates / Of snails, musician of pears, principium / And lex" (CP, 27).[13] Withal, Crispin is a likely novitiate; for he is possessed of a "barber's eye" (CP, 27) that contemplates "Inscrutable hair in an inscrutable world" (CP, 27), tonsorial images for the *prima materia* lodged in the soul.[14] Hence, Crispin embarks on the redemptive quest for the "lost terrestrial," (CP, 28), acquired by the soul's divestment of its profane self—the "mythology of self, / Blotched out beyond unblotching" (CP, 28).

The dissolution of the soul—the first step in the revivification of the Man—is charted against the backdrop of the sea, a metaphor for the "sophic" water which "Severs not only lands but also selves" (CP, 30) in the alchemical rite of purification. Hence, in his pilgrimage toward union, Crispin is "dissolved" (CP, 29), and "annulled" CP, 29), his sullied soul "washed away by magnitude" (CP, 28) in preparation for the double resurrection which reconstructs the divine dyad—a "starker, barer self / In a starker, barer world" (CP, 29). So revivified, he confronts the "veritable ding an sich" (CP, 29), its single harmony a "vast, subjugating, final tone" (CP, 30) which announces Crispin "made new" (CP, 30).

In his initial encounter with cosmic "reality," Crispin raises the question of art, only to repudiate the "poems of plums" that constitute the imagination's evasion of primordial "reality":

> Here was no help before reality.
> Crispin beheld and Crispin was made new.
> The imagination, here, could not evade,
> In poems of plums, the strict austerity
> Of one vast, subjugating, final tone.
> The drenching of stale lives no more fell down.
>
> (CP, 30)

His repudiation, variously affirmed in the course of the poem, is clarified in canto II, which presents a spiritually expanded Crispin "grown in his demesne" (CP, 31) and agitated by "oracular rockings" (CP, 30). In this new-found condition of cosmic afflatus, Crispin grows impatient with the conventional muse, arraigning its music as a "stupor" that while appropriate to "sleepers halfway waking" is of little use to his own illuminated soul, possessed of a "violence" bent on "aggrandizement":

> He was in this as other freemen are,
> Sonorous nutshells rattling inwardly.
> His violence was for aggrandizement
> And not for stupor, such as music makes
> For sleepers halfway waking.
>
> (CP, 31)

As alternative, Crispin offers his own "aesthetic" (CP, 31), scrawled in an "indigenous dew" (CP, 31) and fashioned of "the mint of dirt" (CP, 31), metaphors for the heavenly *lapis*, customarily proposed as a lowly thing, though of inestimable worth.[15] From this "Green barbarism" (CP, 31) arises the poetry of "The fabulous and its intrinsic verse" (CP, 31), typically restated in terms of the luminous dyad—"two spirits parleying, adorned / In radiance" (CP, 31). However, the vision fails to satisfy Crispin's hunger for "aggrandizement"; hence, the poet-hero undergoes a second epiphany, again under the ministrations of the "sophic" water in the guise of a thunderstorm that Crispin boldly seeks to emulate:

> This was the span
> Of force, the quintessential fact, the note
> Of Vulcan, that a valet seeks to own,
> The thing that makes him envious in phrase.
>
> (CP, 33)

The mythic god of the hearth made synonymous with "quintessential fact" recalls the "sophic" fire which distills the alchemical "quintessence." In parallel fashion, the thunderstorm again revives in Crispin's soul the Man made resurrect—"a self possessing him, / That was not in him in the crusty town / From which he sailed" (CP, 33).

Canto III records the third and final transmutation, reaffirming as Crispin approaches America from the south the "matinal continent" of the polar Man, "always north to him" (CP, 34). Suitably, the prospective encounter with deity is prefaced by references to the interior Work, argued as a "book of moonlight" (CP, 33) irradiated by the "sophic" "lunar fire" (CP, 33) and immersed in "sweating changes" (CP, 33), an allusion to the purifying sweat endured by the metals in the transmutative process. So engaged in the redemptive quest, Crispin anticipates the "blissful liaison, / Between himself and his environment," (read Hermetic salvation) affirmed as the soul's "chief motive" and made superordinate to the written artifact—"lesser things / Than the relentless contact he desired":

> How many poems he denied himself
> In his observant progress, lesser things
> Than the relentless contact he desired;
> . . . .
> Perhaps the Arctic moonlight really gave

> The liaison, the blissful liaison,
> Between himself and his environment,
> Which was, and if, chief motive, first delight,
> . . . .
> Moonlight was an evasion, or, if not,
> A minor meeting, facile, delicate.

(CP, 34–35)

The canto concludes with a tribute to the dyadic *imago Dei*, announced in the redemptive "river" that bears the "vessel inward" (CP, 36) to the "marshy ground" (CP, 36) (a variation of the "mud" image Stevens frequently uses for the Man). So "purified" (CP, 36) by the celestial soil, Crispin completes his "rude aesthetic" (CP, 36), typically announced as the "essential prose" (CP, 36) to which "all poems were incident" (CP, 36) to distinguish the pneumatic life of "being" from the written poem of becoming.

With redemption complete, the visionary Crispin considers founding a "colony" (CP, 38) of like souls, subsequently restated as a "polar planterdom" (CP, 40) to announce the hegemony of the icy Man. Suitably a Janus vision compounded of "time to come" (CP, 39) and "backward flights" (CP, 39), the prospective paradise inspires images of humanity assimilated to the natural world ("rainy men" [CP, 37]; "pine-spokesman" [CP, 38]) to which it accords a devotional "sacrament / And celebration" (CP, 39). Such a vision of true being, the revivified Crispin finds, is infinitely to be preferred to the poet's art, disdained as "counterfeit"—a "racking masquerade" of "trash," appropriate perhaps to the "blind" but not to him, a soul "serenely sly," preferring "text to gloss":

> He could not be content with counterfeit,
> With masquerade of thought, with hapless words
> That must belie the racking masquerade,
> With fictive flourishes that preordained
> His passion's permit, hang of coat, degree
> Of buttons, measure of his salt. Such trash
> Might help the blind, not him, serenely sly.
> It irked beyond his patience. Hence it was,
> Preferring text to gloss, he humbly served
> Grotesque apprenticeship to chance event,
> A clown, perhaps, but an aspiring clown.

(CP, 39)

It would appear from canto V that Crispin's visionary dream remains unrealized, though it equally appears that the acolyte, withdrawn from "social nature" (CP, 43), serves a probationary trial, dwelling "in the land" as "hermit, pure and capable" (CP, 40). For reasons that remain ambiguous, rapport with the metaphysical Life proves elusive, tempted, it seems, by the sensuous satisfactions of the sensible world:

> Crispin dwelt in the land and dwelling there
> Slid from his continent by slow recess
> To things within his actual eye, alert
> To the difficulty of rebellious thought
> When the sky is blue. The blue infected will.
>
> (CP, 40)

Crispin therefore determines a "return to social nature" (CP, 43) and, by extension, to poetry. The course, however, occasions for the lapsed poet a bout of self-derision that questions whether, indeed, his active spiritual power would be adequately served by its confinement in the formal images of art:

> Was he to bray this in profoundest brass
> Arointing his dreams with fugal requiems?
> Was he to company vastest things defunct
> With a blubber of tom-toms harrowing the sky?
> Scrawl a tragedian's testament? Prolong
> His active force in an inactive dirge,
> Which, let the tall musicians call and call,
> Should merely call him dead?
>
> (CP, 41)[16]

Repudiation of Hermetic monasticism is subsequently rationalized in a brief couplet that questions whether the poet's personal spiritual experience would serve as model for collective humanity: "Should he lay by the personal and make / Of his own fate an instance of all fate?" (CP, 41). Temporarily resolved, it would appear, to respond affirmatively to his social task, Crispin bids farewell to his original dream, resigning himself to "A Nice Shady Home" (CP, 40) replete with his espoused "prismy blonde" (CP, 42)—the feminine cosmic element suitably associated with the redemptive light. So pledged in divine liaison, Crispin resumes his craft in the "quotidian" (CP, 43).

In the final summation, Crispin's uneasy accommodation to his art is rendered metaphorically in the customary alchemical images of procreation and birth. Thus, following a parodic invocation to the muse, Crispin sets out to chronicle his revived poetic life, conceived as an act of "midwifery" (CP, 43) (to suggest its mediate nature) from which issue four "Daughters with Curls" (CP, 43)—symbols of the hirsute Mercurius, like their primordial counterpart, "Infants yet eminently old" (CP, 43). These "four . . . personae" (CP, 45) of the Hermetic deity Crispin acknowledges as "many mulctings of the man" (CP, 44) to suggest them as the fake images he has perforce to construct in the course of his evangelical pilgrimage. Nevertheless, personal debacle is not without redemptive significance; for if, the poet conjectures, Crispin is a "profitless / Philosopher" (CP, 45–46) whose original "green brag" (CP, 46) concludes "fadedly" (CP, 46); and if his poems are merely "after-shining flicks" (CP, 46) that illuminate the archetypal "apparition" (CP, 46) from which they spring, he remains notwithstanding the instrument of human rebirth—for through his poems constructed of "gulped potions from obstreperous drops" (CP, 46) (the heavenly elixir), he engages in "proving what he proves / Is nothing" (CP, 46)—a tortured allusion to the cosmic void. Since such a condition necessarily entails the dissolution of the written object, Stevens concludes his "Disguised pronunciamento" (CP, 45) by dismissing his own "doctrinal" (CP, 45) creation, inquiring laconically "what can all this matter since / The relation comes, benignly, to its end?" (CP, 46). The one-line coda tersely extends the spiritual experience of the single soul to humanity at large: "So may the relation of each man be clipped" (CP, 46).

Though "The Comedian as the Letter C" is the best surviving record we have of Stevens' spiritual development, it is nevertheless a timeless narrative or, more precisely, a narrative constrained by psychic rather than temporal change. Of actual events in the poet's life, it provides little insight; nor does it hint, even discreetly, of spiritual crisis. If the poem has a center of conflict, it arises not as in the Arnoldian sense from a struggle to accommodate the demands of the spirit to an increasingly skeptical age, but from the soul's effort to preserve the integrity of vision from what would appear to be its supreme antagonist—the written word. To be sure, Crispin the "hermit" capitulates to "social nature" (viz., to the making of the poem), but he does so reluctantly, compelled, it would seem, by the remarkable conviction that he could in some fashion make his "own fate an instance of all fate."[17]

Notwithstanding its biographical limitations, "The Comedian as the Letter C" is of extraordinary interest; for if, as Helen Vendler observes, it may be read as a "semi-ironic confessional"[18]—a view widely shared by Stevens' readers—the poem suggests that Stevens, at some point in his development, experienced a spiritual enlightenment that prompted, at least for a time, the poet's renunciation of his art. The view must of course remain speculative; the reader would comb the corpus in vain to seek an overt declaration to this effect. Nevertheless, it is possible to piece together something of the spiritual climate of Stevens' formative years from several scattered allusions—oblique, to be sure, but of considerable significance when viewed in the context of the poet's repeated delineation of the Hermetic vision. One such casual interpolation arises in the brief essay "Rubbings of Reality," a tribute to William Carlos Williams which first appeared in a 1946 issue of the *Briarcliff Quarterly* and was later collected in *Opus Posthumous*. The title of the piece suggests of course the poet's customary view of the relations between the written artifact and cosmic reality—the first here regarded as a "rubbing" or copy of the second. Stevens' reading of Williams similarly parallels a visionary poetics which accords the poem its usual preliminary function. By this yardstick, Williams, according to Stevens, creates poems that are images of reality, but these images are typically considered "faint or obscure" (OP, 257) "trials" (OP, 258) in the poet's ongoing effort to achieve an "integration" (OP, 257). By no means the parochial task of the poet, this practicing "in order to make perfect" (OP, 258), the poet continues, constitutes a "universal activity" (OP, 258), an observation which allows an instructive spiritual illustration:

> But the world of the past was equally the result of such activity. Thus the German pietists of the early 1700's who came to Pennsylvania to live in the caves of the Wissahickon and to dwell in solitude and meditation were proceeding in their way, from the

chromatic to the clear. Is not Williams in a sense a literary pietist,
chastening himself, incessantly, along the Passaic?   (OP, 258–59)

Though seemingly fortuitous, Stevens' allusion to a unique group
of religious settlers is of considerable interest; for according to historical accounts, the Pietists Stevens names were a group of mystics who
sought to establish in the New World a religious community based on
a blend of Christian and Hermetic doctrine. Established in 1694 on
the banks of the Wissahickon in eastern Pennsylvania, they later
moved in a second resettlement to Ephrata, an area some eighteen
miles southwest of Reading where the young Stevens spent many
summer holidays. There, in the early eighteenth century, they formed
a remarkable religious community which survived to Stevens' day—
albeit in considerable decline—and which he directly acknowledges
in several letters.[19] It seems likely, though the evidence is entirely
circumstantial, that it was this community of gnostics that influenced
Stevens' considerable interest in the Hermetic tradition.[20]

According to Julius Sachse, their chief chronicler, the forty eremites
who constituted the original Rosicrucian Brotherhood of provincial
Pennsylvania sailed from Erfurth, Germany to the New World to establish a "true Theosophical (Rosicrucian) community"[21] grounded in
the esoteric philosophy of the Kabbalah, the speculative theosophy of
Jacob Boehme, and the teachings and art of Hermetism. Protected by
the religious liberalism of William Penn, they settled along the Wissahickon River, establishing in the seclusion of the wilderness a
monastic community devoted to the study of "mystic and occult dog-
mas taught and studied in secret for many previous ages."[22] Their
celibate and cloistered life—unusual in the annals of Protestant religious corporatism—was evidently inspired by the belief that man, in
his primal form, had been "one, not dual and distinguished by sex, or
rather that the male and female sexuality (essence) constituted a single
being."[23] Composed in his femaleness of the divine Sophia, Adamic
man, they believed, had been a spiritual power, but with "the loss of

his divine womanliness . . . he sank down to the level of the dual animal kingdom."[24] To reestablish his wholeness in the human soul required the redemptive restoration of the maiden Sophia, a hope acknowledged in the prayer of Johannes Kelpius, their learned and devout leader:

> At the Creation's dawn thou wort not two but one
> But by the hapless Fall, this oneness was undone.
> Then Sophia thee leads, by penitence and tears
> To her estate again. A ray divine appears
> And streams thee through. A thrilling joy reveals that both are
> one.[25]

In quest of divine reintegration, the theosophists of the Wissahickon practiced the ancient art of "silence, meditation, and intercommunion with one's self," seeking by the mystical condition of "absolute negation" to reach the "unseen . . . spiritual world" of the "nought."[26] Their chiliastic certainty that universal restoration was imminent led to their unique custom of maintaining a watch-meeting every night, in the belief that "the Cry of the Bridegroom's coming" would sound forth at "Midnight," bringing "Evidence of that great Jubelee or Restitation of all things."[27] They also practiced laboratory alchemy for the purpose of distilling the medicinal "Elixir Vitae," which they thought would "remove all seeds of disease from the human body, thereby renewing youth and lessening the infirmities of age, if not repelling death."[28] Indeed, so absorbed were they in their occult speculations that a later chronicler reported them indifferent to either scripture or the sacraments:

> So far as I could gather from acquaintances and old residents, it
> seems to me that most of these former candidates (theological
> students) cared little or nothing for the holy sacraments of
> baptism and the eucharist. . . . So much of the Holy Writ was a
> dead letter to them; but, on the contrary, they busied themselves
> greatly with the Theosophical Sophia, speculation, etc., and at
> the same time practised alchemy.[29]

By the time of the first decade of settlement, the fortunes of the brethren began to decline, spurred largely by numerous defections from their ranks and by a less than rigorous devotional regimen among those who remained. With the death of Johannes Kelpius in 1708, the community virtually disintegrated, though a few of the remaining faithful continued to attract the many religious enthusiasts, visionaries, and separatists who flocked to the Province. Among these was the remarkable Conrad Beissel, a German baker who had been initiated into a Heidelberg Rosicrucian chapter organized in the guise of a Pietist conventicle to escape detection. When one of Beissel's fellow-bakers informed the authorities of Beissel's connection with the proscribed society, the fledgling theosophist was forced to flee. After some months of wandering, he resolved to leave Germany to join the "Chapter of Perfection" established by Kelpius on the Wissahickon, and toward this end sailed for America in the summer of 1720 in the company of several other brethren of like mind.

When on arrival Beissel found but a remnant of the original mystical community remaining, he apprenticed himself briefly to a weaver, but, determined to pursue the contemplative life, he retired in 1721 to a secluded area near Germantown. In 1724, after being baptized into the Baptist fold, he emerged from his solitary existence to form a Conestoga German Baptist congregation which adhered to his newly-formulated conviction that the appropriate day of worship was the old Hebrew seventh-day sabbath.[30] Another Beisselian doctrine—and one that clearly marked him as the spiritual heir of the original Wissahickon brethren—was his belief that the primal Adam—humanity's prototype—had, in his original form, been "coupled with Wisdom and therefore possessed both male and female traits."[31] With the fall of Lucifer, however, Adam had succumbed to prurience, with the result that he lost his divine womanliness. As compensation, God opened Adam's side and gave him Eve. Even then, it might have been possible to propagate the race asexually, but Eve proved as feckless as Adam and the two "fell into a brutish sexuality."[32] Thus, what had been originally one was now divided, but, Beissel held, the divine androgyne had been restored in Christ who, born of the heavenly and virginal Sophia, combined in his being the erstwhile sexual opposites. Salvation was possible if the eremite pursued the work of redemption in his own psyche, for only as he was mystically united with the androgynous Christ would he (if male) regain the divine Sophia, thereby restoring the original primal harmony.

From this curious amalgam of Hermetic and Christian doctrine, Beissel argued for a celibate and ascetic life. In views reminiscent of the alchemical *hieros gamos*, he preached that spiritual reintegration required the abandonment of sex—an "abomination" testifying to man's division—in order that the soul might be wedded to its true and heavenly opposite—for the male eremite, the eternal Sophia, for the female, the "celestial bridegroom," both of whom had returned to their wholeness in Christ. Consecration to this androgynous Christ required that the anchorite not only withdraw from the world—merely an illusory body without genuine substance—but that he cultivate the soteriological imagination, in order thereby to "be drawn back into the *Nichts*, into the divine *Ungrund*."[33] Thus Beissel preached the virtues of renunciation, urging in place of all physical pleasures and earthly pursuits the ecstasy of divine annihilation. "God has overpowered me and I have become a nothing," he advised his faithful adherents, exhorting the mystic death as a "holy nonentity and a holy non-possession."[34] To be so absorbed in the mystic void, he wrote, was not to suffer the sorrow of deprivation but to exult in the joy of plenitude, vouchsafed by the "wealth" of the heavenly "light":

> Since this dark nothingness I chose
> And his lone pathway trod
> No more deterring ramparts rose
> Between me and my God.
> And Oh this wealth of nothingness,
> Won me from creature love,
> For in God's light, I live to bless;
> A pastime 'tis to live and move.[35]

Gradually Beissel assembled a band of faithful disciples willing to follow his demand for celibacy and solitary living. His Sabbatarianism, however, met with considerable opposition from the more orthodox Germantown Baptists; hence, after a few vain attempts at compromise, Beissel led his flock out of the German Baptist church and founded a new congregation, known at its inception in 1728 as the Seventh-Day German Baptist Church. From the first, its organizational pattern was unique, arranged as a communal society which included celibate monks and nuns as well as members of the regular congregation. The arrangement was not, however, immune to factionalism; hence, in answer to the charge that he was partial to the cenobites, Beissel resigned his leadership and retired to a cabin some eight miles away. To the uninitiated, Beissel's choice of habitation appeared peculiar; for the cabin was built on the edge of a stream that notwithstanding its natural beauty, had been studiously avoided, even by the Indians, for it was infested with snakes. In view of the special place of the serpent in Hermetic thought—indeed, in gnostic speculation generally[36]—Beissel's choice appears less than capricious. Hence, he and his followers called the area *Hoch-Halekung*, meaning "Den of Serpents," which later came to be "spelled as pronounced,—Cocalico."[37] This site was later renamed Ephrata, meaning "fruitful land" (Micah 5:2; Ruth 4:11).

Despite Beissel's resignation, members of his former congregation reaffirmed his leadership by following him to Cocalico Creek. In several years, their ranks were swollen by new converts, and by 1735, the congregation was sufficiently stable and prosperous to warrant the building of the first cloister building, Kedar, which housed the sisters and brothers and served as a house of worship. By 1738, their communal organization, following Beissel's original plan, was clearly divided into three orders:

> The women's order was the Order of Spiritual Virgins or Roses of Sharon; the men's order was the Zionitic Brotherhood. These orders took vows of celibacy and lived communally. Besides the solitary sisters and brothers, there was the secular congregation of the married householders, many of whom lived in small houses nearby the cloister. These three orders comprised the church which acknowledged Beissel as their head.[38]

To reaffirm their dedication to the divine androgyne, the cenobites assumed "spiritual names" taken, for the most part, from the Old Testament and from early Christian martyrs. They also donned habits modelled after the style of the Capuchins or White Friars, and consisting of long gowns of unbleached linen or wool to which was attached a pointed cowl or monk's hood. In further pursuit of their original patrimony, the monks let their beards and hair grow, for it was believed that "according to the Jewish literati, Adam was created in the fulness of manhood, and in the first hour of his existence upon earth disported himself in a luxurious black beard."[39]

In an interesting account that outlines the parallels between physical and spiritual alchemy, Sachse tells of how the Zionitic Brotherhood sought Hermetic rebirth through a physical transmutation worked on their own bodies. Accordingly, the candidate seeking regeneration retired for forty days to a hut or cave in the forest where he spent his time in fasting and prayer.[40] Some seventeen days midway in the Operation, the votary had blood drawn and swallowed drops of a white potion known as an "elixir." On the thirty-third day, he took the first grain of *materia prima*, "the same substance which God created to confer immortality upon man when he was first made in paradise, but which, by reason of man's wickedness, was lost to the race, and at the present time was only to be obtained through or by the favor of such adepts as were within the highest circle of the Rosicrucian Brotherhood."[41] The potion evidently had the desired cathartic effect, for the acolyte "lost his speech and power of recollection" and, paralleling the sweat-bath of mercury in which the metals of laboratory alchemy were immersed, experienced "heavy transudation."[42] The next day, he took the second grain of the *materia prima*, losing forthwith his skin, hair, and teeth. After immersion in a purifying bath, he swallowed his third and last grain, upon which he fell into a profound sleep "during which a new skin appeared" and "the hair and teeth . . . were . . . miraculously renewed."[43] When he awoke, he was given "the elixir of life" to signify that he had been "completely rejuvenated and restored to the state of innocence of which mankind had been deprived by reason of original sin."[44] The rebirth, however, was not permanent, for it had to be repeated every "forty years . . . during the full moon of May."[45]

With the arrival of Jacob Martin in 1762, the Brotherhood's effort to regenerate the human organism in accord with alchemical procedures was matched by the laboratory effort to transmute physical substances. Martin, a shadowy figure whom Sachse mentions only briefly, brought with him the alchemical recipes of Michael Sendivogius, a Moravian alchemist and disciple of Alexander Sethon. These evidently guided him in his attempt "to discover the red tincture requisite to transmute baser metals into gold," for which purpose a "laboratory was built somewhere in the vicinity of the Kloster."[46] According to Sachse, the attempt was a "serious one," testified to by Martin's preserved correspondence.

The one feature of the Cloister that perhaps more than any other distinguished it in the eyes of the outside world was the extraordinary hymns composed by Beissel and sung by the cenobites under his direction.[47] The effect of this celestial music—what Beissel's biographer calls an "idiom of angels" possessing a "vitality" absent in the Cloister's other "artistic works"[48]—arose from Beissel's premise—common to the esoteric tradition—that the "spirit of singing" was indistinguishable from the "Holy Spirit."[49] According to one memoirist, the music was patterned on the tones of the Aeolian harp, taking its measure and harmony "after the style of nature":

It is very peculiar in its style and concords, and in its execution.
The tones issuing from the choir imitate very soft instrumental
music, carrying a softness and devotion almost superhuman to
the auditor. . . . All the parts save the bass, which is set in two
parts, are led and sung exclusively by the females, the men being
confined to the high and low bass. The latter, resembling the
deep tones of the organ, and the former in combination with one
of the female parts, the contrast produces an excellent imitation
of the concert horn [hautboy]. The whole is sung in the falsetto
voice, which throws the sound up to the ceiling, and the melody,
which seems to be more than human . . . appears to be
descending from above and hovering over the heads of the
assembly.[50]

In the view of the cenobites, Beissel's music belonged "more to
the angelic world than to ours," its harmonic principles the "rules"
which "the angels themselves" had observed "at the birth of Christ."[51]
Indeed, his "Paradisiacal Wonder Music"—so described on the title
page of the *Turtel Taube*, a collection of hymns issued in 1754—was
itself a "prevision of the New World" which his chiliastic disciples
regarded as imminent.[52] Hence, in an effort to prepare humanity for
the final restoration, Beissel wrote in the preface to the *Turtel Taube*
that the Cloister's "high and precious gift" was not to be kept "alone
for ourselves" but was to be shared, thereby to "favor other lovers of
the divine and celestial comedy."[53]

Despite some internal wrangling, the community flourished for
some thirty years, even inspiring three satellite orders—the result of a
number of evangelical forays periodically undertaken by the Brotherhood. But with the death of Beissel in 1768, the community rapidly
declined, until in 1814 only four members of the two orders remained.
In that year, the congregation was incorporated and administration of
the land fell to the secular householders.[54] At the turn of the century
when Stevens knew it, the congregation numbered only twenty and in
1941, 210 years after its founding, the Cloister was taken over by the
Commonwealth of Pennsylvania and turned into a museum open to
the public.

Though the Cloister's formal organization disappeared, its
spiritual legacy evidently inspired the formation of the Ancient and
Mystical Order Rosae Crucis (AMORC), an American Rosicrucian
society founded in 1909. According to H. Spencer Lewis, its Grand
Imperator, the Order traces its descent to the "first Rosicrucian colony" established "first at Philadelphia, then at Ephrata, Pennsylva-

nia."[55] Initially a body "of considerable importance," Lewis writes in his preface to a document outlining Rosicrucian principles, the organization came to a close in 1801 (some 108 years after the Kelpius' colony of 1694) in accord with an "ancient law" that decreed that "each 108 years was a cycle of rebirth, activity, rest, and waiting."[56] Though the Cloister was defunct for the next 108 years, its esoterica was preserved, known only to "certain *descendants of the last initiates*" (Lewis' emphasis) who passed "to one another the rare records and official documents"[57] in preparation for the 1909 revival (the beginning of a new 108-year cycle).

The privatism at which Lewis hints is followed by a theosophical glossary containing an entry identical to the title Stevens chose for his first volume of poetry:

> *Harmonium* — A state of harmony. The metaphysical meaning when applied to the relationship of humans is unity of thought, agreement of purpose, the direct communion or kinship of souls. As applied to the relationship of the Cosmic to the human soul, it means that state of ecstasy where the human becomes conscious of the attunement of the natural forces of his being with the Absolute or the source from which they emanate.[58]

Though we may perhaps never know the extent of Stevens' indebtedness to this particular formulation of Hermetic doctrine, there can be little doubt that it records a vision of human transcendence very close to one the poet never tired of describing in the course of his remarkable poetic career.

ℭ *Notes* ℭ

Introduction _____ ℭ

1. C. Ronald Wagner, "A Central Poetry," in *Wallace Stevens*, ed. Marie Borroff (Englewood Cliffs: Prentice-Hall, Inc., 1963), p. 73. The essay first appeared in *The Hudson Review*, 5 (Spring 1952), 144–48.

2. Stevens' disavowal of humanism is explored in chapter 4.

3. Roy Harvey Pearce, *The Continuity of American Poetry* (Princeton: Princeton University Press, 1961), p. 381.

4. Louis Martz, *The Poem of the Mind* (New York: Oxford University Press, 1969), p. 203.

5. J. Hillis Miller, *Poets of Reality* (New York: Atheneum, 1969), p. 259.

6. Pearce, *The Continuity of American Poetry*, p. 415.

7. Harold Bloom, "'Notes toward a Supreme Fiction': A Commentary," in Borroff, *Wallace Stevens*, p. 76.

Chapter 1 _____ ℭ

1. For a contrary view, see Roy Harvey Pearce, *The Continuity of American Poetry*. According to Pearce, Stevens' poems are to be regarded as processes revealing the mind's potential capacity to annihilate all determinate forms in order "to abstract forward, as it were, and to partake, through the abstraction, of its own potentiality to make more poems and to realize itself in all its humanity" (p. 408). The "ultimate poem" is thus only a possibility, pointing not to any final and conclusive order but to the mind's unceasing effort to touch the rock of selfhood.

2. Joseph N. Riddel, *The Clairvoyant Eye* (Baton Rouge: Louisiana State University Press, 1965), p. 37.

3. Those who have addressed Stevens' theology have generally agreed that the imagination is Stevens' substitute for God. See Ralph Mills, "The Image of the Rock," in Borroff, *Wallace Stevens*, pp. 96–110; Doris L. Eder, "The Meaning of Wallace Stevens' Two Themes," *Critical Quarterly*, 11 (Summer 1969), 181–90; Adalaide Kirby Morris, *Wallace Stevens: Imagination and Faith* (Princeton: Princeton University Press, 1974); H. W. Burtner, "The High Priest of the Secular: The Poetry of Wallace Stevens," *Connecticut Review*, 6 (October 1972), 34–45.

4. Stevens speaks of Ananke as "an importation from Italy" (L, 370), a reference generally traced to a 1934 letter from the Italian philosopher Mario Rossi, in which Rossi mentions "the imperscrutable Ananke." Portions of the letter are excerpted in Stevens' commonplace book, *"Sur Plusieurs Beaux Sujets,"* The Wallace Stevens Manuscript Collection at the Huntington Library, Cahier I, p. 8.

5. Pearce, *The Continuity of American Poetry*, p. 413.

6. William Van O'Connor, *The Shaping Spirit* (New York: Russell & Russell, 1964), p. 64.

7. Stevens' preoccupation with the future appears frequently in the poetry. For a brilliant account of the implied futurity of Stevens' linguistic modulations, see Helen Vendler, *On Extended Wings* (Cambridge: Harvard University Press, 1969), chapter 1.

8. Stanley Burnshaw, "Turmoil in the Middle Ground," *New Masses*, 17 (October 1935), 41–42. Apparently dissatisfied with "Owl's Clover," Stevens substantially revised it for its reappearance in *The Man with the Blue Guitar and Other Poems* (1937) and subsequently dropped it from *The Collected Poems* on the grounds that it was "rhetorical" (OP, xxiii). Samuel French Morse reprinted it in its entirety in *Opus Posthumous*. For an account of Stevens' revisions, see A. Walton Litz, *Introspective Voyager* (New York: Oxford University Press, 1972), pp. 317–19.

9. Merle E. Brown, *Wallace Stevens* (Detroit: Wayne State University Press, 1970), p. 89.

10. W. K. C. Guthrie, *A History of Greek Philosophy* (Cambridge: Cambridge University Press, 1965), II, p. 164.

11. According to Peter Brazeau, Stevens' copy of Freud's *The Future of an Illusion* contains the notation in Stevens' hand (in the margin and on the dust jacket) that "Freud identifies Ananke with external reality" ("Wallace Stevens at the University of Massachusetts: Check List of an Archive," *The Wallace Stevens Journal*, 2 [Spring 1978], 50). Though there is no way of knowing whether Stevens intended this as confirmation of his own use of the figure, the observation coincides with Ananke's traditional significance.

12. The serpent, a common symbol of the unconscious, is identified with Ananke in "Like Decorations in a Nigger Cemetery" (CP, 152).

13. The peroration calls to mind Stevens' oft-noted disdain for the aesthetic object and for the imagination that creates it. In this connection, it is worth noting that the title "Owl's Clover" appears to reflect Stevens' skepticism towards art; for as Holly Stevens accurately observes, owl's clover is the common name for "the genus *Orthocarpus*, a weed and herb" that resembles clover but is, in fact, "false clover" (L, 311). Since Stevens was unusually scrupulous about his titles (see L, 297), we may reasonably conclude that this one, too, was chosen to reflect the intention of the poem.

Chapter 2

1. Brown, *Wallace Stevens*, p. 90.

2. Riddel, *The Clairvoyant Eye*, p. 135; Martz, *The Poem of the Mind*, p. 211. Critics are divided on the merits of "Owl's Clover." William Van O'Connor sees the poem as "one of the best long poems in English published during the first half of the twentieth century" (*The Shaping Spirit*, p. 60). Less lavish but nonetheless positive is Henry W. Wells' judgment that the poem is "one of the most rewarding flights of Stevens' art" (*Introduction to Wallace Ste-*

vens [Bloomington: Indiana University Press, 1964], p. 195). In contrast, Louis Martz regards the poem as unsuccessful, often depending on "a rhetoric of empty assertion" (*The Poem of the Mind*, p. 210). Joseph Riddel and Helen Vendler have provided the fullest exegeses, but for neither is the poem successful. Vendler finds its basic style "florid," its concepts "squeamish," its language "notably strained," the poem of a man "embarrassed by his own rhetorical excesses." She concludes that the social theme of "Owl's Clover" was unsuited to Stevens' poetic talent (*On Extended Wings*, chap. 4). Riddel also sees the poem as a failure, "contentiously defensive, impenetrably opaque, and gracelessly hortatory" (*The Clairvoyant Eye*, p. 134), concluding that at this moment in his career Stevens did not have the "political acumen" to understand the point at which poetry had to divorce itself from ideological controversy (pp. 121–22). "Owl's Clover" is certainly flawed, but to dismiss it for its stylistic lapses is to miss the more crucial matter of its "rhetorical" intent. Indeed, so eager was Stevens to be understood that he lavished considerable exegetical energy on the poem (the glosses for "Owl's Clover" are exceptionally generous and unusually [for Stevens] straightforward) and even revised and reissued it, so according it an attention enjoyed by no other poem in the corpus.

3. Riddel, *The Clairvoyant Eye*, p. 136.

4. *Ibid.*, p. 153.

5. Joseph Riddel acknowledges that the hero is Stevens' subman "projected outward" (*The Clairvoyant Eye*, p. 152).

6. Litz, *Introspective Voyager*, p. 317.

7. Wallace Stevens, *Mattino Domenicale ed Altre Poesie*, trans. Renato Poggioli (Torino: Giulio Einaudi, 1954), p. 180.

8. It is worth noting that in Stevens' copy of John Lubbock Avebury's *The Pleasures of Life*, the passage recording this myth (Aristophanes' story of the halving of bisexual man) is heavily marked (*The Pleasures of Life, Complete Edition* [Philadelphia: Henry Altemus, 1894], p. 181 in the Wallace Stevens' Manuscript Collection at the Huntington Library). Milton J. Bates suggests that these notations are "probably" not in Stevens' hand but offers no evidence for this conjecture ("Stevens' Books at the Huntington: An Annotated Checklist," *Wallace Stevens Journal*, II [Fall 1978], 55).

9. Riddel, *The Clairvoyant Eye*, p. 32. A number of studies have suggested the influence of the French Symbolist tradition on Stevens' work, though Stevens disclaimed such a connection (L, 391; 635). See Hi Simons, "Wallace Stevens and Mallarmé," *Modern Philology*, 43 (May 1946), 235–59; Haskell M. Block, "The Impact of French Symbolism on Modern American Poetry," in *The Shaken Realist: Essays in Modern Literature in Honor of Frederick J. Hoffman*, eds., Melvin J. Friedman and John B. Vickery (Baton Rouge: Lousiana State University Press, 1970), pp. 165–217; René Taupin, *L'Influence du Symbolisme Francais sur la Poésie Américaine* (Paris: H. Champion, 1929), pp. 276–77. Michel Benamou suggest a more ambiguous relationship in view of Stevens' attachment to the natural world (*Wallace Stevens and the Symbolist Imagination* [Princeton: Princeton University Press, 1972]).

10. R. P. Blackmur, *Form and Value in Modern Poetry* (New York: Doubleday & Co., Anchor Books ed., 1957), p. 202.

Chapter 3 _____ ⟰

1. For a lucid account of the connection between alchemy and chemistry, see F. Sherwood Taylor, *The Alchemists: Founders of Modern Chemistry* (New York: Henry Schuman, 1949). Spiritual alchemy is a complex affair distinguished by a literature that records two parallel processes (the transmutation of natural substances and the metamorphosis of the soul) in a cryptic and allusive symbol system designed to maintain a modicum of secrecy. In my exploration of this arcane "science," I have encountered no single text that provides an adequate critical and scholarly exegesis, though, to be sure, the pioneering work of Carl Jung, to which I am thoroughly indebted, contains a rich sampling of alchemical texts and an equally penetrating interpretation, when not marred by Jung's own theory of individuation. I have attempted a reconstruction of alchemical "theoria" as well as of its allegorical system which, lest it appear arbitrary, has required the frequent support of quotation.

2. Taylor, *The Alchemists: Founders of Modern Chemistry*, pp. 143–44.

3. Mircea Eliade, *The Forge and the Crucible*. trans. Stephen Corrin (New York: Harper & Row, Harper Torch Book, 1971), p. 163. Carl Jung similarly describes the alchemical Work as a psychic operation which "was always understood as a kind of rite after the manner of an *opus divinum*" (*Alchemical Studies* [Princeton: Princeton University Press, 1967] p. 123).

4. Mary A. Atwood, *Hermetic Philosophy and Alchemy: A Suggestive Inquiry into the Hermetic Mystery*, rev. ed. (New York: The Julian Press, 1960), p. 162.

5. H. J. Sheppard suggests that Greek alchemy and Gnosticism, contemporaneous movements "strongly associated with each other," drew their philosophical ideas from Stoic and Oriental doctrines current in their time ("Gnosticism and Alchemy," *Ambix* 6 [December, 1957], 93). Carl Jung similarly traces Christianized European alchemy to "pagan, and more particularly . . . Gnostic, sources," (*Psychology and Alchemy*, 2nd ed. [Princeton: Princeton University Press, 1968], p. 357). It is well to emphasize that the gnostic view of deity as absolutely transmundane differs substantially from alchemical doctrine, which proposes matter (and man) as emanations of the cosmic soul and hence sacramental. The alchemist sought not to transcend matter but to restore it to its original "glorified" body.

6. Jung, *Psychology and Alchemy*, p. 293.

7. Walter Leslie Wilmhurst, "Introduction," to Mary Atwood, *Hermetic Philosophy and Alchemy: A Suggestive Inquiry into The Hermetic Mystery*, p. 26. Subsequent references to this "Introduction" will be cited as Wilmhurst, (I), *Hermetic Philosophy*, followed by page number.

8. Hans Jonas, *The Gnostic Religion*, 2nd ed., rev. (Boston: Beacon Press, 1963), p. 155.

9. Carl Jung, *Mysterium Coniunctionis*, 2nd ed. (Princeton: Princeton University Press, 1970), p. 49.

10. Jung, *Psychology and Alchemy*, p. 232. Jung suggests that the figure of the Anthropos enters alchemical thought in the third century A.D. with the work of Zosimos of Panopolis (*Mysterium Coniunctionis*, p. 410).

11. Leo Schaya, *The Universal Meaning of the Kabbalah* (Baltimore: Penguin Books, 1973), p. 128. In the fifteenth century, Pico della Mirandola's analysis of Kabbalistic literature contributed to the synthesis of Hermetism and Kabbalism.

12. Titus Burckhardt, *Alchemy*, trans. William Stoddart (Baltimore: Penguin Books, 1971), p. 149.

13. Jung, *Alchemical Studies*, p. 92.

14. *Ibid.*, p. 131.

15. Arthur Edward Waite, ed., *The Hermetic and Alchemical Writings of Paracelsus* (Berkeley: Shambhala Publications, 1976) I, p. 135.

16. Wilmhurst, (I), *Hermetic Philosophy*, p. 60.

17. Franz Hartmann, *Paracelsus: Life and Prophecies* (New York: Rudolf Steiner Publications, 1973), p. 34.

18. Wilmhurst, (I), *Hermetic Philosophy*, pp. 32, 33.

19. Jung, *Psychology and Alchemy*, p. 319.

20. Ronald D. Gray, *Goethe the Alchemist* (Cambridge: The University Press, 1952), p. 20.

21. Jung, *Psychology and Alchemy*, p. 320.

22. Mircea Eliade, *The Myth of the Eternal Return*, trans, Willard R. Trask (Princeton: Princeton University Press, 1974), p. 17.

23. Jung, *Mysterium Coniunctionis*, p. 45.

24. *Ibid.*

25. Gray, *Goethe*, p. 26.

26. Jung, *Mysterium Coniunctionis*, p. 47.

27. Jack Lindsay, *The Origins of Alchemy in Graeco-Roman Egypt* (New York: Barnes & Noble, 1970), p. 331.

28. Jung, *Alchemical Studies*, p. 125.

29. Gray, *Goethe*, p. 26.

30. Jung, *Alchemical Studies*, p. 147.

31. Gray, *Goethe*, p. 13.

32. Burckhardt, *Alchemy*, p. 94.

33. Lindsay, *The Origins of Alchemy*, p. 111.

34. Jung, *Mysterium Coniunctionis*, p. 18.

35. Jung, *Psychology and Alchemy*, p. 74.

36. A succinct summary of Mercurius' numerical value is afforded by a sixteenth-century adept: "But know that the Stone is composed out of one, two, three, four, and five. Out of five—that is the quintessence of its own substance. . . . Out of four, by which we must understand the four elements. Out of three, and these are the three principles of all things. Out of two, for the mercurial substance is twofold. Out of one, and this is the first essence of everything which emanated from the primal fiat of creation." (Cited in John Read, *The Alchemist in Life, Literature and Art* [London: Thomas Nelson and Sons, 1947], p. 10.)

37. Jung, *Alchemical Studies*, p. 219.

38. Walter Pagel, *Paracelsus: An Introduction to Philosophical Medicine in the Era of the Renaissance* (Basel: S. Karger, 1958), p. 267.

39. F. Sherwood Taylor traces the alchemical air-spirit to the ancient idea of the *pneuma* or breath thought to have been an original emission from God by virtue of which all living things existed (*The Alchemists*, pp. 10–17).

40. Jung, *Alchemical Studies*, p. 292.

41. *Ibid.*, p. 214.

42. *Ibid.*, p. 209.

43. Jung, *Mysterium Coniunctionis*, p. 449.

44. Wilmhurst, (I), *Hermetic Philosophy*, pp. 13–14.

45. *Ibid.*, p. 27.

46. Jung, *Psychology and Alchemy*, p. 277.

47. *Ibid.*, p. 278.

48. Wilmhurst (I), *Hermetic Philosophy*, p. 37.

49. Gershom G. Scholem, *Major Trends in Jewish Mysticism*, 3rd rev. ed. (New York: Schocken Paperback, 1961), p. 25.

50. Atwood, *Hermetic Philosophy*, xiv.

51. *Ibid.*, p. 260.

52. Pagel, *Paracelsus*, p. 51.

53. Wilmhurst, (I), *Hermetic Philosophy*, p. 61.

54. Pagel, *Paracelsus*, p. 63.

55. Atwood, *Hermetic Philosophy*, p. 260.

56. Wilmhurst, (I), *Hermetic Philosophy*, p. 45.

57. H. Spencer Lewis, *Rosicrucian Manual*, 8th ed. (San Jose: Rosicrucian Press, 1941), VIII, p. 170. First published in 1918.

Chapter 4

1. The image of a "Universal Superman" arises in the journal of the young Stevens: "We go slumming in a quarter, we help starving Asiatics — true; but we do not pursue the idea of the Universal Superman — at least not to-day. But we may the day after to-morrow" (L, 89). A variation of the superman, associated this time with revivification, arises in the figure of the "super-animal" of "Owl's Clover," sought as a "man of folk-lore" who "shall rebuild the world" (OP, 63). Equally, the "super-man" (CP, 262) of "Montrachet-le-Jardin" appears in a poem dedicated to a hero who beckons humanity to a purified world "purged" of "The poison in the blood" (CP, 262). Milton J. Bates correctly points out that Stevens' superman appears variously in the poetry in the guise of Ananke, the hero, "major man" and the "supreme fiction" ("Major Man and Overman: Wallace Stevens' Use of Nietzsche," *The Southern Review*, 15 [Autumn 1979], 818–19).

2. "A Thought Revolved" first appeared in *New Directions* (1936). It was subsequently collected in *The Man With the Blue Guitar and Other Poems* (1937).

3. Carl H. Kraeling, *Anthropos and Son of Man* (New York: Columbia University Press, 1927), p. 51.

4. *Ibid.*, p. 49.

5. *Ibid.*, p. 109.

6. Jung, *Alchemical Studies*, p. 232.

7. *Ibid.*, p. 96. In his careful analysis of the Fourth Gospel, C. H. Dodd suggests parallels between the "Son of Man" and the archetypal Anthropos of the Hermetic tradition (*The Interpretation of the Fourth Gospel* [Cambridge: Cambridge University Press, 1953], pp. 10–49; 241–49). Carl Jung affirms that the *lapis* concept assimilated to Christ in Christianized alchemy was "from time immemorial . . . this same Anthropos or Son of Man, appearing in the gospel of St. John as the cosmogonic Logos that existed before the world was" (*Mysterium Coniunctionis*, p. 290).

8. Jung, *Mysterium Coniunctionis*, p. 92.

9. *Ibid.*, p. 395.

10. *Ibid.*, p. 92.

11. *Ibid.*, p. 7; Jung, *Alchemical Studies*, p. 226.

12. Jung, *Mysterium Coniunctionis*, p. 132. The "animal" of alchemical symbology is a counter for the anima-soul, an equivalence Stevens suggests in his gloss to poem vii of "The Man with the Blue Guitar": "Anima= animal=soul." He goes on to say that "The body has a shape, the soul does not. The soul is the animal of the body. Art deceives itself in thinking that it can give a final shape to the soul" (Poggioli, *Mattino Domincale ed Altre Poesie*, p. 179). Stevens' disdain for art as a final spiritual form is explored in chapter 7.

13. Jung, *Alchemical Studies*, p. 214.

14. Jung, *Psychology and Alchemy*, p. 195.

15. George S. Lensing, " 'From Pieces of Paper': A Wallace Stevens Notebook," *Southern Review*, 15 (Autumn 1979), 894. The notebook entry "All Men in One Man" (Lensing, 879) similarly reaffirms the Man as the "one" and "all."

16. Michel Benamou correctly notes the alchemical imagery of this poem, considering it a symbolic analogue of the poet's individual quest for psychic reintegration (*Wallace Stevens and the Symbolist Imagination*, p. 126).

17. Jung, *Mysterium Coniunctionis*, p. 40.

18. Henry Corbin, *Spiritual Body and Celestial Earth*, trans. Nancy Pearson (Princeton: Princeton University Press, 1977), p. 99.

19. The motifs of death and war are considered in chapter 7.

20. Jung, *Psychology and Alchemy*, p. 428.

21. Burckhardt, *Alchemy*, p. 41.

22. A similar use of "transparence" arises in "Owl's Clover," where the poet recalls a former condition of life characterized by "solitude":

> There each man,
> Through long cloud-cloister-porches, walked alone,
> Noble within perfecting solitude,
> Like a solitude of the sun, in which the mind
> Acquired transparence and beheld itself
> And beheld the source from which transparence came . . .
> (OP, 54)

For an account of a monastic community of solitaries to which the passage possibly alludes, see chapter 9. The Hermetic doctrine of transcendental perception is considered in chapter 8.

23. Jung, *Mysterium Coniunctionis*, p. 97.

24. Jung, *Psychology and Alchemy*, p. 317.

25. In alchemical thought, the feminine archetype in one of her guises represents the black earth that composed the body of the original macroanthropos and from which he is said to be begotten (Jung, *Alchemical Studies*, p. 232). The Great Mother is as well a component of the psyche corresponding to the anima in man—his *soror mystica* embedded in the imagination and associated with moon, night, and shadow and with the divine transformative waters (symbolically rendered as clouds, rain, and dew). Frank Doggett correctly notes that the feminine archetype in Stevens' poetry is both an "earth image" and "a latent feminine element of the self," a symbol of the "unconscious" (*Stevens' Poetry of Thought* [Baltimore: Johns Hopkins Press, 1966], pp. 23; 43).

26. Jung, *Mysterium Coniunctionis*, p. 112.

27. *Ibid.*, p. 113.

28. Glauco Cambon points out "the emphasis on the number three (three sections, three-line stanzas, albeit unrhymed)" in "Notes toward a Supreme Fiction" (*The Inclusive Flame* [Bloomington: Indiana University Press, 1965], p. 100). It may be that this triadic structure, especially prominent in the late major poems, is patterned after the triune stone, which represents body, soul, and spirit. In the sixteenth century, Paracelsus gave the trichotomous doctrine wide currency: "Know, then . . . that all the seven metals are born from a threefold matter. . . . Mercury is the spirit, Sulphur is the soul, and Salt is the body . . . the soul, which indeed is Sulphur . . . unites those two contraries, the body and spirit, and changes them into one essence." (Cited in Read, *The Alchemist in Life, Literature and Art*, p. 7.)

29. Jung, *Alchemical Studies*, pp. 286; 213.

30. *Ibid.*, p. 290.

31. *Ibid.*, p. 230.

32. C. Kerényi, *Hermes: Guide of Souls*, trans. Murray Stein (New York: Analytical Psychology Club of New York, Inc., 1976), p. 80. Helen Vendler suggests the similarity of the "dead shepherd" and the Orphic Christ (*On Extended Wings*, p. 173). The suggestion is not amiss, since in the mystery religions with which alchemy has much in common, Dionysos, Hermes, and Orpheus were at times considered companion gods. See C. Kerényi, *Dionysos: Archetypal Image of Indestructible Life*, trans. Ralph Manheim (Princeton: Princeton University Press, 1976), pp. 195; 240–42.

33. The distinction is between the historical past and the primordial past. Stevens of course disdains the historical past.

34. Erich Neumann, *The Origins and History of Consciousness* (New York: Harper and Brothers, Harper Torchbook, 1962), I, p. 11.

35. Though "Notes toward a Supreme Fiction" is dedicated to Henry Church, a long-time friend, Stevens was at pains to dissociate the name of Church from the dedicatory poem, acknowledged as "the most important thing in the book" (L, 538). Wishing to make clear the distinction, he urged a separate page for the title (with the inscription to Church). These instructions, Holly Stevens notes, were observed in *Transport to Summer* but were disregarded in *The Collected Poems* (L, 538). After examining the correspondence

between Stevens and Harry Duncan, the proprietor of the Cummington Press which first published "Notes toward a Supreme Fiction," Roger Mitchell concludes that the dedication to Church was an "afterthought, though the writing of the dedicatory poem was not" ("Wallace Stevens: The Dedication to 'Notes toward a Supreme Fiction,' " *Notes and Queries*, 13 [November 1966], 418).

Chapter 5

1. Harold Bloom, "'Notes toward a Supreme Fiction': A Commentary," in Borroff, *Wallace Stevens*, p. 77.

2. Bernard Heringman, "Wallace Stevens: The Use of Poetry," in *The Act of the Mind*, eds. Roy Harvey Pearce and J. Hillis Miller (Baltimore: Johns Hopkins Press, 1965), p. 6.

3. Statement from the front flap of dust jacket, *The Man with the Blue Guitar and Other Poems* (New York: Alfred A. Knopf, 1937).

4. Martz, *The Poem of the Mind*, p. 183.

5. The kitchen and its utensils are a familiar metaphor for the laboratory in alchemical texts and iconography. For a discussion of this motif in connection with seventeenth-century engravings based on alchemical themes, see Read, *The Alchemist in Life, Literature and Art*, p. 63.

6. Corbin, *Spiritual Body And Celestial Earth*, p. 32.

7. Jung, *Alchemical Studies*, p. 93.

8. Read, *Prelude to Chemistry*, p. 54.

9. Stevens experimented with several endings for "A Collect of Philosophy." Evidently eager for a more direct expression of the divine androgyne whose being the essay "philosophically" defends, Stevens devised in one version an "image of the imagination" represented by a crowned and irradiated "blue peacock" (a variation of the *cauda pavonis* whose many-colored plumage stood as symbol of the completed Work) which stands in the "center" of an "aerial floor," its "gold and silver fans" (the metals of the Work) "commanding" a group of "scholars" attached to the floor by means of "ceremonial ropes"—a common symbol in the esoteric tradition signifying the affinity of the soul for its source and the interrelatedness of all things ("Three Manuscript Endings for 'A Collect of Philosophy' " in *Wallace Stevens, a Celebration*, eds. Frank Doggett and Robert Buttell, [Princeton: Princeton University Press, 1980], p. 55).

10. Frank Doggett has pointed out the prominence of apposition in Stevens' later poetry ("Wallace Stevens' Later Poetry," *English Literary History*, 25 [June 1958], 146). Apposition is of course eminently suited to a vision which seeks to outline in emphatic catalogue the multiple powers and features of a single divine force.

11. Martz, *The Poem of the Mind*, p. 216.

12. Morris, *Wallace Stevens: Imagination and Faith*, p. 31.

13. Corbin, *Spiritual Body and Celestial Earth*, p. 4.

14. Stevens' structural coherence has eluded his critics who, persuaded that he is committed to existential process, read the poems as collections of discrete, albeit associative, units of thought. Helen Vendler considers "the poetry of disconnection . . . Stevens' most adequate form" (*On Extended Wings*, p. 65). Joseph Riddel suggests that "An Ordinary Evening in New Haven," like "Notes toward a Supreme Fiction," develops by "discontinuity and *divertissement*, and is ultimately tied together only by the mind itself and its natural habits of reflection" (*The Clairvoyant Eye*, p. 256). J. Hillis Miller similarly reads the later poems as "open-ended improvisations" that "begin in the middle of a thought" and end "arbitrarily" (*Poets of Reality*, p. 260). For R. P. Blackmur, "Notes toward a Supreme Fiction" is "not a system, or even an organization . . . but a set of notes brought together and graphed by the convention of [Stevens'] triad" (*Form and Value in Modern Poetry*, p. 215).

15. S. Angus, *The Religious Quests of the Graeco-Roman World* (London: John Murray, 1929), p. 342.

16. Evelyn Underhill, *Mysticism* (New York: E. P. Dutton & Co., 1961), p. 359. Underhill regards alchemy's symbolic system an accurate account of the mystic's yearning for "the unutterable perfection of the Absolute Life" (p. 140).

17. When questioned by Sister Bernetta Quinn as to the intent of the "centre" that appears so frequently in his poetry, Stevens evades a direct answer, even as he casually invokes the image of the divine stone, the "sophic" Man in turn synonymous with the "centre":

> It is a relief to have a letter from some one that is interested in understanding. However, I don't want to turn to stone under your very eyes by saying "This is the centre that I seek and this alone." Your mind is too much like my own for it to seem to be an evasion on my part to say merely that I do seek a centre and expect to go on seeking it. I don't say that I shall not find it or that I do not expect to find it. It is the great necessity even without specific identification. (L, 584)

18. It is common in emanationist theories to propose deity as both essence and attribute—that which is anterior to the phenomenal world and that which is manifest therein. When considered the first, the divine principle is the eternal and unchanging element underlying all transitory forms. In its second manifestation, it represents the generative principle of multiplicity and change. Stevens epigrammatically captures this two-fold character of deity in the sprightly "Adult Epigram": "It is the ever-never-changing same, / An appearance of Again, the diva-dame" (CP, 353).

Chapter 6 ⟲

1. Miller, *Poets of Reality*, pp. 258–59.

2. Harold H. Watts, "Wallace Stevens and the Rock of Summer," *Kenyon Review*, 14 (Winter 1952), 125–26.

3. *Ibid.*, p. 132.

4. Jung, *Mysterium Coniunctionis*, p. 463.

5. Vendler, *On Extended Wings*, p. 13.

6. Poggioli, *Mattino Domenicale ed Altre Poesie*, p. 183.

7. Idries Shah, *The Sufis* (New York: Doubleday & Co., 1971), p. 214.

8. In an uncollected letter to William Van O'Connor (March 31, 1949), Stevens identifies Hoon as "a mental abridgement possibly for who knows . . . everybody; more accurately anybody" (Benamou, *Wallace Stevens and the Symbolist Imagination*, xx). Though typically indirect, Stevens' explanation affirms that Hoon, like the "sophic" Man, is a universal being created in the mind.

9. In Chinese alchemy, the stone is known as the pill of immortality (*tan*) and is represented by cinnabar, a bright-red mineral which, in combination with gold, is the major ingredient of the laboratory Operation. The spiritual (internal) counterpart of physical alchemy is known as " 'internal cinnabar' (*nei tan*) as opposed to practical alchemy, called 'external cinnabar' (*wai tan*)" (Max Kaltenmark, *Lao Tzu and Taoism*, trans. Roger Greaves [Stanford: Stanford University Press, 1969], p. 132). It is likely that the Canon Aspirin of "Notes toward a Supreme Fiction" is Stevens' whimsical personification of the Chinese spiritual pill. Stevens' notebook entry "Still Life With Aspirin" ("Lensing, 'From Pieces of Paper,' 907) further manages to associate the "Aspirin," suitably capitalized, with its equivalent, the cosmic Life.

10. Walter Scott, *Hermetica* (London: Dawsons of Pall Mall, 1968), I, p. 275.

11. Read, *Prelude to Chemistry*, p. 251.

12. John Hollander, "The Sound of the Music of Music and Sound," in *Wallace Stevens, A Celebration*, eds. Doggett and Buttel, p. 235; 236.

13. Hargrave Jennings, *The Rosicrucians, Their Rites and Mysteries* (New York: Arno Press, 1976), p. 387. In the harmonic theories of Marsilio Ficino, a Renaissance Neoplatonist deeply influenced by Hermetism, musical sound is viewed as a "living, 'spiritual' animal" (D. P. Walker, *Spiritual and Demonic Magic from Ficino to Campanella* [Notre Dame: University of Notre Dame Press, 1975], p. 25).

14. Schaya, *The Universal Meaning of the Kabbalah*, p. 162.

15. The image of "clappers going without bells" recalls a similar image in the work of Michael Maier, a seventeenth-century German alchemist who writes in connection with the alchemical sun and its shadow, "For what in the end . . . is this sun without a shadow? The same as a bell without a clapper" (Jung, *Mysterium Coniunctionis*, p. 98). Maier was a central figure in German Rosicrucianism. Stevens' interest in a Rosicrucian community is discussed in chapter 9.

16. Jung, *Alchemical Studies*, p. 209; 421.

17. Stevens' icy sovereign appears to be patterned after the following alchemical formula: "Now the final result of the alchemical Operation is exactly this *coincidentia oppositorum:* once a body has been treated and perfected by this Operation, it is in the state of 'solid' (or 'congealed,' 'frozen' . . .) liquid" (Corbin, *Spiritual Body and Celestial Earth*, p. 99).

18. Though Stevens notes that " 'concupiscent curds' have no genealogy," he goes on to explain that they "express the concupiscence of life, but, by contrast with the things in relation to them in the poem, they express or

accentuate life's destitution, and it is this that gives them something more than a cheap lustre" (L, 500). Though characteristically ambiguous, the observation associates "concupiscent curds" with "life" and with light ("lustre"), both attributes of the Man.

19. Stevens uses this phrase in his recently discovered letter to R. P. Blackmur. See Holly Stevens, "Flux," *Southern Review*, 15 (Autumn 1979), 773.

20. Stevens notes that "the poem is obviously not about icecream, but about being as distinguished from seeming to be" (L, 341).

21. Holly Stevens, "Flux," p. 774.

22. The "fantails" signify "fantail pigeons," Stevens explains in his note (L, 340).

23. Jung, *Psychology and Alchemy*, pp. 293—95.

Chapter 7

1. Pearce, *The Continuity of American Poetry*, pp. 412–13.

2. *Ibid.*, p. 413.

3. Joseph N. Riddel, "The Contours of Stevens Criticism," in *The Act of the Mind*, p. 272.

4. Pearce, *The Continuity of American Poetry*, p. 413.

5. Jung, *Mysterium Coniunctionis*, p. 104.

6. *Ibid.*, p. 17.

7. Kraeling, p. 108. In the first treatise of the *Corpus Hermeticum* ("Poimandres"), the Primal Man is similarly characterized as nameless: "He is bodiless, and yet has many bodies, or rather, is embodied in all bodies. There is nothing that He is not; for all things that exist are even He. For this reason all names are names of Him, because all things come from Him, their one Father; and for this reason He has no name, because He is the Father of all" (Scott, *Hermetica*, I, p. 163).

8. Lensing, "'From Pieces of Paper,'" 899.

9. Stevens dismissal of belief originates in the Hermetic view that the cosmic Man transcends parochial manifestations of traditional faith. The distinction is summed up in the declaration, "We believe without belief, beyond belief" (CP, 336) of "Flyer's Fall." The desire to escape all manifestations of the divine mistakenly projected onto external gods leads Stevens to characterize "The Man with the Blue Guitar" as an "anti-mythological" poem (L, 778).

10. Doggett, *Stevens' Poetry of Thought*, p. 131.

11. Vendler, *On Extended Wings*, p. 250.

12. The apocalyptic note of the passage is especially prominent in the second canto of "Owl's Clover" (retitled "The Statue at the World's End"). In its earliest form, it arises in one of the terse couplets of "New England Verses": "Civilization must be destroyed. The hairy saints / Of the North have earned this crumb by their complaints" (CP, 106).

13. Read, *Prelude to Chemistry*, p. 136. The alchemist often used the metaphor of combat to suggest the conflict of opposites that precedes the resurrection of the Man. See Jung, *Mysterium Coniunctionis*, p. 353.

14. The notion that the parasol shields the soul from the common sun, thereby allowing the onset of transcendental vision, is clarified in "Certain Phenomena of Sound": "Eulalia, I lounged on the hospital porch, / . . . and opened wide / A parasol, which I had found, against / The sun. The interior of a parasol, / It is a kind of blank in which one sees" (CP, 287).

15. The Old Man is a common alchemical name for Saturn, who is often portrayed as Mercurius' father (Jung, *Mysterium Coniunctionis*, p. 224; *Alchemical Studies*, p. 227). The image recurs in the late poem "A Child Asleep in Its Own Life" (OP, 106), similarly used to project the vision of a brooding figure hovering over the beds of sleepers. In its earliest form, the figure of the Old Man concludes the sketch, "A Day in February," published when Stevens was a special student at Harvard (*The Harvard Advocate*, 66, 9 [March 6, 1899], 135–36).

16. Jung, *Mysterium Coniunctionis*, p. 241.

17. Stevens often characterizes the Hermetic Man as "final." Ananke, for example, is a "final god" (OP, 59); the "central man" of "Asides on the Oboe" invites a "final belief" (CP, 250); "Credences of Summer" offers the Man as a "natural tower" who is the "final mountain" (CP, 373); the giant of "A Primitive Like an Orb" is a "roundness that pulls tight the final ring" (CP, 442). And since the Man is a creature of the mind evoked in meditation, it is likely that he is Stevens' "interior paramour" (CP, 524), his voice a "final soliloquy" confirming that "God and the imagination are one" (CP, 524).

18. Jung, *Alchemical Studies*, p. 228.

19. *Ibid.*, p. 87.

20. In his letter to Oscar Williams to whom he submitted "Extracts from Addresses to the Academy of Fine Ideas" for publication in *New Poems: 1940*, Stevens has this to say of the poem: "One of the characteristics of the world today is the Lightness with which ideas are asserted, held, abandoned, etc. That is what this poem grows out of" (L, 380). Though Stevens' explanation is characteristically ambiguous, the reference to "Lightness," suitably capitalized, recalls the heavenly light of the Man.

21. Stevens often uses the point or dot (the alchemical scintilla) to symbolize the Man. Considered in "The Rock" the "space . . . contained" in the "mind" (CP, 528), he is characterized as "The starting point of the human and the end" (CP, 528). The redemptive journey undertaken in "Prologues to What Is Possible" moves to "a point of central arrival" (CP, 516). The object perceived through transcendental perception—what Stevens calls "The poem of pure reality" (CP, 471)—is said to be "the exactest point at which it is itself" (CP, 471). In "Someone Puts a Pineapple Together," the alchemical scintilla appears as a "dot" which the poet defines as "the pale pole of resemblances" (NA, 88).

22. The passage recalls the conclusion of "The Man with the Blue Guitar," which similarly summons humanity to the sacramental "bread," reaffirmed in the image of the Hermetic stone: "Here is the bread of time to come, / Here is its actual stone. The bread / Will be our bread, the stone will

be / Our bed and we shall sleep by night. / We shall forget by day . . ." (CP, 183–84).

23. Jung, *Psychology and Alchemy*, p. 340.

24. Jung, *Mysterium Coniunctionis*, p. 197.

Chapter 8

1. John Malcolm Brinnin, "Plato, Phoebus and the Man From Hartford," *Voices*, 121 (Spring 1945), 33.

2. Sister M. Bernetta Quinn, "Metamorphosis in Wallace Stevens," in Borroff, *Wallace Stevens*, p. 68.

3. Joseph N. Riddel, "Wallace Stevens," in *Sixteen Modern American Authors*, ed. Jackson R. Bryer (New York: W. W. Norton and Co., 1973), p. 549.

4. Scott, *Hermetica*, I, p. 193.

5. Corbin, *Spiritual Body and Celestial Earth*, p. 14.

6. *Ibid.*, p. 12; 11.

7. *Ibid.*, p. 12.

8. *Ibid.*, p. 78.

9. *Ibid.*

10. *Ibid.*, p. 56.

11. *Ibid.*, p. 83.

12. Jung, *Alchemical Studies*, p. 197.

13. Yvor Winters' celebrated reading of this poem places special emphasis on the sterility suggested by the poem's final lines. Not recognizing Stevens' special doctrine, Winters concludes that the poem expresses "the corrupting effect of the intellect upon natural beauty" (*In Defense of Reason*, 3rd ed. [Chicago: The Swallow Press, 1947], p. 437).

14. According to S. K. Heninger, Jr., the view of metaphor as cosmic correspondence was widely held in the Renaissance—the legacy of Pythagorean doctrine as interpreted by Plato and the Church Fathers (*Touches of Sweet Harmony: Pythagorean Cosmology and Renaissance Poetics* [The Huntington Library: San Marino, California, 1974], pp. 325–363).

15. The number suggests the twelve signs of the Zodiac, often used to represent the twelve successive stages of the Operation (Read, *Prelude to Chemistry*, p. 136).

16. Jung, *Mysterium Coniunctionis*, p. 7.

17. Brinnin, "Plato, Phoebus and the Man From Hartford," p. 32.

18. Jung, *Mysterium Coniunctionis*, p. 4.

19. "The Snow Man" has received extensive comment. For a reading closest to my own, see William Bevis, "Stevens' Toneless Poetry," *English Literary History*, 41 (Fall 1974), 257–86.

20. Scott, *Hermetica*, I, 191.

21. Vendler, *On Extended Wings*, p. 270.

22. Jung, *Alchemical Studies*, p. 315. In Shiïte Gnosticism, the palm tree serves "as a symbol of the celestial Earth and of resurrection" (Corbin, *Spiritual Body and Celestial Earth*, p. 136).
23. Scott, *Hermetica*, I, p. 193.
24. *Ibid.*, p. 241.
25. *Ibid.*, p. 221.
26. Joseph Riddel dismisses the *"Regulae mundi"* of the poem as an ironic statement "of very unclear proportions" (*The Clairvoyant Eye*, p. 160).

Chapter 9 ───────────────────────────── 🌀

1. Stevens' reputation as a "mysterious figure," even to his fellow poets from whom, on the whole, he lived apart, has been chronicled by William Van O'Connor, (*The Shaping Spirit*, pp. 7–22). No biography of the poet exists and, apart from Michael Lafferty's bare description of Stevens' early life ("Wallace Stevens, A Man of Two Worlds," *Historical Review of Berks County*, 24 [Fall 1959], 109–13; 130–32), little is known of Stevens' formative years. Reviewing the biographical material available, Joseph Riddel concludes that "broad and important periods of Stevens' life remain vague and mysterious" ("Wallace Stevens," in *Sixteen Modern American Authors*, p. 537).
2. According to Holly Stevens, the letters to Elsie Moll dated before 1907 were destroyed, although passages from them were excerpted (L, 77). Of the heavily excised "Journal," Holly Stevens conjectures that the excisions may have been made either by Stevens' widow or by Stevens himself (*Souvenirs and Prophecies: The Young Wallace Stevens* [New York: Alfred A. Knopf, Inc., 1976], p. 115).
3. That Stevens experienced a degree of tension between a felt need for secrecy (traditionally the mode of Hermetic speculation) and an equally insistent need for direct acknowledgment of his spiritual purpose seems to be implied in a curious passage in "The Noble Rider and the Sound of Words," which considers the "inherent nobility" of the imagination. Eager to acknowledge the source of this "inherent nobility" but equally shy of direct statement, the poet resorts to circumlocution (what he calls "evading a definition") to image humanity's "spiritual height and depth" (the traditional "above" and "below" of Hermetic correspondence). What emerges is a reluctant presentation of the divine "nothing" (used ambiguously, in Stevens' customary fashion) which, oddly enough, inspires a confession of "shame" and "horror"— perhaps, we can only speculate, because the poet felt a degree of betrayal in attempting definition without the convenient disguise of symbol:

> This inherent nobility is the natural source of another. . . . I
> mean that nobility which is our spiritual height and depth; and
> while I know how difficult it is to express it, nevertheless I am
> bound to give a sense of it. Nothing could be more evasive and
> inaccessible. Nothing distorts itself and seeks disguise more

quickly. There is a shame of disclosing it and in its definite pres-
entations a horror of it. But there it is. The fact that it is there is
what makes it possible to invite to the reading and writing of
poetry men of intelligence and desire for life. . . . I am not thinking of the solemn, the portentous or demoded. On the other
hand, I am evading a definition. If it is defined, it will be fixed
and it must not be fixed. As in the case of an external thing,
nobility resolves itself into an enormous number of vibrations,
movements, changes. To fix it is to put an end to it (NA, 33–34).

4. Critics have usually followed Hi Simons' view that the poem is an
autobiographical "fable" intended to generalize "the author's experience and
point of view" ("'The Comedian as the Letter C': Its Sense and Its
Significance," *Southern Review*, 5 [Winter 1940], 454.) An earlier version of the
poem (presumed lost) was submitted to Harriet Monroe in 1921 in competi-
tion for the Blindman Prize. A typescript copy of the poem (entitled "From
the Journal of Crispin") has recently been recovered. See Louis A. Martz,
"'From the Journal of Crispin,'" in Doggett and Buttel, eds., *Wallace Stevens, a
Celebration*, pp. 3–45.

5. Jung, *Alchemical Studies*, p. 278. Persuaded that Stevens' antecedents
are literary rather than religious, some readers have sought the origin of Stevens' Crispin figure in the Italian and French comic traditions. Others, mindful of the final stanza of "Anecdote of the Abnormal," in which Crispin is
addressed as "Crispin-saint" (OP, 24), conjecture that Crispin is patterned
after Saint Crispin, an early Christian martyr.

6. Jung, *Mysterium Coniunctionis*, p. 59.

7. *Ibid.*, p. 56.

8. *Ibid.*, p. 59.

9. Joy, laughter, gaiety, and pleasure—all aspects of the comic—
similarly arise in connection with the Man. The red colossus of "Notes
toward a Supreme Fiction" appears in the poem's final canto entitled "It Must
Give Pleasure" to signify the blissful beatitude of union which the alchemist
imaged in the *serpens mercurii* "rejoicing in itself" at the culmination of the
Work (Jung, *Mysterium Coniunctionis*, p. 504). Similarly, the marble horses of
"Owl's Clover" are said to be the "drafts of gay beginnings and bright ends"
(OP, 57), a common designation for the alchemical Mercurius, who stands "at
the beginning and end of the work" (Jung, *Psychology and Alchemy*, p. 293). At
times, Stevens uses the clown image to represent the comic, as in "Jumbo,"
renamed the "Cloud-clown" and represented as "the transformer, himself
transformed" (CP, 269)—the Man's double virtue. Note 53 below explores
the motif of the comic in Rosicrucian lore.

10. Lensing, "'From Pieces of Paper,'" 902.

11. *Ibid.*, 889.

12. Lindsay, *The Origins of Alchemy*, p. 215.

13. In "From the Journal of Crispin," the poet questions whether Crispin
is a fit "sceptre of the unregenerate sea" (Martz, "'From the Journal of Crispin,'" p. 30). The line was subsequently dropped from the published version.

14. The tonsorial image recurs in "From the Journal of Crispin" in allusions to "barber-poles" (Martz, "'From the Journal of Crispin,'" pp. 39; 40;

41). The image has precedent in alchemical lore. According to Jack Lindsay, the barber figure in the writing of Zosimos, an alchemist of the third century A.D., was associated "with cosmetics and beautification, which were regarded as works of transformation"; hence, he represents the elegance and artistry attributed to the entire transmutative process (*The Origins of Alchemy*, p. 346). Stevens' adaptation of the alchemical barber arises in his frequent allusions to hair artificially arranged in coiffures, wigs, curls, and braids. The "tailor" of "The Man with the Blue Guitar" is another of Stevens' artisans who "clips" and redesigns the natural world.

    15. Jung, *Alchemical Studies*, p. 146.

    16. This passage Yvor Winters glosses as "Crispin's taking leave of his art . . . because the art is, after all, futile and contemptible" (*In Defense of Reason*, p. 433). Though Winters' assessment of the poet's attitude towards his art is accurate, the passage is not a valedictory but a grudging acceptance of art as a halfway redemptive measure. Winters' view that Crispin's (and Stevens') animus towards art is inspired by the desire for direct experience is not amiss, if the experience to which Winters alludes is interpreted as the mystical condition of Being.

    17. There is some evidence that Stevens considered his belief in the Hermetic Man an alternative object of faith for the collective. He explains to one correspondent, for example, that it was a "habit of mind" with him to seek "some substitute for religion" that would replace "the sort of God in Whom we were all brought up to believe" (L, 348). Equally, he describes "Notes toward a Supreme Fiction" as an effort "to create something as valid as the idea of God has been" (L, 435). Moreover, when the appeal is direct, as it is in "Asides on the Oboe," the poet affirms the need for a "final belief" intended to supersede traditional faith and made concrete in the image of the "philosophers' man." That Stevens thought his poetry could indeed transform the collective seems to be implied in a curious passage in "The Figure of the Youth as Virile Poet," which alludes in the first person plural (a device which affirms shared perception), to the possible discovery of the sacred "center," the culmination of Hermetic meditation. The observation is accompanied by a version of Hermetic dissolution and resurrection, this time, however, made the function of the poet who, Stevens claims, has the "power to destroy us," thereby "to reconstruct us by his transformations" (NA, 45).

    18. Vendler, *On Extended Wings*, p. 54.

    19. In a letter to Barbara Church, Stevens mentions reading "two volumes on the early German Sectarians of Pennsylvania" (probably the work of Julius Sachse; see n. 31 below), noting, too, that "At Ephrata one of these groups built the earliest monastery ever built in this country" (L, 511). The letter concludes with a tribute to the Ephrata community and an acknowledgment that as a boy, Stevens had met one of the cenobites: "The whole story of the early Pennsylvania Pietists is precious. When I was a boy I met one of these sisters in Ephrata. She was then 90 and her father could very well have gone back to the time when the vital characters were still alive" (L, 511).

    20. Conceivably, Stevens' interest in Hermetism could have been influenced by the French Symbolists, whose poetic assimilation of esoteric doctrine has been chronicled by Gwendolyn Bays (*The Orphic Vision: Seer Poets*

from Novalis to Rimbaud [Lincoln: University of Nebraska Press, 1964]). I have suggested otherwise, not because Stevens was indifferent to the major poetic movement of his youth—he certainly knew and admired the Symbolist poets, though he disclaimed their influence of his work (L, 391; 635)—but because his poetry reflects a doctrinal loyalty beyond the merely eclectic. Not only does it draw liberally on traditional Hermetic symbols but, more importantly, it repeatedly proffers the image of the "sophic" Man within the pattern of Hermetic meditation—the major mode of Hermetic salvation. Such strategies argue the religious, rather than literary, roots of the poet's faith.

21. Julius Sachse, *The German Pietists of Provincial Pennsylvania* (New York: AMS Press, 1971), p. 38. First printed for the author in 1895.

22. *Ibid.*, p. 7.

23. Abraham H. Cassell, "John Kelpius, The Hermit of the Wissahickon" (n.p., 1897), p. 15. TS, Library of the University of Pennsylvania, Philadelphia, Pennsylvania.

24. *Ibid.*

25. *Ibid.*, p. 16.

26. Sachse, *The German Pietists*, p. 64.

27. *Ibid.*, 129–30. The nocturnal "Bridegroom" of the Wissahickon hermits recalls the "hero of midnight" (CP, 466) of "An Ordinary Evening in New Haven." Stevens' cryptic notation "The Identity of the Bridegroom" (Lensing, " 'From Pieces of Paper,' " 906) may also be related to this figure.

28. Sachse, *The German Pietists*, p. 111.

29. Report of Rev. Heinrich Melchior Mühlenberg, as cited in Sachse, *The German Pietists*, p. 148. A prominent Lutheran pastor and leader, Mühlenberg arrived in Pennsylvania in 1742. Stevens mentions him twice in his letters (L, 479; 664), in each instance noting that he married a daughter of Conrad Weiser. Weiser was a prominent member of the Ephrata Cloister for some years before leaving to assume administrative duties in the Province.

30. Walter Conrad Klein, Beissel's biographer, attributes the Hebraic impulse of the Ephrata community to the influence of several religious sects in the area that observed the Hebrew sabbath (*Johann Conrad Beissel: Mystic and Martinet* [Philadelphia: University of Pennsylvania Press, 1942], pp. 67–68). In view of Beissel's theosophical beliefs, a more likely source of his Sabbatarianism is Rosicrucianism, which traces its pedigree to the Hebrew Essenes—a gnostic sect which strictly observed the ordinances of the Hebrew sabbath (Arthur Edward Waite, *The Brotherhood of the Rosy Cross* [New York: University Books, n.d.], p. 5). Sachse acknowledges the Essenes as one of the spiritual models of the Wissahickon Brotherhood (*The German Pietists*, p. 38).

The Hebraism of the Ephratists appears to be echoed in Stevens' interest in the rabbi, whom the poet considers "exceedingly attractive . . . because it is the figure of a man devoted in the extreme to scholarship and at the same time to making some use of it for human purposes" (L, 786). Stevens' meaning is clarified in "Things of August," where the rabbi is associated with *gnosis:* "We'll give the week-end to wisdom, to Weisheit, the rabbi" (CP, 492). In "The Pure Good of Theory," Stevens links the *anima mundi* to the Jew, perhaps a reference to the Kabbalistic Adam Kadmon: "This platonic person discovered a soul in the world / And studied it in his holiday hotel. / He was a Jew from Europe or might have been" (CP, 331). The Kabbalah is mentioned twice in "The Auroras of Autumn" in connection with a heavenly imagination crowned with a "diamond cabala" (CP, 417) and further described as "Goat-leaper, crystalled and luminous" (CP, 417) to suggest the Hermetic Mercurius for whom the goat (the sign of Capricorn) stands as symbol.

31. Klein, *Johann Conrad Beissel*, p. 192. Adam's bisexuality Beissel called *Tinktur*, echoing in his phraseology the alchemical *tinctura philosophorum* — another name for the *lapis* which Christian alchemists associated with Christ (Jung, *Mysterium Coniunctionis*, p. 345). The same esoteric terminology appears in the work of Jacob Boehme, whose speculation was heavily indebted to Hermetic teachings; and, indeed, Oswald Seidensticker, an early historian of the Ephrata community, speculates that Boehme was the source of Beissel's religious views ("Ephrata: The Story of an American Monastery" [n.p.; n.d.], p. 56. TS, Library of the University of Pennsylvania, Philadelphia, Pennsylvania). However, on the basis of a number of books discovered at Antietam, a branch of the Ephrata Cloister, Julius Sachse holds that the influence of Behmist theosophy on Beissel's thought was filtered through the mystical teachings of Gottfried Arnold, a seventeenth-century theologian and historian whose emphasis on celibacy as a required condition of union with the celestial Sophia Beissel adopted as his own (Julius Sachse, *The German Sectarians of Pennsylvania, 1708 – 1800*, [New York: AMS Press, 1971], II, p. 163. First printed for the author in two volumes in 1899, 1900). For a succinct summary of Arnold's thought, see F. Ernest Stoeffler, *German Pietism During the Eighteenth Century* (Leiden: E. J. Brill, 1973), pp. 175 – 81.

32. Klein, *Johann Conrad Beissel*, p. 193.

33. *Ibid.*, p. 194.

34. Seidensticker, "Ephrata," p. 52.

35. *Ibid.* The resemblance of Beissel's *"Nichts"* to Stevens' "priest of nothingness" (OP, 88) is noteworthy. Walter Klein speculates that Beissel's doctrine of nothingness was influenced by the quietism of Madame de Guyon, a Roman Catholic mystic whose work was read by many Pietists (*Johann Conrad Beissel*, p. 114). Madame de Guyon's chief disciple was Francois Fénelon, whose name arises in Stevens' "Journal" in the cryptic but somewhat rhapsodic entry, "Fénélon. — The name is enough" (L, 105).

36. In gnostic thought, the serpent is the creature that induces knowledge; hence, it represents the "powers of redemption" and "the beginning of all *gnosis* on earth" (Jonas, *The Gnostic Religion*, p. 93).

37. Sachse, *The German Sectarians*, I, p. 183.

38. Charles M. Treher, "Snow Hill Cloister," *Publications of the Pennsylvania German Society*, II (Allentown: The Pennsylvania German Society, 1968), p. 24 – 25.

39. Sachse, *The German Sectarians*, I, p. 297. Stevens often paints the Man as bearded. His appearance in "Like Decorations in a Nigger Cemetery" is so described in conjunction with the "sophic" fire: "His beard is of fire and his staff is a leaping flame" (CP, 150). Elsewhere, he appears as the androgynous "bearded queen" (CP, 507); or as "The Well Dressed Man with a Beard" (CP, 247). In "Owl's Clover," the beard is linked to the Ananke-artist, from "whose beard the future springs, elect" (OP, 64).

40. Wood, tree, and forest were evidently numinous to the theosophists. According to James E. Ernst, the Ephratists built the Kedar "entirely of wood, even to the pins, hinges and latches, for mysticism and theosophy forbade the use of iron" (*Ephrata: A History* [Allentown, Pennsylvania: Schlechter's, 1963], p. 107). The reliance on wood extended—at least for some—to diet. Julius Sachse tells of discovering recipes for coffee, bread, and tonics made from acorns, the fruit of the oak. This habit, Sachse notes, derived from the Rosicrucian belief that "the oak furnished the first food for mankind, the acorn as meat and the honey-dew (*honigmeth*) as drink. . . . It was further firmly believed that when the time of Philadelphian restitution should come, it would once more bring about the primeval simplicity when the oak would furnish unto man his entire sustenance" (*The German Sectarians*, I, p. 195). The Rosicrucian reverence for the oak probably stemmed from the synonymity in the alchemical system between Hermes-Mercurius and the "sophic" oak—the "king of the forest" (Jung, *Alchemical Studies*, p. 199). For this belief in a tree deity, the Hermetist had precedent in the classical Hermes; for scholars now believe that Hermes "has a certain connexion with tree-cults," since "his famous staff, the caduceus, was in all probability originally of wood, and is sometimes depicted as having leaves and therefore living" (W. K. C. Guthrie, *The Greeks and Their Gods* [London: Methuen, University Paperback, 1968], p. 92). The clearest expression of Stevens' use of the cosmic oak arises in the brief lyric "Solitaire under the Oaks," which employs the "sophic" tree to describe the onset of vision—an "escape / To principium, to meditation" (OP, 111).

41. Sachse, *The German Sectarians*, I, p. 360.

42. *Ibid.*, p. 361.

43. *Ibid.*

44. *Ibid.*

45. *Ibid.*, p. 362. The account recalls the spiritual pilgrims of "The Pediment of Appearance," who similarly retire to the woods in the month of "full-blown May" (CP, 362) in search of the "savage transparence" (CP, 361). Crispin's "sweating changes" (CP, 33) suggest another version of this regenerative process, as does the "bodiless" head of "The Men That are Falling," said to experience "More than sudarium" (CP, 188) in the cause of mystical death. In "Credences of Summer," the regenerative ritual is enacted in the woods by anonymous acolytes who repeat the trichotomous order of Hermetic rebirth (CP, 376).

46. Sachse, *The German Sectarians*, II, 175.

47. Beginning in 1745, these hymns were published at Ephrata by the Brotherhood Press. An early collection and the first book published by the Cloister was owned by Stevens but was sold at auction by the Parke-Bernet Galleries of New York shortly after his death. See Parke-Bernet Catalogue Sale #1895, April 7 and 8, 1959, No. 150. The Parke-Bernet Catalogue of April 7 and 8 lists another of Stevens' books bearing the Ephrata imprint (*Ibid.*, No. 151).

48. Klein, *Johann Conrad Beissel*, p. 144.

49. Sachse, *The German Sectarians*, II, p. 138.

50. *Ibid.*, pp. 134–35. The comparison between the cenobites' singing and the tone of a hautboy or oboe suggests Stevens' title "Asides on the Oboe," the poem in which the "philosophers' man" is carefully described.

51. Lamech and Agrippa, *Chronicon Ephratense: A History of the Community of Seventh Day Baptists at Ephrata, Lancaster County, Pennsylvania*, trans. J. Max Hark (Lancaster: S. H. Zahm & Co., 1889), p. 160. This book was completed in 1786 by two Ephrata brothers. Though it is generally regarded as an apologetic for Beissel, it provides a firsthand account of many of the social and economic problems Beissel and his disciples encountered in their attempt to fashion a communal life based on religious principle. Of theosophic doctrine, it has little to say.

52. Sachse, *The German Sectarians*, II, p. 150.

53. *Ibid.*, p. 151. Beissel's allusion to the divine restoration as a "comedy" is obviously of interest to the student of Stevens' work. The allusion is reaffirmed in the correspondence of Christopher Sauer, a printer who published a number of Ephrata manuscripts before the Cloister acquired its own press. One such manuscript (the *Weyrauchs Hugel*, a hymnal compiled by Beissel and his associates) contained a Beisselian hymn which Sauer read as Beissel's effort "to portray himself as Christ" (Klein, *Johann Conrad Beissel*, p. 96). Evidently offended, he wrote to Beissel asking for clarification, in the course of which he referred to Beissel as a "Martial and Mercurial spirit" who wished to appear as a "Pillar of fire and clouds" (Sachse, *The German Sectarians*, I, p. 331). Beissel's haughty response so enraged Sauer that he charged the Superintendent publicly with being under a "strange . . . conjunction of stars . . . from Mars he has his great severity, from Jupiter his friendliness, from Venus that the female sex ran after him, Mercury taught him the art of a comedian, etc." (Sachse, *The German Sectarians*, I, pp. 332–33). Sauer's characterization not only echoes the ancient astrological belief that the soul in its descent to earth acquired the dispositions and qualities of the seven planets but suggests that according to the Cloister's arcana (Sauer was not a member of the Cloister but was familiar with its doctrines), the planet associated with the Hermetic deity was accorded the quality of the comic. The attribution has its echo in Rosicrucian lore: according to Frances Yates, Johann Valentin Andreae, the reputed author of the Rosicrucian allegory *The Chymical Wedding of Christian Rosencreutz*, repeatedly referred to the R. C. Brotherhood as "an admirable Fraternity which plays comedies throughout Europe" (*The Rosicrucian Enlightenment* [London: Routledge and Kegan Paul, 1972], p. 142).

54. In 1934, when proceedings were started by the Commonwealth of Pennsylvania to acquire the Cloister, one of the Cloister's trustees was William K. Bechtel, the father of Edwin De Turck Bechtel—a childhood friend of Stevens with whom Stevens maintained a lifelong friendship. Two other trustees of this period bear the surname Kachel (Milton H. Heinicke, *History of Ephrata, Supplement to Booklet Seven* [The Historical Society of the Cocalico Valley, February, 1974], p. 12). Kachel was the maiden name of Mrs. Stevens (she took her stepfather's surname Moll when her mother remarried). According to Daniel Kachel, a surviving householder (and a later trustee), Mrs. Stevens was the second cousin of his father, Reuben Kachel, one of the householders (Interview with Daniel Kachel, 207 South Reading

Road, Ephrata, Pennsylvania, August 5, 1977). Apart from this distant relationship, there is no evidence that Mrs. Stevens was in any way connected to the Cloister.

55. H. Spencer Lewis, *Rosicrucian Manual*, p. 5.
56. *Ibid.*, pp. 5–6.
57. *Ibid.*, p. 6.
58. *Ibid.*, p. 170.

ℭ Indexes ☉

————————— *Works by Wallace Stevens* —————————

A

"Adagia," 13, 16, 18, 60, 82, 118, 129
"Adult Epigram," 174 n 18
"Anecdote of the Abnormal," 180 n 5
"Anecdote of the Jar," 131–32, 149
"Asides on the Oboe," 37, 66–68, 74, 120, 177 n 17, 181 n 17, 185 n 50
"The Auroras of Autumn," 110, 111, 112–14, 182–83 n 30

B

"The Bagatelles the Madrigals," 111
"Bantams in Pine-Woods," 92
"Belgian Farm, October, 1914," 115
"The Bouquet," 135–36
"Burghers of Petty Death," 116

C

"Certain Phenomena of Sound," 117 n 14
"Chocorua to Its Neighbor," 34, 37, 38, 69, 98, 109, 112, 133
"A Collect of Philosophy," 13, 16, 37, 78, 173 n 9
The Collected Poems, 78, 172 n 35
"The Comedian as the Letter C," 147–54, 155
"Credences of Summer," 88, 177 n 17, 184 n 45

D

"A Day in February," 177 n 15
"Dezembrum," 88
"A Duck for Dinner," 29–31. *See also* "Owl's Clover"
"Dutch Graves in Bucks County," 115, 117
"The Dwarf," 97

E

"The Emperor of Ice-Cream," 98–99, 137
"Esthétique du Mal," 119–20
"Evening without Angels," 95
"Examination of the Hero in a Time of War," 19, 34, 38, 39, 42, 64, 66, 81, 97, 112, 115, 117
"Extracts from Addresses to the Academy of Fine Ideas," 10, 121–26, 177 n 20

F

"The Figure of the Youth as Virile Poet," 79, 119, 181 n 17
"Five Grotesque Pieces," 118
"Flyer's Fall," 176, n 9

G

"Gigantomachia," 115
"The Greenest Continent," 17, 23, 29, 40, 64, 111. *See also* "Owl's Clover"

187